THE SECRETS OF BENJAMIN FOX

AMERICAN FOX TALES

JAMES ROYAL FOX JR

Print ISBN: 978-1-64719-690-5
Ebook ISBN: 978-1-64719-691-2

The information in this book is true to the best of the author's knowledge. The author disclaims any liability in connection with this information. Those who can add to this educational narrative are invited to contact the author who reserves the right to expand the facts contained herein in subsequent printings.

James Royal Fox Jr
21575 Highway 101 South
Cloverdale, Oregon 97112

Published by BookLocker.com, Inc., Trenton, Georgia.

Printed on acid-free paper.

Library of Congress Cataloging in Publication Data
Fox Jr, James Royal
The Secrets of Benjamin Fox: American Fox Tales by James Royal Fox Jr
Library of Congress Control Number: 2021913022

BookLocker.com, Inc.
2023

TABLE OF CONTENTS

INTRODUCTION

My Grandma Bessie Fox was born in 1906 and passed away in 1993. She left behind to her grandchildren handwritten notes detailing the genealogy of our family. Compiled over her lifetime in an age well before the internet, only three errors have ever been discovered in the many dossiers. Besides names, birth dates, marriages and deaths, were sometimes home addresses of those yet living when she was investigating. Some notes found among the pages might be considered gossip, but it is still important historically. These notes kindled a fire of curiosity that led to a hobby that after retirement in 2017 led to a full time job.

In the beginning of my research, those notes were a guiding light. Able to utilize technology Grandma could never have imagined, a veil began to lift and our dead kin began to speak again. Heroes and vagabonds and everything in between harboring lost stories of triumph and tragedy; adoption, divorce and murder. Yet secrets remained.

Just beyond Grandma's handwritten trail I found Ephraim Fox, who she had not yet identified. I found his father was Nicholas and believed his father was named Benjamin, but there was no consensus of which Fox family they came from. Despite genealogical research quickly evolving from a hobby to a full time job, I could not identify Nicholas or Benjamin Fox. DNA was the answer, but as it cast light into shadows, it created others.

Initially choosing to use FamilytreeDNA,[189] I found their platform hard to decipher, partly because I did not recognize any of the surnames I was directly related to. Since I already had a well-developed family tree on Ancestry.com, I then submitted to their DNA test. Before I received those results, Fox group administrator, renowned Fox researcher Joe Fox from the FamilytreeDNA website informed me I was, genetically speaking, not a Fox.[215] This news was a broadside that caused me some level of uncomfortable agitation and confusion.

Joe and other administrators were asking questions as if I had been adopted. The idea made my head swim. At first I thought I read his email wrong. Besides a well-documented paper trail, I had the living memories of my family going back over 100 years. All of that I had to accept, means little in the face of DNA proof. I cannot stress enough how much this news unsettled me.

My reality shifted a little, faced with questions about my heritage I never thought I would ever wonder about. I was surprised how deeply the news affected me. It was a stark, unexpected lesson about how the news of adoption at any age, in any era can blindside a person.

Only a few days after these email exchanges with Fox admins at Familytree.DNA, Ancestry.com results were posted and I did not qualify to have a family tree! Ancestry.com provides a feature called Thrulines; a software program that uses family trees created by members and cross references the DNA relationship of others who have DNA tested in order to establish relationships. Initially I had no results from this software either. I had hit a dead end. I knew the identity of Nicholas and Benjamin would solve this mystery, but in 2017 I seriously doubted that would ever happen.

By this point I was committed to doing all I could to get some answers, so I went back to FamilytreeDNA, where hundreds of dollars were spent to specifically test my paternal bloodline. Their Big Y500 test did not yield answers. Undeterred, I bit the bullet and paid a few hundred more for their Big Y700 test. These tests focus on the Y chromosome that is passed generation to generation almost unchanged from father to son.

Results of the Big Y700 test were shocking and as I found out, well worth the investment. The test established a biological relationship with John J. Cobb born 1822 in Knox County, Kentucky.

In this initial phase, researchers believed Benjamin was a direct *descendant* of Ambrose Cobb, The Emigrant, The Planter. In addition, a gentleman named Ronald Martin who has since passed, was identified as also sharing a common father from probably 1100-1200 years ago.[178]

As I grappled with this new information, the Thrulines software on Ancestry.com posted results that multiplied quickly. To my surprise, my DNA was traced back through Ephraim Fox and his father Nicholas, to Benjamin Kendrick Fox of Virginia. In a matter of days Thrulines pointed out a DNA relationship to all 9 children of Benjamin K. Fox; between two wives.

It was Familytree.DNA that established there is no DNA connection between Benjamin and William Fox, whom historical documents claim was his father. YDNA proved that at some point Benjamin, likely early in his life, was adopted by William and Mary (Kendrick) Fox. Genealogist Joe Fox termed it a 'DNA crossover'.

There is no indication who Benjamin's true father is. Due to that fact, one could say both this Fox bloodline and the country itself began at the same time.

By 2021 as more people were DNA tested, results were refined until currently only a handful of men, including myself and Ronald Martin, share the designation of YDNA Haplogroup R-BY60440[189] Another living male Cobb would likely share this designation if he were to take the BigY700 test.

The most impactful DNA discovery was made in 2022, when it was proven John J. Cobb was not biologically a Cobb, but was sired by a Fox; and Ronald Martin and I were not related over a thousand years ago, but instead his 3rd great grandad was fathered by a Fox.

These 'DNA crossovers' occurred about 300 years ago, in the colonial era that Benjamin and Nicholas Fox lived. The families of John J. Cobb and Ronald Martin suddenly realized their biological father was a Fox and I realized one of my grandfather's had at least two children out of wedlock. The plot thickened as everybody's reality shifted - again.

Discovery of the adoption of Benjamin seriously altered the initial mission of this book, which was to simply create a light work of historical fiction about my family. DNA discoveries that defied 250 years of commonly held beliefs convinced me it was important to correct the record, and relate the story truthfully.

Meanwhile research revealed I was the last living ancestor of Ephraim Fox, the grandson of Benjamin Fox who came to Oregon in 1852. That emotional discovery left it to me to document the lives of my family before I am gone. I cannot let eight generations of my family be lost because I didn't have a son to carry our name forward. I owe them that. I owe us that.

Stories have been lost or disconnected and need to be organized for the record and wove back into the fabric of history. It became necessary to historically detail the Fox, and to some extent the Cobbs and Martin families.

Despite all the added aims of my research, from the beginning this was a story about how Benjamin's adoption affected the arc of my family that resulted in his grandson Ephraim leaving everything behind to cross the Oregon Trail.

This document lives, just as the dead it chronicles continue to speak. Memories fade and family history is lost to time but I have done my best to restore everything I can. The American Fox Tales are works of historical and genealogical significance to many besides the Fox family.

The Virginia Fox's might be the most studied of Fox families, but revelations made by DNA alter long accepted paper trails. Despite the depth of research on the Fox's of Virginia there are also quite a number of disagreements in the research. While DNA ends centuries old questions, it poses others.

Here the lineage of the Virginia Fox's is revealed from all available information in a way not able to have been done before. The Cobbs and Martin families are well-documented on paper also, however the ties they shared with Benjamin Fox's family have been easily overlooked, prior to recent DNA findings.

Each genealogist approaches information from a different point of reference, according to their family history. My family history was lost but due to DNA testing I was able to identify connections between the Fox, Cobb and Martin families.

"The Secrets of Benjamin Fox" is the first in a series of books about the family of Benjamin Fox of Virginia. Beginning in England to the New World; from Virginia and then Kentucky and Tennessee, to Missouri where all ties between Benjamin Fox and the Virginia Fox family ended. From vast cotton plantations in South Carolina including Monticello to colonial Georgia and back to Kentucky where John J. Cobb and Henry Franklin Martin were born. This is the story of a very particular Fox family, with source citations that include my own blood, placed on paper; lost and forgotten no more.

After deciding to write a true account, I felt it necessary to study how fathers affect sons generationally. One of the most important goals in this first book is to determine how the life experiences of Benjamin impacted the life and decisions of his son Nicholas and grandson Ephraim, who was 20 years old when Benjamin died; old enough to know him well.

Besides the easy stuff like how occupations were passed from father to son, a search is conducted to find what character and personality traits were passed forward. I want to understand how these men manifest in me. I'm looking for some form of similarity, to understand myself better; to make sense of who and why I am.

For every generation, a son's first hero is his father. Every move that man makes and emotion he feels is seen by his son who himself does not realize he is absorbing everything. Without being conscious of it sons walk like their father and act like them in many aspects.

That said, maternal influences cannot be disregarded. The men of each generation; their fears and fearlessness; reasons for grievances and ability to forgive; all the feelings they had throughout the seasons of their lives, were tempered or exacerbated by the feminine influence of wives, mothers and daughters.

While DNA proves and disproves biological lineage, it does indicate what personal adoptive relationships that people shared; documents do. This was an issue I never thought I would face and the distinction is no less important in respect to the long dead than it is for the living.

It is inaccurate to state adopted children "are unrelated", when in fact, they were named after their adoptive parents and were treated equally with their step-siblings in the wills of their adoptive parents. 'Not biologically related' is a far more descriptive, accurate description, and it indicates there was a relationship between adoptive parents and the children.

The historical events these men lived through are vital to understanding how each formed the other. Bits and pieces of disconnected information, far flung, have been found only because a handful of men happened to get their YDNA tested. A story forgotten over 200 years ago is brought to life while a study is slowly conducted to determine nature vs nurture questions that formed an American family, from its beginning.

Besides historical documents, for hundreds of years families commonly used Bibles to record births, marriages, offspring and deaths. Given as wedding gifts, the information was often transcribed; parts anyway. The rest learned, which was a lot, was simply by word of mouth, told by parents and relatives. Random articles, books and columns can be located to fill in the blanks.

Then of course, there are notes left behind like Grandma Bessie's. But while Grandma's notes and other various Family Bibles recorded information, when the information became too personal, it surely was not recorded. I think Grandma Bessie, if not always proud of the facts, would be both entertained and amazed at the detailed results her grandson discovered, all due initially to her humble, handwritten notes.

It is in those days long ago when bibles became available to the public to become dog-eared, yellow-paged genealogical histories that would otherwise be forgotten, that our story begins.

CHAPTER ONE

JOHN FOXE

In about 1450 the printing press was invented in Germany. Before that all books, bibles notices and news were hand written. The invention had an immediate affect that allowed much information to be accessed by people unlike anything previous generations had known. It wasn't used for ill until 1513 when over-indulgent Catholic Pope Leo X who had massive, grand plans for beautifying the Vatican used it to create a printed piece of paper, called 'Indulgences'.

These printed papers promised relief from eternal penalties in the Hereafter. Martin Luthor rose to significance challenging the idea that the Pope was able to offer eternal life and challenged the Indulgences forcefully. The Reformation era had begun.[222] In addition, up till now the Bible had only been printed in Hebrew, Aramaic and Greek and only scholars and the church could disseminate its truths. William Tyndale is credited for deciphering and printing into English, the first Bible. The literature was immediately forbidden. About the same time, King Henry VIII of the House of Tudors who had taken the Throne in 1509, was often at odds with the Catholic Church in England, due to his many wives.

In this turbulent time was born the son of a family of middling prominence with long roots in England, an unusually devout and studious young man, named John Foxe, born in Boston, Lincolnshire, about 1516. His father died when he was young and the relationship he had with his step-father was cool. These events shaped the young man, who poured himself into scholastic pursuits and exhibited an "indefatigable zeal and industry" for them. Letters found from about 1544 show him to be *"a man of friendly disposition and warm sympathies, deeply religious, an ardent student, zealous in making acquaintance with scholars."*[342] He talked theology with William Tyndale and Martin Luthor and counted as friends the fathers of the Reformation movement. John Foxe was a man with as deep of a sense of conviction as was his desire to learn.

With English, Irish and German origins, the animal itself is the root of the surname Fox. Beginning as Fuchs in Germany, it was at its earliest Foxe, in England and bore its origin in Ireland from the Anglo-Norman de Bosque or Old Gaelic, "Mac a'tSionnaigh", which meant "son of the fox". It is also said that the decidedly English sounding name of Fox, originated from the French word Vaux, the plural form of val; meaning valley or dale. For this reason, it is believed, that those that originally used the name, 'Vaux', were valley dwellers. Ancestry.com identifies my ethnicity as 48% English Northwestern European, 12% Germanic European and 40% Scottish.[86]

Surnames became common in the 11th century and it's said that the prominent 11th century noble, a Norman Knight named Robert I de Vaux of Petney can be traced to the beginning of the name. The Fox and Cobb lines chronicled here are both descendants of Norman invaders, who descended from Vikings and secured a settlement on Frankish soil, in the valley of the lower Seine. In this regard, the story of being 'valley dwellers' would concur with DNA results that show the Virginia Fox line began with Norman invaders in 1066. First mention of the Fox surname came in 1273, when the name of John Fox was listed in the "Hundred Rolls of Yorkshire". The line of Fox's whose lives are detailed here have their origins mainly in England but also Scotland.[217]

The Anglo-Saxon origin of the Cobbs name was originally derived from the Old English word, Cobba, that described large, impressive features and great strength. DNA indicates the Ambrose Cobbs family originated in Scotland, where Jon Cob in Ardoch appears as witness in 1479.[176]

In Europe as the Reformation began, in 1525, there were those believers that did not want to reform the church, but wholly restore it to its initial purity and simplicity. They called themselves, the Anabaptist Movement. They were persecuted greatly by the Catholic Church.

King Henry VIII had an infamous appetite for wives during this era, but as a Catholic he had the Pope to answer to. When his first wife would not bear him a male heir, he wanted to marry Anne Boleyn, but this was forbidden. It's important to note Henry met Anne, through her sister, Mary, whom he was already having a relationship with. When Henry married Anne despite opposition, he was excommunicated from the Catholic Church and so created the Church of England, wherein he made the rules, thereby ending the country's association with Catholicism. When the new church made many of the same trappings of Catholicism, the Reformation movement began in earnest to purge all traces of Catholicism from the church.

In this search for purity of religion, the Puritans were born. In retaliation, William Tyndale, credited for making the forbidden literature of the Bible available to the masses, was strangled, while tied to the stake and his body burned, in 1536. In 1538 William Cowbridge joined hundreds of others who were sentenced to death during the deadly reign of King Henry for exercising their beliefs. Cowbridge too, was sentenced to death, *"for being involved in the publication of the Bible in English".*[358] Sentenced by Longland, Bishop of Lincoln, he was burned to death in Oxford. In the crowd, listening to his screams and howls until the flames extinguished his cries, was John Foxe. There was no doubt, that for those that practiced the dissemination of information, that if they were caught, they would share the same grisly, tortuous murder in front of a howling crowd screaming for blood.[342]

An educated man of conviction, knowing the repercussions of his decisions, John became a Protestant in 1545 and summarily resigned his position from his college as he understood his beliefs were now condemned by the Church of England. One of the main reasons that John turned away from Catholicism was for the fact that in about a year he would have been obliged to take holy orders by Michaelmas, requiring clerical celibacy. In letters he described the practice to friends as self-castration.

Under King Henry VIII, coming out as a Protestant was by no means done without risk and John's decision angered his stepfather, fracturing their already weak relationship. He fell on hard times and was taken in by a friend. With his job lost and his family not speaking to him, John turned to tutoring for a living and it was here that he began to work in that regard for Thomas Lucy of Charlecote, near Stratford-on-Avon. Because of the political climate, Lucy hid John in the house for his safety.

Despite his living conditions, while employed by Lucy, John married Agnes Randall, on February 3, 1547 and in the ensuing years would share the birth of reportedly 6-12 children, of whom only 6 reached adulthood. Of his children, he had two named Samuel and two named Thomas. It was a common practice in that time to name children similarly, if one had died, or was the product of another marriage.

As a leader of the Reformation movement, John Foxe was a marked man for much of his life. John used the new technology of the printing press well before the pen was believed more powerful than the sword. In March of 1563 John published an 1800 page English version of *Actes and Monuments*, also known as *The Book of Martyrs*, that he dedicated to the Queen. It made him instantly famous and in doing so, he became the first literary celebrity in history.

It was read as widely as the Bible itself among Puritans. The Catholics, however, brought vast amounts of criticism on the work and detested the martyrs that John wrote about. When he published the second edition he omitted some material but bolstered other claims that resulted in the second edition being 2300 pages, in two great tomes. This second edition was so well received by the English church that copies were ordered to be placed in every church and in the homes of all church leaders for the use of their servants and visitors. As his contemporaries were jailed, John often took their place at the pulpit. On one such occasion he preached a fiery Good Friday sermon at Paul's Cross, which was so well received that it was expanded upon and published later as *A Sermon of Christ Crucified.*[342]

John led a life that was by no means easy and studied often to the detriment of his health, in fact toward the end of his life, those that saw him, hardly recognized him. As an old man, it was some consolation no doubt, that he lived to see the first Reformation church gathered at Norfolk, England, in 1581.

John Foxe died April 18, 1587 and was buried at St Giles's Cripplegate. Through his works promoting the Reformation and Puritan movements, John inadvertently ended up being among those who took part in the creation of the New World and religious freedom in America. Agnes his wife, likely lived until 1605 and his son Samuel was to prosper greatly after his death while another son named Thomas, became a doctor. A grandson or nephew named Thomas, is suspicioned to have been an investor who, if for financial gain, would build upon his grandfather or uncle's work, promoting a settlement in America.[342; 307]

In John's waning years, specifically in the year 1583, Sir Humphrey Gilbert drowned while returning from a fishing expedition to Newfoundland. In his death, a charter was left unfulfilled that he had been given by Queen Elizabeth I.[289] In turn, his half-brother, Sir

Walter Raleigh worked to assume the charter, for the colonization of The New World. A settlement had to be established in order for Raleigh to not lose the charter, intended to bring great wealth to those involved. It called virtually for the establishment of a military base meant to thwart the efforts of Spain and provoke them as well.

Raleigh himself did not go along in the spring of 1584 when he sent Philip Armadas and Arthur Barlowe to explore the coastline for a suitable site. The group landed at what would become Roanoke Island on the Virginia shoreline, where they established relations with the native Croatan Indians. When Armadas and Barlowe returned to England they brought along Manteo and Wanchese, two of the natives they had met, who were able to describe in flamboyant accuracy, the geography and native tribes that inhabited the area.

A year later in 1585, based on their information, a second expedition comprising of five main ships, left Plymouth, England to establish a colony in the New World.[350] The expedition led by Sir Richard Grenville was separated by a storm but had made a contingency plan to meet at Puerto Rico in such an instance. *The Tiger*, commanded by Grenville, separated from the others, sailed for the agreed meeting site. While waiting, they encountered Spanish residents and put up a fort from which Grenville simultaneously traded with and conducted raids upon the Native people.

Tiring of waiting, Grenville abandoned the fort and sailed for their original settlement site. Striking a shoal in the Ocracoke Inlet, *The Tiger* lost most of its storage of food, but were able to effect repairs and yet meet up with Roebuck and Dorothy that had been there for some weeks. A fourth ship, The *Red Lion*, had dropped its passengers off already and departed for privateering activities in Newfoundland.[350]

By the time *The Tiger* arrived on scene, settlers had already landed onshore and in their initial scouting of the area, had encountered a village of Aquascogoc Indians. Despite initially being friendly, at a point the colonists believed one of the natives stole a silver cup and accused them of the crime. When the accusation was denied, the colonists set upon the Indians, sacking their village and setting it afire. When *The Tiger* arrived and heard the news, there was yet little trepidation about the confrontation and so after unloading the remaining colonists and supplies, they sailed away on August 17, 1585 intending to return the following year.

Led by Ralph Lane, 107 people were left alone on an unexplored shore, on an unexplored continent, to set about and build a colony. Bad blood between the colonists and the Indians over the treatment of the Aquascogoc village increased throughout the year. By the following April in 1586, Grenville had not arrived and tensions increased until in June the Indians attacked the colonists new-built fort. Shortly after the colonists successfully repelled their attackers, Sir Francis Drake stopped by on his way back from a successful time of raiding Spanish ships in the Caribbean. Offering to take the besieged colonists home, many quickly jumped into row boats, though many did not.[350]

As it turned out, Grenville's relief fleet arrived shortly after Drake had departed. But when a landing party went ashore, they found no sign of colonists. Those left behind were simply gone. In order to protect Raleigh's claim to Roanoke Island, Grenville left 15 men behind to maintain an English presence.

The following year Raleigh sent Simon Fernandez to lead ships back to the New World where he would drop off 115 colonists to re-inhabit the abandoned fort. Anchored offshore, their longboats approached the quiet settlement. The landing party thought it was curious when at least some of the 15 men that had been left behind, didn't come out on the beach to greet them. As the explorers and settlers made their way across the coarse dark sand to the fort, they encountered no one and heard nothing but the sounds of the sea and the birds upon it. Inside the fort was empty but for a single skeleton. With growing fear, the colonists returned to the ships with news they wanted back aboard and to leave the island. Fernandez denied them access to the ships and insisted they return to the colony. He then sailed away, leaving them to their own survival.[350]

The colonists were led by John White, who had been among the first group of colonists; he assumed the title of governor. In the next month's relations were established between some Native Indians, but those whose village had been burned harbored deadly intentions for the White men. While crabbing by himself, colonist George Howe was murdered by Indians shortly after White had tried to hold a meeting of Indians and colonists. The colonists were alone and they were scared. By the following year they had talked Governor John White into returning to England to explain the dire situation they faced. Despite a treacherous time of year, the leader of the colonists disembarked to procure his people relief.[350]

Rushing to return with relief for his family and friends White procured supplies and a ship, but his captain refused to sail to the New World at a dangerous time of year so the relief mission was canceled. John White was stuck in England while his family was isolated thousands of miles away on a continent inhabited by deadly natives. Then the Spanish Armada attacked England and every ship was needed for the Anglo-Spanish War, making his procurement of passage impossible. By the spring of 1588 White had managed to procure two small ships and began for the colony with supplies. On the way, the ship's captain spotted several Spanish ships and intending to fatten his profit, set upon them. To the dismay of John White, the Spanish defeated the attempt and in fact took both his ships captive and sacked them for their supplies, sailing away.

With no supplies left, White returned to England. It was three more years before he could persuade another ship to attempt to take relief to the colonists. Walter Raleigh and John Watts were upon a privateering expedition to the Caribbean and gave White passage, promising to stop on their way back from their plunder.

Ironically, White set foot back onshore of Roanoke Island on August 18, 1590; the third birthday of his granddaughter whom he had left behind with the other colonists. Just as before, White walked up the stony beach, leading members of the relief party as he had done before, when Fernandez abandoned them. And just as before, no one ran out to meet them. The group fell gravely silent the further they walked into the tropical island forest, until they came upon the fort. Just as before, it was abandoned. Ninety men, 17 women and 11 children, all gone without a trace. The only evidence they had ever been there was the abandoned structure and dilapidated wood fence that surrounded it. On the fence they found the word "Croatoan" and nearby on a tree, the letters, CRO. History would call them the Lost Colony. For John White, they were his lost family.[350]

Twelve years went by before in 1602 Walter Raleigh financed his own expedition to investigate what had happened to the colonists. Still intending to make money on the voyage, Raleigh landed near the Outer Banks to gather aromatic wood, like sassafras. As fate would have it, by the time they were ready to go to the colony on Roanoke Island the weather had turned and it was time to go back to England, where Raleigh was promptly arrested for treason.

Bartholomew Gilbert made a final attempt in 1603 to investigate the disappearance of the colonists, but bad weather forced their ship to shore in an unknown location and a landing party led by Captain Gilbert was completely wiped out by a party of Natives. The crew sailed home alone.

Meanwhile, the Spanish had received rumor that the English colony was successful and were hunting its location as well. Consequently, when the Spanish stumbled onto the remains of the

Roanoke Colony in 1590, they didn't realize they had found it and believed it to be an abandoned outpost of a larger colony at Chesapeake Bay. By a twist of fate, the Anglo-Spanish War that prevented John White from returning with aid, also kept the Spanish from being in a position to pursue their assumptions about locating an English colony.[350]

Sir Thomas West, the 2nd Baron de le Warre died in late March of 1601, subsequently his 24 year old son, also named Thomas, just cleared of charges of insurrection against Queen Elizabeth, became the 3rd Baron De La Warre, a member of the Privy Council. The West name had become established in the 1300's by ancestor Sir Thomas West, 1st Lord West, a knight who came to be favored at the time by King Edward and his successor. Through peerage and marriage the title joined with the De La Warr title. Despite the vast contributions the West family had historically made, its greatest roles were yet to be played.[20]

Following the death of Elizabeth I in 1603, her first cousin, twice removed, the King of Scotland, James IV succeeded to the English throne and became James I in an event known as the Union of the Crowns. Persecution continued and Separatists who refused oversight of the Church of England were actively hunted, leading them to look to the New World as a home for religious freedom.[289]

CHAPTER TWO

THOMAS FOX of the VIRGINIA COMPANY OF LONDON

On April 10, 1606, a commercial enterprise was established by The Society of Adventurers patented to Sir Thomas Gates, Sir George Somers and their associates, including Thomas Fox, who acquired interest in the company paying money, rendering service or settling on land themselves, in Virginia. The Virginia Company of London was decreed by the King to be two separate companies that were given two separate territories to colonize. Their initial charter gave the two companies identical goals and while their territories overlapped, they were to keep a 100 mile buffer zone between them. Thus, late in 1606 two more groups of colonizers were on their way to America.[361]

Of those original investors, Thomas Fox, born in 1580, was a businessman with some degree of wealth and as a member of the initial "adventuring investors" that created the renowned, Virginia Company of London, was in part responsible for English settlement in the New World.[170; 361] The likely grandson or nephew of John Foxe, took an active role in facilitating the religious freedom John had begun. Thomas Fox and his fellow investors were not alone with sights on the New World. In 1608 a group of Separatists Puritans attempted on their own to escape England with intentions of creating a colony in the New World. Betrayed and their possessions taken, they spent a month in prison but they could not be deterred. A year later these Pilgrims tried for escape again, but were pursued and the women caught, while the men escaped, reaching Holland. Eventually the women were freed and reunited with their families in Amsterdam, residing in nearby Leiden. It didn't take long before Pilgrim values were at odds in what was known as a city of free thinkers.[225]

During this era, the area known as Virginia in the New World was considered to be that area from current day Florida to Maine. The Virginia Company of London landed on shore on April, 26, 1607 at a place they named Cape Henry after stopping first in the Canary Islands and then at what would become Puerto Rico.[361] They explored the immediate area and named an outlet of Chesapeake Bay, the James River, while searching for a secure location. They settled on a large piece of ground 40 miles from the ocean on a peninsula that provided natural defense from attack by limiting access by land. The area was inhabited by the Paspahegh Indians of the confederated tribes of the Powhatan. However, they found no Indians in the marshy area they chose, finding out later that the Indians had abandoned the ground for being a mosquito infested swamp with nothing to drink but tide water.[361] Travel in the untamed frontier was simplest on the water and so Chesapeake Bay offered the colonists ease of travel while also isolating them from unfriendly Natives. Trails created by both Indians and wildlife offered the only established means of travel. As many of those in this group were gentlemen and their man servants that were unused to physical work, the demands of building a colony were far more than they were used to. Of note among these emigrants was Chaplain Robert Hunt. In the matter of a few months, over three quarters of them were dead. Perhaps provoked by their presence or another expedition up the James River by Captain Christopher Newport, the Indians who had initially welcomed the colonists, now began a series of attacks that began the end of May and lasted until the middle of July.[169]

Meanwhile, the second company of this endeavor, the Plymouth Company of the Virginia Company of London, landed ashore far north in present day Maine. This colony was abandoned a year later and the Plymouth Company discontinued its efforts at colonization. This was not the case with the Virginia Company of London to the south. Even so, the settlers in Jamestown never believed they were expected to grow all their food and be self-sustainable and nearly didn't survive the initial couple years. They yet relied on shipments that were infrequent at best. By 1608 when ships brought eight Polish and German craftsmen to join the colonists in Jamestown along with the first two European women, most of the James Fort colonists were dead or had defected to nearby Indian settlements. Many of the first colonists were employee's that worked for The Virginia Company of London that were supplied firearms, clothing and food for their work. After seven years they would be paid in land, dividends or other stock. The colony was governed first by a president and seven member council named by the King. The first two leaders faced class warfare among their own, attacking Indians and sickness. Following a successful recruiting campaign, 600 colonists settled in Virginia between the spring of 1608 and 1609.[361]

As the colony took shape, a unique idea was hatched in England by the investors of the Virginia Company of London, who began construction on a ship called *The Sea Venture*, built specifically for their purpose to resupply and deliver more emigrants to the colonies. The 300 ton ship was the first of its kind, built by the Company, specifically for the purpose of transporting emigrants and supplies to the colonies. In its maiden voyage, *The Sea Venture* became the flagship of a fleet of seven ships transporting vital items of relief to the colonies. On June 2, 1609, the fleet brought a greater amount of supplies than had ever been brought before, thanks to the urging of the colonists third leader John Smith and work behind the scenes of Lord Thomas West, who was always the colonists best advocate. There were many important individuals in this trip and many of them were aboard the flagship. By late July, the fleet unfortunately ran into a hurricane that separated the ships and *The Sea Venture* was stranded upon a reef in modern day Bermuda. While the remainder of the supply ships limped to shore, the crew and passengers of their flagship never arrived. Among those stranded in the Caribbean islands, was the newly appointed deputy governor of Virginia, Sir Thomas Gates as well as John Rolfe and many other individuals important to the future of the colonies. In fact there were over 150 survivors and a dog that became residents of the cluster of tropical islands. In the colonies the remaining ships of the relief party limped to the James River. Despite their harrowing journey, the supplies and people the armada brought did the job of raising morale and for a time, it looked as if the fledgling colony was getting a foot hold.[361]

Then came, “The Starving Time”, in the winter of 1609-1610, when the Powhatan Indians began a series of assaults that isolated the colonists from tending their crops or hunting. Concurrently, a severe drought laid siege upon the land and the combination of factors created a famine. The Starving Time took the population from 500 in the fall to tragically only 60 by the following spring. The hostilities between the native people and the colonists would last four more years and become known as the First Anglo-Powhatan War. When 9 months later, the survivors of the shipwrecked *Sea Venture* finally arrived in Virginia months after their ship had wrecked, only a fraction of the colonists were alive. Trapped and starving, the desperate colonists had resorted to cannibalism to survive. The shipwrecked survivors, believing the colonies were flush and prospering, had brought no food along and now found themselves joining the ranks of these meager, starved and dying Virginians. Of those having survived being shipwrecked in the Caribbean John Rolfe carried in his pockets tobacco seeds brought from Bermuda, where the stuff grew wild since the Spanish had planted it many years before. His plan was to see how it would grow. No one knew those simple seeds would change everything for the colonists and in doing so, alter the future of the world.[306]

When spring came, the desperate survivors boarded ships, abandoning the settlement and sailed for Chesapeake Bay. Here they were intercepted by a convoy of supply ships led by Sir Thomas West, 3rd Baron De La Warre. Though they weren't pleased about it, they were given escort back to Jamestown. Along the way they were given news that the previous year in 1609 the Company had received a new, second charter that allowed them to elect a president from their shareholders. Sir Thomas West, 3rd Baron De La Warre was the newly appointed governor-for-life and captain-general of the Virginia colonies to replace the governing council. [361] The fleeing colonists had lost all hope of survival and his escort was not well received, but the colonists found in time they began to fare much better under his leadership. It was a turning point for those isolated settlers in a land never cultivated; the home of fierce native people that were just as likely to kill as not. Captain John Smith, locked up by his political foes, was released from the brig and was elected as the third governor of the colony. In contrast to the previous leadership, Smith immediately and forcefully invoked the biblical principle, *"he that will not work, shall not eat"*.[245] Under this new leadership, strife began to ease for the colonists. John Smith made no secret of his disgust with the work ethics of many of the colonists. In no uncertain terms he told them, *"the labors of 30 or 40 honest and industrious men shall not be consumed to maintain 150 idle loiterers"*.[245] This was not England and there were no servants, there was only work and that work had to be divided in order for all to survive. The idea may have been met with disdain by those accustomed to class-rights, but its logic was indisputable in this naked frontier. In England, the upper crust was horrified that the well-to-do had to work alongside their servants in the colonies. However in fact, though everyone was made to labor, there were still indentured servants, both White and Black. Twice ships brought emigrants with some supplies, however it was not really enough to truly bolster them. Despite that, the colonists under John Smith's direction, were gaining ground in establishing their settlement and the beleaguered and ragged emigrants began to see their hope grow.[346]

Back in England, the rug was pulled from under the Virginia Company of London as many new investors reneged on their subscriptions and a handful of lawsuits tied them up in court, even as they were compelled to take hundreds more to the colonies. As the company imploded, it threw itself into a massive publicity campaign to publicize the virtue of colonization. Street signs on every corner and bits in newspapers extolled the promises of the New World. Several pamphlets, books and articles were written and the clergy was even compelled to extol the virtues of colonization. Everyone was talking about The New World. For God, King and England the public became consumed in the publicity and investing once again soared. However, unknown to those in England, back in the colonies life was no better and the mortality rate remained high.[361]

Just as uniquely American ideas were being planted one at a time in the psyches of the colonists heads, seeds of tobacco from John Rolfe's pockets were growing in brush-cleared meadows. By 1614, Rolfe was very successfully harvesting tobacco and married the daughter of Pocahontas. Their union brought peace between the Indians and colonists and contributed to their overall success as much as the new tobacco crop.[361]

CHAPTER THREE

JOHN FOX, MARINER

Little else is left known of Thomas Fox, investor in the Virginia Company of London, except that he supposedly had a son named John, in 1615 who became a ship's captain. John Fox was the first Fox to set foot on the North American continent.[20; 78] Additionally it appears that this merchant ship Captain John Fox used the name Richard when he served in the military.[78] Family stories related without prior knowledge of what scholars accepted as "fact" include the exploits of a "Richard Fox", that are nearly identical to known historical facts. Indeed, when John Fox disappears from historical record, Richard Fox appears without a past and when his military service ends, Richard disappears and John Fox reappears. While we may never know what the reason for a change in names was, it might be that John Fox was simply a man who had an identity to hide. In any event, young John Fox was educated, ambitious, rebellious and willful; the eldest of his siblings, he was the only one that would choose and then survive to make America his home. In his time, though John was born in England he was prominently known as one of "the Irish Fox's".[78] When John Fox was born, James VI had ruled Scotland for nearly 50 years and England and Ireland for 12 as James I.

The other Englishmen besides the Virginia Company of London that had their sights on the New World, the Pilgrims, finally had an opportunity for colonization. In 1608 church Separatists called Pilgrims, escaped England desiring to colonize in the New World to practice their puritanical religion. Leaving their temporary home in Holland, the Pilgrims were unable to colonize that year when they landed on shore but were afraid to be inside the King's jurisdiction, so returned to personal exile in Holland. They remained there for eight years working together toward the goal of still creating a colony of their own before in desperation they reached out to the country they had escaped from. Some were so desperate that they joined groups going to Virginia, but most wanted more privacy and anonymity, fearing a replication of the politics in England. Finally, in 1616, as the second charter for the Virginia Company of London was nearing expiration, the Puritans sailed for England to negotiate for rights to colonize and freely practice their religion. While the idea was greeted with great acceptance by the Company, the King was hesitant to relinquish any power over controlling the colonizers. Despite royal concerns, emissaries from the Virginia Company of London were able to get an agreement wherein they granted the Pilgrims a 'patent' on the land as long as the Pilgrims would recognize the King's authority.[225] While it might have seemed like a capitulation, when the Pilgrims sailed away from England there was little the King could do, until a ship showed up. From this compromise was realized in the minds of Americans, the idea of religious freedom.

As the Virginia Company of London's debts soared, they were given a third charter that allowed them to run a lottery and allow the Virginia assembly to act as their own legislature and added 300 leagues of ocean to the colonies which made Bermuda part of Virginia. As the company struggled to stay afloat, in 1616 the original colonists finished their 7 year stint and wanted paid. The company was forced to renege on cash payments and instead offer 50 acre parcels in payment. The following year the company came up with the 'headright' system. Investors and residents were able to acquire land in paying the passage of new settlers. In most cases these new emigrants would work for a period of time on the companies land before being released. This system brought the wealthy and their servants as well as brought common people willing to be indentured servants for a time. In this transaction the idea that the ownership of land was money, began.[361]

Following some internal disputes in the Virginia Company of London about how strictly to control the colonists, The Great Charter was passed. Instead of adhering to strict British controls, the Company endeavored to make the colony more attractive, by allowing more freedoms and bringing more women to the colonies so more English families would be established there. While the company was concerned about the success of their venture, their promotion of freedom in the colonies were laying the cornerstones of something far bigger.[361]

In 1619 a general assembly was held in the Jamestown Church, the first in the New World. While they joined to simply agree to form a loose government that would ensure their happiness, they only allowed Englishmen to vote. The recently arrived Polish artisans found that rule unfair and so staged the first labor strike in the New World; no vote, no work. The Poles and Slovaks were given their vote and the assembly went on to separate the colony into four distinct boroughs that they called ‘cities’, of 1500 acres each. They were chief county Jamestown, Charles, Henrico and Kiccowtan. The boundaries were drawn so that land owners were inside the colonies. In addition, plantations could be cultivated if they were five miles from an established colony. The policies themselves encouraged spreading out, which led to violence with Indians that felt the policy foul. In this assembly the idea of individual land ownership was made the law. While each of these small events proved to burgeon their little colony, they also created pride among them and the simple idea that they were there to own land and be happy. The rules they made would set the stage for what would become the conquering of the last frontier on the planet. By establishing the idea of individual land ownership, there were no Natives consulted and so it would also become the death knoll of the Native Indians. The colonists did not set out to displace Indians, but were simply looking for peace and felt the natives were not utilizing the land and there was plenty of it they could move to. Unfortunately, the peace and happiness of the colonists was at the cost of land that the Indians did not appreciate giving up.[444]

Having held up in Holland for some time, the separatist Pilgrims feared their children were in danger of losing their English heritage and their religious beliefs and so in September of 1620, finally set sail in the Mayflower, landing at Plymouth Rock as winter was setting in. Separated widely from other colonies, with little time to prepare for winter weather, their first months were dismal. In time, however, they began to thrive.[225]

By 1621 the Virginia Company of London had held so many lotteries and reneged on so many promises that investors were more than wary. To complicate matters, on March 22, 1622 the uneasy peace between the colonists and the Powhatan Indians was ended when Chief Opchanacanough and his Powhatan Confederacy staged an uprising intending to kill every colonist in the New World. Beginning in the outlying plantations and communities that had grown along the James River, the Indians killed 300 people; fully a quarter of the population of the colonies; one third of all English speaking colonists. It was a blood-bath. If it hadn't been for a timely warning from an Indian employee, Jamestown itself might have been wiped out too. It became known as the Indian Massacre of 1622, or the Second Anglo-Powhatan War.[293; 300] In response to unfavorable conditions, the Virginia Company of London was offered a fourth charter that severely reduced the companies rights to make decisions in the governing of Virginia. The shareholders rejected it and in turn, in 1624, King James revoked the charter and Virginia became a royal colony that would be led by a governor named by a King.[361]

In 1625 King James VI died, leaving his son Charles I, as heir to the throne. Charles was of the belief in the divine right of kings and clashed with parliament. He was known to be contrary and it ruffled feathers. When he levied taxes without consulting parliament, he raised the ire of many subjects who saw him as a tyrant. In 1634, by order of King Charles, the colonies in the New World were divided into eight shires, in the style common to England. Jamestown became James City shire and over time, as shires became counties, it became known simply as James City.[337]

Married to a French catholic, Charles supported high church Angelican ecclesiastics and failed to aid Protestant efforts in The Thirty Year War, developing distrust between himself and Reformed groups like the English Puritans and the Scotch Covenanters who believed he was too Catholic. Finally, his attempt to force those Angelican practices upon the Church of Scotland led to the Bishop's War. By 1640, parliament was calling for the impeachment of Charles' leading councilors for treason and in turn the King began to arrest those who opposed him. Facing opposition from the Scotch, the Irish and his own government, tensions rose until rumors began to circulate that Parliament might raise an army in opposition. When Charles wanted to raise money to put down Irish rebellion, his parliament was hesitant to help for fear the ruler would use the army he raised to slaughter them. Instead, they passed the Militia Ordnance, intending to wrest control of the military from the King. The move raised the ire of the English Lords, who rallied to Charles side.[337]

In America in 1630, some Pilgrims founded the town of Boston. It was soon to become a political, financial, commercial, religious and educational center in the New World. South of the New England Pilgrim colony, in the Virginia colony, the population reached 5,000 by 1634 and the General Assembly found it more efficient to divide the colony into eight counties, including the four they had created in

1619. Including established counties of Henrico, Charles, Jamestown and Kiccowtan that was deemed a heathen name so was renamed Elizabeth City, Charles River county became the county of York and the counties of Accumack, Charles River, Warrosquyoake and Warwick River were established, altering names and boundaries as the years passed. Just three years later Warrosquyoake was renamed Isle of Wight. The boundaries for counties on the mainland were broad stretching west and reached well into what was still deemed a limitless frontier.[169]

Connecting the colonies of New England and Virginia was The Great Path, called the War Path in places along the Ohio River, or the Mohawk Trail in the Connecticut valley. The paths were ancient native thoroughfares that were adopted by the Europeans who found them all along the coastline and connecting inland to the Great Lakes region. Used for commerce, hunting and general travel by both Whites and Indians, the trail could be dangerous, but vital.[296]

Growing to manhood with benefit of private schools and exposure to his father's business dealings including summers in Wales on the family farm, it might be considered that John Fox had a silver spoon in his mouth. But that would not be the whole story, for the boy was naturally adventurous, inquisitive and hard working as well. By the time of the English Civil War, John had become the commander of the merchant ship, *The White Horse And Curry Comb*, which conducted trade with the English colonies in Virginia.[20] While Capt. John Fox might thank his father for his initial opportunities to learn his trade and indeed in part for a trade route to Virginia, he became a ship's captain of his own volition, earning respect and his title, with his honesty and hard work.

He was married in London, England to a woman named Anne, who may have been a cousin, but her surname cannot be proven. The couple had a daughter they named Anne. Strong of limb as he was of will, Captain John Fox was a proud and accomplished mariner. His actions in life prove he was a man of opposing positions. While patriotic and politically connected, his decisions in life in effect pushed him out of England, to the American Colonies. Though a supporter of the King, he was forced by his decisions ironically to leave England, to the New World, where people went to escape the Monarch. He was a family man, but his vocation kept him at sea much of the time.[78]

It can't be denied that as captain of a merchant vessel John saw first-hand the settlements in America before he settled there. He was keenly aware of the deception in advertising that was being conducted by the Virginia Company of London of which his father was invested in. He had to have seen for himself, the colonists were struggling, but given the position he was in, decided the frontier of the New World colonies was preferable to what life offered in England.

CHAPTER FOUR

AMBROSE COBBS, THE PLANTER & JOHN PUNCH, THE SLAVE

Predating the Fox family being established in the New World, were the Cobbs family. Ambrose Cobbs was born in Kent, England in 1603, the son of Ambrose Cobbs and Angelica Hunt. His mother Angelica was the sister of Robert Hunt who was chaplain in the first permanent colonies in Virginia in 1607. Ambrose married before 1627 to Anne White and they would soon have four children. Two of the children died very young and by 1633 the couple sold their farm in Kent to make ready to move their family across the ocean, to the colonies. They arrived in Virginia in 1635 and on July 25, 1639 Ambrose Cobbs patented 350 acres at the mouth of the Appomattox River, to pay the headright to migrate for himself, his wife Anne, daughter Margaret, son Robert as well as Richard and Hugh Barker and Thomas Harvey. Ambrose Cobbs was not poor when he came to the New World and he prospered there, but probably not like he thought he would. In time Ambrose and Anne had two additional sons named Ambrose and Thomas who would prosper greatly.[78]

If prostitution was the oldest profession, slavery was the next. By the time the English colonized the New World, slavery had been practiced for over 3000 years in many different forms, by all races and was a common, accepted institution all over the planet. In the English colonies that first settled Virginia they practiced the common form of chattel bonded labor. This was usually to settle debt and had a time limit. Spanish colonies, established in the New World prior, practiced chattel slavery in which there is no end to the servitude. In the English colonies most of the chattel servants were White Europeans and only few were Black.[304] At this time, stepping out of the shadows and into the history of mankind, came indentured servant, John Punch.

By the year 1640 in Virginia, along the Charles River, there lived a wealthy landowner named Hugh Gwyn; a justice of the peace and member of the House of Burgesses for Charles River Shire. One of his indentured servants serving a limited chattel service bond was a Black man named John Punch.

At that time there was little stigma attached to the idea that Punch was married to a White woman. She was also an indentured servant and the couple had a son named John. In 1640, John Punch and two fellow indentured servants, a Dutchman and a Scotsman, ran away to Maryland. Securing a legal order, Gwyn went armed and retrieved the men from where they had taken refuge; returning them to the fate of local courts.

Keenly aware of common law that held a Christian could not enslave a Christian, the two White men were sentenced to 30 lashes each and to serve out their terms of indenture, plus four additional years for their infraction. With no such common law boundary to protect non-Christian Black man John Punch, the court cited his "being a negro" as their excuse and sentenced him to the punishment of 30 lashes but additionally condemned him to work until his death, for Hugh Gwyn.[244]

While the line between indentured chattel servant and slave might have been blurred before, this life-sentence surely made John Punch the first slave in the English colonies. This was the first time of record that a Black man was treated differently than a White, setting off 200 years of bitter debate that would culminate in a bloody Civil War in America that ended the practice, though it continues around the world still today.[345; 244]

Reformation continued mainly in Europe and with it the Church of England suffered dozens of defections, spawning new ideas of ideologies. The decade from about 1640 to 1650, saw many new religions give rise. George Fox who is of no relation to those detailed here is given responsibility for having begun the Quaker movement during that period. As the population struggled with the subject of religion, another congregation began that appropriately called themselves, The Seekers.[236]

CHAPTER FIVE

BRITISH CIVIL WAR

British colonies were solidly established by 1640; their encroachment displacing many tribes of Indians. Despite the unsure relations between settlers and Indians, settlers needed the Natives and some tribes fared better than most others in this regard. The Cherokee migrated southwest from Virginia as the colonial population grew while the Iroquois began a lucrative trade in furs with the colonials that continued for over 100 years.[308]

In 1642 as John Fox returned to England from a typical trip to Virginia, he found his country preparing for war and was immediately drawn into it. Both the King and his parliament were arming for a confrontation that had been building for years. The combination of Thomas Fox, holding an elevated social position with the Royals as well as the education he had been given, provided his relative John, a means to become a cavalier officer under Prince Rupert, a nephew of the King. From this point on until his service ended, John used the name Richard, which may have been his formal name, though it's more likely he used it to allow some level of anonymity considering the nature of civil war, pitting friends and family against one another. Regardless, he distinguished himself in a number of important engagements in the rank of Captain.[78]

By 1643 the combatants were engaged and King Charles instructed the 7th Earl of Derby, James Stanley, to fortify the Isle of Man against a Scottish invasion and then move to join the northern campaign. This left Stanley's wife Charlotte de la Tremouille in command of the impressive fortification of the family home, Lathom House. Setting in the lowest point of a naturally vast 'bowl', surrounded by an eight yard wide moat and six foot thick walls, there were impressively, nine towers with six cannons in each, with three pointing each direction and another Eagle Tower situated in the center, providing an unobstructed view of the open expanse all around.

It was here Richard Fox served as one of six captains protecting the vital fortification. As fighting intensified, Her "she-Majesty generalisima over all", the Countess of Derby, prepared for certain siege. When the city of Warrington, on the River Marsey fell to the Parliamentarians, Sir Thomas Fairfax immediately demanded the Countess acknowledge Parliaments authority and surrender her house. She refused in no uncertain terms. The scene was set and inside Richard Fox, as one of the six captains bracing for imminent attack, took his assignment by means of a lottery.[78]

The siege began in February with snipers taken from the ranks of the best marksmen around who had hunted with the Earl of Derby, placed in the towers of the castle. Before them, the ground sloped upward giving them a naturally convenient view of the entrenchments of the enemy. Hunters and woodsmen rained deadly fire upon the Parliamentarians, slaying officers coming and going from cover of their encampment.

On Wednesday, April 10, 1644 the enemies engaged with Capt. Fox flying colors from the Eagle Tower to direct the movement of the Royalist troops. From the elevation of the imposing tower Capt. Fox was able to direct his troops in such a way that the enemy was stymied by their very movement. Reduced to cannon and mortar fire against the Lathom House, the Parliamentarians did little or no damage and each time they tried to relocate a battery closer to the castle, they were shot upon to such effect they were forced to retreat.[78]

Finally mortars were placed that had deadly effects and for some time the Royalists were taking a beating. A plan was hatched and at 4am on Saturday, April 27th, men poured out of the castle into the early morning light, to capture the mortars.

A bloody conflagration raged that day and many Parliamentarian positions were lost to the Royalists. Capt. Fox distinguished himself and his men when the captured artillery they were sent after, was lifted from its rest and drug back to the Lathom House with nothing but the strength of desperate and determined men. When the mortar had been drug across the moat and into the court yard, the raging battle quieted as if in response.

In the odd quiet, all eyes turned to look at the great artillery piece and the battle bloodied men that had not only captured, but removed it from the enemies arsenal. In that sudden and odd silence of an otherwise chaotic battlefield, inside the great walls, men began to grin. Then a roaring shout rose up from those beleaguered Royalists, as stares of awe became smiles and shouts of celebration. It was a great exploit and one that would be remembered by everyone that lived to see it, recorded in history by the written word.[78]

Outside the thick walls of the Lathom House, the Parliamentarians were beside themselves with frustration. That evening, in response to the shellacking he had taken, Fairfax ordered a day of fasting and prayer. One of the Parliamentarian chaplains invoked Jeremiah 50:14 "*Put yourselves in array against Babylon on every side: all ye that bend the bow, shoot at her, spare no arrows: for she hath sinned against the Lord.*"[357]

To avoid any more loss, the second night of the siege the Parliamentarians pulled all their cannons back except one, which they spiked, to ruin. When Fairfax procured a letter from Lord Stanley that asked for his wife's safe passage in surrender of the Latham House, he sent a messenger, producing it to the Countess, who bluntly refused the offer. When a messenger from Colonel Alexander Rigby gave her a post asking for her honorable surrender, she tore it up and told the messenger, *"Carry this answer back to Rigby, and tell that insolent rebel, he shall have neither persons, goods nor house. When our strength and our provisions are spent we shall find a fire more merciful than Rigby; and then, if the providence of God prevent it not, my goods and my house will burn in his sight; and myself, children and soldiers, rather than fall in his hands will seal our religion and loyalty in the same flames."*[354]

Then she threatened to hang the messenger from the front gate and sent him back to his superiors. Not one for good humor, the Countess was uncharacteristically satisfied with herself and her people to such degree she called for a day of thanksgiving saying that God Almighty called for it. Captain Fox was promoted to the office of Major.[354]

With the castle surrounded, from a safe distance, on May 23, Col. Rigby made a similar ultimatum to the ensconced Countess, who sent the reply, *"The mercies of the wicked are cruel..."* and that unless they *"treated with her lord, they should never take her or any of her friends alive."* Four days later the House of Latham was saved when the Royalist General Rupert arrived with thousands of infantry and cavalry. Colonel Rawstorne took command of the besieged house as Charlotte and her household departed for the Isle of Man and Major Fox was given a new assignment under Prince Rupert. [357]

The House of Latham lasted another year before the Parliamentarians returned with four thousand infantry and cavalry besides ordnance. The second siege lasted about six months before Col. Rawstorne accepted that his supplies were low and aid was not forthcoming. By the summer of 1644, the general Prince Rupert, rode north to provide support to Newark and York, which were under serious threat from Scottish Covenanter and Parliamentarian armies. King Charles remained in the south, engaging the army of the Earl of Essex and battling at Newbury before winter closed in and the fighting turned to the negotiation table.

Nothing was gained during the winter and so in the spring, the combatants engaged again. This time Rupert and Charles combined their forces and attacked Parliaments New Model Army, with varying levels of effectiveness.

Inexplicably at the onset of a major engagement, in one fateful moment, the King rode forward to rally his troops, but as he advanced, Lord Carnwath, believing the monarch in danger, grabbed hold of his reigns. Seen from a distance, the retreat of the King was taken as a sign to move back and when they did, their position collapsed. It was the last major engagement of the war that year and was soon followed by a number of defeats for the Royalists.[337]

Meanwhile, in the colonies, in 1644, the Powhatan Indians staged another large scale attack upon the colonists, in what became the third Anglo-Powhatan War.[308] Using weapons fashioned from the woods around them and painted fearfully, screaming with such shrill effect it rose the hair on ones scalp; the Natives were seen as savages.

In the eyes of colonists, the Indians were doing nothing with the land and therefore saw it within their rights to live there and do something with it. If the Indians wanted a fight over the land, they were gonna get one, because there was no backing up for these people; there was no retreat and no one was coming to save them. Once a colonist watched a ship sail away, it quickly became clear they alone were responsible for their own safety and that of their family and friends. Survival was their responsibility. Self-defense; being clannish; individualism and pride in surviving together were natural traits shared almost immediate by colonial Americans.

In 1646, the Indian Chief Opchanacanough was captured and against orders, was shot in the back by an English guard, killing him. The murderer coerced his successor to sign the first peace treaty between the colonists and the Powhatan Confederacy, rather than start a war.

Opchanacanough had held great position for the Powhatans and when he was killed their tribes began to slide into decline. The treaty they signed required the Indians to pay yearly tribute payment to the English colonists and restricted them to reservations. The acquiescence of the Powhatan Confederacy saw the last chance that Native Americans might have been able to expunge the threat of Englishmen from their shores. It would, however, not nearly be the last effort by Native Americans.[300; 308]

By the spring of 1646 in England, Parliament laid siege to Oxford and Charles was only able to escape, disguised as a servant. Finally surrounded, Charles gave himself to the Scottish Presbyterian army that laid siege to the city and was taken north to Newcastle upon Tyme. The Scots held Charles for nearly a year while they negotiated with the English for the monarch as well as the ground they had fought for and won. After nine months, the Scots arrived at their price for the King and Newcastle and delivered him to them in January 1647.

Originally held at Holdenby House, in Northamptonshire, Charles was taken by threat of force, by Cornet George Joyce of the New Model Army who were seeking a larger role in government. His imprisonment changed location a number of times before Charles realized his best bet was escape. On November 11 he snuck out of Hampton Court, making contact with Colonel Robert Hammond who he felt was sympathetic. His assumptions were wholly wrong and instead Hammond locked Charles in Carisbrooke Castle and notified the Parliament where they could fetch him. Negotiations began again for the rights to King Charles I and this time, he signed an agreement with the Scots that would have them restore him to power if he would see Presbyterianism established in England for three years.[337]

The Second Civil War in England broke out in May of 1648 as great risings-up occurred when the Scots invaded England and rebellions occurred in Kent, Essex, Cumberland and in South Wales.

By August at the Battle of Preston, the Royalists were defeated and the Second Civil War was over. Charles reached back out to the negotiations table with Parliament and on December 5 they voted overwhelmingly to begin talks with him again. This drew the ire of the New Army and Oliver Cromwell, who replaced Hammond as governor of the Isle of Wight and placed him in the custody of the Army the following day. Members of Parliament were arrested or excluded from entering the building. The New Army had taken control of the English government.[337]

By the end of the year, Charles was lodged at Hurst Castle and afterwards, to Windsor Castle. In January of 1649, the Rump House of Commons indicted the King, but the Chief Justices of the three common law courts of England came down against the indictment, calling it unlawful.

When the House of Lords rejected the indictment the Rump House of Common declared their sovereign ability to legislate alone, creating a separate court for a trial of the King. Despite opposition and the ire of Royalists, the Act was passed and established 135 member commission to pass judgment. Over half of those named refused their appointment and many more were too frightened to attend. As events transpired, it became clear that it was a mock trial and Charles was being taken for a ride.

His supporters seethed. Men that had served to defend the Monarch were incensed at his treatment. In effect, there had been a coup with such effectiveness that all looked lost to most.[337] But there were three men, who believed that they might cheat the hands of death and rescue the King.

When the war was lost, John Fox escaped to Holland, where he met fellow veterans Colonel Henry Norwood and Major Francis Morrison. There, a scheme was devised to rescue the King from Carisbrooke Castle on the Isle of Man and spirit him to safety. Time and secrecy were of the utmost importance for such a plan but these were men who had friends in many places from low to high. In short order they had raised the funds to purchase a yacht and found 18 veterans with similar commitment to their purpose. When the men heard that Charles had been moved for trial in London, their plan was altered, but undeterred and they set sail for Westminster Hall, England.[115]

Because they were at sea it was unknown to the rescuers that on January 20, Charles was formally charged with putting the interests of himself and his family over that of his people and his kingdom. Parliament charged that he "*traitorously and maliciously levied war against the present Parliament, and the people therein represented*".[337]

While the idea of putting a King to trial was a new one, so was the concept of command responsibility in which Charles was charged with each act of violence committed in the war; every murder, burning, raping and spoil stolen. Considering that 300,000 had died in the conflict, the charges were multiplied.

In answer, for three days Charles refused to plead to the charges and declared a Monarch could not be tried. At the end of the third day of the standoff, Charles was removed from the court room and over the next two days, 30 witnesses against the him were heard without any representation or cross examination.

Of the 135 member commission, only 68 attended the trial and the day of Charles judgment he was sentenced to death by only 59 individuals who were hard-core Parliamentarians. His sentence was passed in a public session and reported widely in periodicals and by word of mouth. For his rescuers at sea, there was no way to know the monarch had only days left to live, and for those at Westminster there was no way to know that a rescue party was speeding toward them.[337; 78]

Charles was sentenced to death January 30, 1649. A son and daughter who were still in England, under the control of the Parliamentarians, visited their father the day before his execution, to share a tearful farewell. On the morning he was to be hanged, a cold chill lay across the land. From his chamber Charles requested two shirts so that he would not be chilled to shiver, as he did not want spectators to mistake it for fear, *"I would have no such imputations made"*. Walking under guard from St. James Palace to gallows constructed inside the confines of the Castle of Whitehall, the King was kept separated from the people by a large concentration of armed guards.[337]

Colonel Norwood and Majors Morrison and Fox arrived in London the same day Charles was beheaded, only hours before the deed was done. As they took to shore it was all people were talking about and their hearts fell, for they knew they were too late.

Rushing through the city in cloaks to obscure their identities, they made their way through Whitehall streets that became increasingly more crowded until they reached the Palace itself. The crowd spilled out into the street, tightly cramping themselves inside the walls, with those at the door standing on their toes, peeking above the mass of humanity.

In fact, the guards held the crowd back so far that no one could hear the King's last words but those on the gallows with him. Having pushed forward as far as they could, conspirators Fox, Morrison, Norwood and many of their hired muscle, were forced to watch their King speak his final words, but could not hear them.

Firstly he blamed his downfall on his failure to prevent the execution of Strafford, his faithful servant. Secondly, Charles defended the idea of Kings and subjects, when he said that while he desired liberty and freedom of the people as much as any, that their liberty resides in having a government, "*It is not their having a share in the government; that is nothing appertaining unto them. A subject and a sovereign are clean different things.*" He finished by saying, "*I shall go from a corruptible to an incorruptible Crown, where no disturbance can be.*"[337] With that King Charles lowered his head and said a prayer.

At about 2pm, the King stepped forward, knelt and placed his head on the block and when he was ready, signaled by holding his hands outstretched. He was beheaded in one stroke by an obviously experienced swordsman, the result of which drew a moan from the gathered crowd that haunted those that heard it.

The man that typically executed people had refused to do the deed, so another had disguised himself, under cover of his dreaded hood. Many conjectured of who he was. The guards ceased holding the crowd back, allowing onlookers to dab handkerchiefs into the Kings blood, for souvenir. Customarily for such an event the executioner held the head of the executed into the air, presenting them to the crowd and saying the words, *"Behold! The head of a traitor!"* however the words were never said, for the executioners fear of exposing his identity.[337]

The following day, Charles head was sewn back onto his body and he was moved to Windsor, as his burial at Westminster Abbey was refused by the commission. He was buried after a private ceremony on February 9, in St. George's Chapel at Windsor Castle and placed in the Henry VIII vault, alongside the coffins of Henry VIII and wife.

Though the Parliamentarians had succeeded in changing the government from a monarchy to a commonwealth, they had created a martyr. Angelicans formed devotional societies like, The Society of King Charles the Martyr and services were held on the anniversary of his death.[337]

There was no time to watch and see what might transpire for those that had conspired to save the King. The eighteen men gathered for the purpose, scattered for jobs on vessels that would take them home or at least away from England. Fearing for their own safety, Fox, Norwood and Morrison signed up for passage on the vessel, *The Virginia Merchant*, a ship owned by the West family, which would leave England in September, taking emigrants to America.

John Fox might have thought himself running away, but actually he was running toward his destiny. In the interim the men had to keep their heads down and not bring attention to themselves. The collaborators were concealed by Royalist sympathizers like Charles West, the 5th Baron de le Warre, who owned the vessel they planned to escape upon and was incidentally the grandson of Thomas West the 3rd Baron de le Warre, who had sailed to the relief of the colonists after The Starving Time, many years prior.[37]

John Fox left England from the Downes, with friends Norwood and Morrison on September 23, 1649 along with 130 other emigrants. Low on provisions, the ship stopped at Fyall on October 22 and then continued, slicing through known dangerous trade winds to Bermuda, where they found the weather refused to let them land. With little choice left them, they continued to Cape Hatteras, where the ship became grounded. They were able to work the vessel free and continued toward their destination but when storms rose for some days, the ship was dismasted, except the shorter mizzen mast.

Crippling along, *The Virginia Merchant* was then hit by another vessel, *The Mighty Sea*, which tore the upper deck forecastle off. Yet able to float, the crippled vessel made land on January 4, 1650. Major Morrison went ashore with the ship's mate and found water, so they sent for the crew. Leaving a skeleton crew, Colonel Norwood, Major Fox and others, took longboats to shore.

Inexplicably the following day, for no reason, the ship sailed away, leaving the landing party stranded. Desperation was such that an immediate cloud of misery surrounded them. People died and survivors were forced to cannibalize the dead before ten days later the abandoned party was found by a friendly party of Native Americans who took them in their canoes back to their village of Kickotank. Using sign language to overcome the language barrier, Norwood recognized the word "Accawmacke" as being a place in the Virginia colonies and knew they were close to other White men, but not where.

The Indian Chief sent word to the White settlement whereupon the Governor of the Colony, Sir William Berkeley sent Jenken Price, a man keen as a scout, to lead the stranded White men back to Jamestown.

Meanwhile, *The Virginia Merchant* had limped on to the James River, near the colony of Jamestown. Price, a colonial trader and early mountain man, found Norwood, Fox, Morrison and the other survivors in a ready state to leave the friendly Indian village and the group quickly made the trip back to civilization, such as it was, until they had reached what was at that time, Northampton County. Here the party rested at Price's camp on Littleton's Plantation before they traveled to Yeardley's Plantation and on across Chesapeake Bay and to the York River at Ludlow's Plantation. Across a creek, the party was met by an old acquaintance of Colonel Norwood's, who thankfully offered the use of a mount for him to continue the trek. Finally reaching colonial Jamestown in the middle of February and taking some rest, the group soon arrived at Green Spring Plantation, the home of Governor Sir William Berkeley.[37]

While family lore would sympathetically say that Berkeley was impressed by who the men were in England, therefore he gave them all appointments, Col. Norwood himself later admitted his collusion with Governor Berkeley that yielded him the title, Escheator, Treasurer and Receiver of Quit Rents in Virginia. The position meant little except for a steady stream of income that Norwood need not live in the colony to collect.

Major Morrison took a post at Point Comfort. By some accounts Major John Fox took an allotment of 640 acres and built a brick home on land in York County, that about a year later became Gloucester County, Virginia. Records indicate far less, in fact he may never have built a home on the land. The difficulty is that there were no records kept of men who paid their own charges to the colonies, rather than coming as an indentured servant.

A land grant of 200 acres dated September 20, 1650 was conveyed to Thomas Lisle, John Fox and Gilbert Thornborough. This could be additional land, or part of the 640 acre allotment John had been given. Fox, Morrison and Norwood were by no means alone in their position, in fact so many veterans of hostilities in England moved to the colonies after the execution of Charles I that 1649 was referred to as "The Great Cavalier Exodus"[12]

Both Fox and Morrison recognized good fortune when it smiled upon them, but Henry Norwood kept himself involved in intrigue, albeit while his fortune and credit suffered. From Holland to England Norwood continued his life of adventure and backstage political maneuvering, at one point being arrested for complicity in the assassination of Dr. Isaac Dorislaus for his involvement in opposition to the late King Charles I.

When no evidence was found and Norwood was not convicted, he was then caught running firearms as part of preparation for the Penruddock uprising and imprisoned first in the Tower and interrogated by John Thurloe and then Cromwell, himself. Despite no evidence found, he was deemed a dissident and imprisoned until the state was forced to pay his debtors. At some point, Cromwell ordered Norwood sent to New Jersey and forbid him to ever return to England but the banishment did little good. Norwood found passage back to England and continued his lifelong war against those in the English government. He became involved in a plot to kill the King, but the plan failed to materialize. Henry Norwood died single in 1689, never having been married to anything other than his job as a soldier. Norwood's account of the shipwreck with Fox and Morrison published in a broadsheet in his lifetime, entitled, *A Voyage To Virginia*, was widely popular at the time and is still fascinating to read.[37; 314]

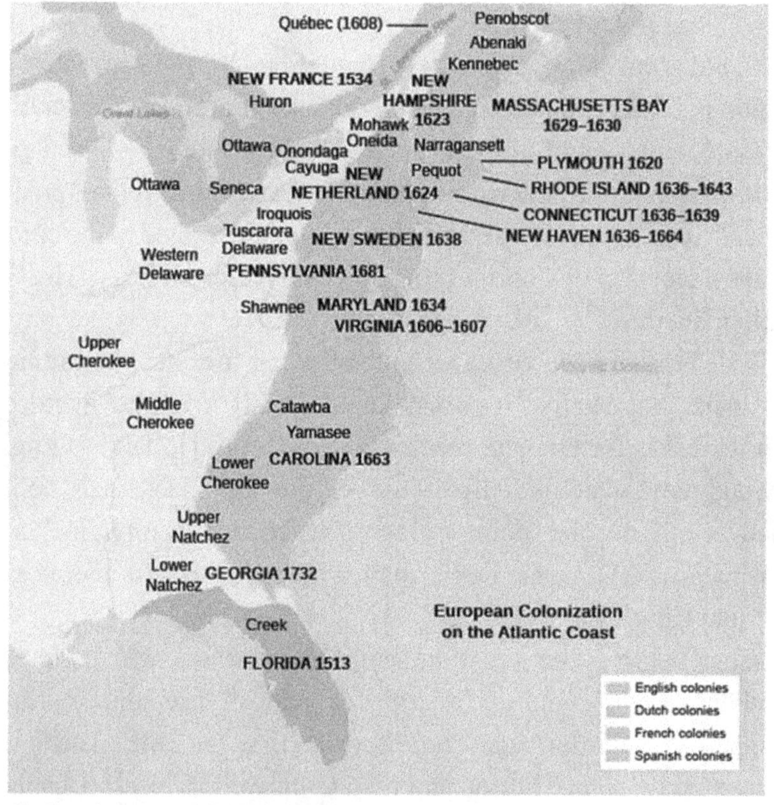

Colonies and Native American locations in the New World. John Fox, the mariner, came to America in 1650. (1)

CHAPTER SIX

GENTLEMAN HENRY FOX I, SECOND GENERATION AMERICAN

John Fox continued to be a mariner despite establishing a home in the Virginia colony of the New World. He used the title 'Captain' rather than 'Major', likely as a means to gloss over his military and international intrigue.

In about 1650 a son named Henry was born in London, Middlesex, England to John Fox and his wife Anne.[20] The same year, following the failed rescue of the King, the family arrived in the colonies where John took possession of his acreage allotment and subsequently became a part-time farmer.

Gloucester County had only been safe for settlement since about 1644 but other ancestors of notable people were taking property there as well. The great grandfather of George Washington took a land patent in the area in 1651, shortly after John Fox had done so. It is apparent that John either brought money or had a credit line that extended to his wealthy relative, Thomas, in England. It was not inexpensive to move a family across the Atlantic with enough cooking supplies, tools, seeds, ammunition and weapons, building materials and livestock.[78]

It was here, right from the beginning, that pioneer families adopted rituals of buying allotments of land and "proving up". These allotments were always at the edge of civilization and initially getting settled was life threatening; be it from accident or from Indian hostility. For these reasons communities rose dominated by growing families that by simple logistics inter-married.

These were the first generation of Americans and while some came with money, there was no aristocracy. These were simply men from across the ocean who wanted better lives for them and their families. They worked beside and knew each other only as men, generations before any of their ancestors had distinguished themselves in the contributions they would make in the great experiment they had begun.

Among the tight knit colonies were families that had known each other from England; others met when they landed in America. In either case, it was here that so many families inter-married and later migrated together, spreading out for 250 years, until the West was settled by the same families that had in most cases, forgotten the earliest special relationships that brought them to where they were.

Their crops mainly tobacco, were vast and indentured servitude or slavery in some form or another was common and necessary. Trading labor, services or possessions was the only form of currency.

To the north in New England lied another British colony established by the Pilgrims, and between the colonies were the Dutch and small Swedish colonies.

It was a double edged sword for the Indians who benefited from the technology and commerce the White men brought, but saw a constant encroachment taking place and more Whites arriving in ships all the time. Despite the hardships, the colonials were expanding their influence and their communities were growing.

In 1654 Virginia, New Kent county was carved out of York county and settled by William Claiborne whom with many others, had been evicted from their settlements when Maryland was formed.[33] His relatives would cross the Oregon Trail in conjunction with members of the Fox family, some 200 years later.

When Anne passed away in the latter 1650's, John Fox remarried a 26 year old widow, named Margaret Elizabeth Thomas. Margaret and her parents had arrived in the British Colony of Virginia in 1654 and she had no previous children. The will of John Coneur proved May 1, 1654 left to his *"lovinge friend Capt. John Fox 5 lbs (for a ring) he to be overseer and also my legal attorney and to receive all my debts in Virginia and to dispose of my cargo of goods in the ship called the* Thomas And Anne*..."*[20p.9] Coneur left John's wife Elizabeth 20 shillings for a ring as well.

The following May 1655 Henry Fox arrived in England aboard the *Thomas And Anne*, with his father John, commanding. Considering that Henry's birth is estimated about 1650, he would have been just a small boy.[20]

In Virginia by 1658, Robert Cobbs, the son of "Ambrose the Planter" that had been born in England, lived in Marston Parish, in York County and served as the church warden there when the first brick place of worship was built. When Marston Parish was absorbed by Bruton Parish, he became the vestry of the new parish. He was but the first offspring of Ambrose that would continue to elevate the family as they became established in the colonies.

Some of the original children died or had children that died; such as it was for the Cobbs, it was for all emigrants. Despite adversity, in time the family grew and some ancestors took similar positions to Robert, in the church but many others remained farmers. They spread out, each amassing more land in the process in York, James City, Chesterfield, Amelia, Louisa, Bedford, Spotsylvania, Halifax, Campbell and Granville Counties in both Virginia and North Carolina. They were chaplains, justice of the peace, farmers, laborers and politicians.[78]

In a letter written in 1662 to Capt. John Fox by his brother Stephen, who died at sea en route from the New England colonies to London, were listed the siblings of the two Fox brothers. The list cited Thomas, William, Peter and Mary. While none of these children but John are suspected of living in the Virginia colony, the letter provides proof that Stephen Fox was in New England and had holdings in Virginia as well.

It appears Thomas Fox of the Virginia Company of London, provided the family means of travel to and from the colonies. In the letter, Stephen gives his brother John direction for the dispensation of his tobacco holdings on the James River in Virginia. For those genealogists looking for Fox's in New England, these are important clues.[78]

In 1662, due to some of the children of racially mixed marriages in the colonies between English and Blacks being unlawfully enslaved, the principle of *partus sequitur ventrem*, was written into slave law. It over ruled English common law and provided that children in the colonies were born into the social status of their mother not their father.

There were 300 African and 4000 indentured slaves effected, but those numbers were changing. As England's economy improved, less White's volunteered for servitude in the colonies.

While initially the act freed many people, it was designed to take advantage of slaves. In many cases however, this law freed those born in slavery and made it possible regardless of nationality to establish free families, breaking a racial caste that was associated with people of African ancestry and provided for a more equitable freedom in Virginia colonies.

By about 1800, 80% of free Blacks had used this law to gain liberty.[304] This included the sons and daughters of John Punch, who altered their surnames to Bunche and Bunch, to avoid the association with their Black father. These offspring avoided passing on details to their children and little information was passed on to the next generation. Within a few years Bunch family bibles could only elude to the first Bunch in America being unmarried and 17 years old at the time of his arrival; there was no mention of him being Black.

In his lifetime John Punch suffered greatly for his escape attempt and could never have known how pivotal his part was in history for both his adopted country and his descendants. Like most true stories, the story of John Punch is a sad one. That said, the Bunch family would grow vastly, propagating far and wide as they took part in building America.[65]

Ironically, one particular descendant of John Punch did his best not to build America, but to "fundamentally transform America". Barack Obama's White mother is a descendant of John Punch.

The White population in Virginia increased from 15,000 in 1649, to 38,000 in 1670. Native American Indians reluctantly tolerated Europeans initially, when their settlements were along the coastline. As colonials built further inland they ate a lot of game and their farming activities spread out, impacting the way the Natives lived.

By 1675 the son of the first Indian chief to make a peace treaty with the pilgrims was being pressured by his people, the Wampanoags, to make war on the "Bostons". Chief (or Sachem) Metacomet was known to the English as King Philip. He was not as committed to peace as his father had been, after a generation of tolerating the invading Europeans.

When a Christian Native American and interpreter for Metacomet was murdered by his tribe because he had acted as an English informant, the English executed three Wampanoags. Sachem Metacomet responded by launching a war on the colonists in which over half of all English settlements in southern New England were attacked, resulting in the bloodiest conflict between the English settlements and Native Americans in the 17th century.

The hostility took a new tone when an allegiance was reached between the Wampanoags and the Nipmunk. Finally when some Narragansett Indians gave refuge to Wampanoag women, children and elderly, a large force of Englishmen attacked the village in current day Rhode Island. Despite their attempt to remain neutral, the attack brought the Narragansett into the hostilities as well; the result was all-out war.[235]

The Europeans had begun decades earlier converting Natives to Christianity and these were known as "praying Indians". These praying Indians lived in communities between the White settlements and the Native American villages, creating a buffer zone.

The colonists utilized a few of their Indian allies in the conflict, but not many because they held little trust in Natives. King Philip's War, as it was known, lasted 14 months, until the Indian sachem (chief) was killed. Despite the meager population, thousands on all sides of the hostility were killed.

The war took place in the New England colonies, and in the aftermath, it took the colonies in southern New England many years to rebuild what had been lost in the war. In addition, many Indian villages moved further west, while others had already been destroyed. This was a second opportunity to expunge Europeans from the New World that failed, but there would be more attempts.

The lasting impact of King Philips War was that it put the English in complete control of southern New England. In the wake of King Philip's War, was the first time that "military bounty lands" were offered to veterans for their service defending the colonies. It was a practice that would become more and more common as a lure to service, first by the Crown and eventually by colonial governments.

Giving away Native American land was a convenient way for governments to pay the debts of their military actions without impacting their economy. Ironically, hostilities inevitably began when White men began to inhabit land held by Indians and the answer was in order to defend them, was offering more Indian land. It was a cycle created by the English, perpetuated by the American government that would be repeated for about another 150 years until the Indians were wiped out or contained on reservations. These governments used White men, abused Red men, and yet hundreds of years later the hate they caused is blamed on the combatants they manipulated.[235]

CHAPTER SEVEN

THE ROYAL CONNECTION

The Fox family enjoyed some level of prestige among the early population and society of the colonies, in fact John's son Henry Fox I married Anne West, the daughter of Colonel John West who served as Governor of Virginia 1635-37 and whose brother was Thomas West, 3rd Baron De La Warre.

John was the third West to serve as Governor and though the colonists did not practice aristocracy, the family was as close as they could be without formal declaration of it. In addition, the West brothers were descendants of English Royalty. Their grandfather, Sir Thomas Leighton West, 2nd Lord De La Warre had been married to Anne Knollys, whose grandmother was Mary Boleyn, who had been a mistress of King Henry VIII (in the days when being a mistress of the King was not to be frowned upon). Mary introduced her sister, Anne Boleyn, to the King who then became obsessed with Anne until he got rid of his wife and married her. Anne became Queen of England from 1533-36, but Henry had her beheaded so he could remarry. The prolific King had six wives, two of which including Anne, he had beheaded in order to continue his serial marriages.

The West family descended from Norman Vikings as did the descendants of ship's Captain John Fox and Ambrose Cobbs the Planter. This Royal connection has been the purpose many Fox family genealogists seek to establish a relationship.[20; 215]

The marriage of Henry Fox I and Anne West took place in 1673 and their first child, Henry Fox II was born the following year; the first Fox born in America. The couple had a second son named Thomas two years later early in 1676.

"Mary Boleyn, Sister of Queen Anne Boleyn, maternal first cousin of Katheryn Howard" (2)

These third generation Americans were the first to never experience life in England; whose memories were uniquely 'American' because none of their memories would be of England.

Though the colonies had thus far survived, the New World was still wild and dangerous and their survival was not guaranteed. These children would grow up hearing distant tales of their grandpa being a merchant seaman and that he had brought the family to Virginia in the New World. Fewer stories about England were related as time went on.

Tales their father and grandfather endured to establish their homes in America, were what these sons heard. It was about there in that third generation when any love and dedication to England naturally slipped away, replaced by pride and loyalty to the American colonies and their ideals.

Henry I and his wife Anne had their fourth child in 1684, a daughter they named Anne. Three years later in 1687, merchant captain, first American settler and patriarch John Fox passed away at 56 years old.

Like his contemporary soldiers in service to the King, Norwood and Morrison, Captain John Fox remained forever faithful to the Monarch they had tried to save. John's second wife Margaret's, death date is unknown. During his life John lost some of the trepidation he had about relating his experiences with Henry Norwood when he was young.

Memories of his stories were written down at some point by someone but they were incomplete and vague. Notes were placed into a bible and passed forward. Henry I and Anne had a fifth child that year, a son named John, but sadly he died shortly after birth. Rumor persists that a son David was born to them later but it's never been proven.[20]

In 1690-91, King and Queen county was cut out of New Kent county and a year later Edmund Tunstall, whose father Richard had been born in Surrey, England (as John Fox had been), donated an acre of land for the court house to be built upon. Edmund's daughter Mary Polly Tunstall married Col. Thomas Fox, second son of Henry Fox I, in 1707.

In 1695 Henry I served as a vestryman in St. John's Parish in King and Queen county and in 1699 served as a justice of the peace. During this latter period of Henry I's life he bore the title, Gentleman Henry

Fox's on The Mattaponi River; built by either Henry Fox (1650-1714) or by his son, Col. Thomas Fox, who received a Royal Grant on the Mattaponi in 1713. (3)

Fox on many documents, denoting the Fox family laid claim to a coat of arms; the bearer of arms being a gentleman. These titles were vestiges left over from English aristocracy and would mostly be forgotten over the course of the next couple generations.[20]

The history of men and countries is replete with non-intended consequences. The New World was the focus of many attempts at colonization that were initiated to generate wealth but instead brought death and doom for governments. In the late 1690's the Scottish Kingdom devised the Darien Scheme, in which they would colonize the Isthmus of Panama and therefore control trade in the area, but the scheme failed and led to the Kingdom of Scotland signing the Act of Union 1707, that established the United Kingdom and saw the end of Scottish ruling their homeland. By 1713, after a number of years of hostile exchanges for turf, Britain captured Nova Scotia from the French.

Despite the establishment of the colonies the prospect of making a life there was still no small feat. For emigrants, such isolation demanded great preparation and most failed to understand that the land would give up riches only if one survived long enough. Long winters and irregular visits from ships bringing scant supplies were the end of many hopeful colonists who died miserable deaths of starvation or murder by Native savagery.

In 1701, seeking to expand their reach, the British Crown offered land for a nominal fee for 20 years to those who would move to armed settlements on the Indian frontier. Why not? It wasn't their land.[339]

As the Church in Europe offered compromise to the government, the population went into spiritual decline. A spontaneous movement arose among the Reformation churches, first in Germany, then Sweden, then the Netherlands, called Pietism. Sects like Moravians, Mennonites, Quakers and the Brethren of German Baptists concurred in these puritanical beliefs, though Mennonites were known as Anabaptist for their practice of denying infant baptism and re-baptized converts. In August 1708, the first Baptism was given, as an outward signal of their new faith. Their ordinances included threefold baptism by immersion, a communion combining feet washing with an evening meal, called a Love Feast, anointing and use of a "ban" on wayward members. It wasn't long before the persecution endured by the Catholic Church drove the sect to the Netherlands.[349]

Back in America, by 1702 due to inconvenience in travel across the Mattaponi River to attend court, Pamunkey Neck was declared its own jurisdiction and became named King William County. The property for the first courthouse was donated by Henry Fox I and Richard Littlepage. When the new county of King William was formed, a list of men to become the counties first sheriff was created and Henry Fox was first on the list; commissioned sheriff February 17, 1702.

Henry I is listed on many documents of the time, purchasing, selling and trading property, some of it small lots, some nearly 1000 acres. Recorded transactions he made include indenture agreements for property, and though no records were found directly relating to his owning slaves, he surely did. From 1702-12 he served as a Burgess (political representative) of King William county. As an administrator of Richard Johns will in 1703 Henry I served as arbitrator when the deceased left his estate for the schooling of the poor.[20]

At St. John's Parish in 1705 Henry I joined other notable men John West and Thomas Claiborne (the elder, born in 1647, whose son of the same name would marry Henry I's daughter, Anne), in protesting the new minister. With as little disdain as they could muster, they said it wasn't that they didn't like him for his Scottish ancestry, but an Englishman would be much preferred. Their protest was met by the Governor who requested the minister come to terms with the men, re-establishing peace. On December 20, 1705, a meeting at the St. Johns Parish in which the minister and six of the vestrymen filled two vacant positions in the vestry with two men they had chosen, two of the church wardens and Mr. Henry Fox "not only dissented, but went away in some heat, carrying with them the Vestry book… the order of the Vestry could not be entered." He was obviously a man of conviction and 'heat'.[20]

Henry I was an active participant in King William county politics and at St. John's Parish, until he passed away in 1714, having led an exemplary public life. He had prospered and propagated and his sons would do likewise.[20] He was the last Fox born in England, raised as an American. His sons, born in the colonies, held less allegiance to the Crown, though surely heard first-hand stories of their mariner grandfather Captain John Fox as well as their own father's lives of service to the British Throne.

Perhaps the unintended consequence was the colonial-born boys grew to men adulating their fathers, hearing about their sense of duty and bravery for England, but began to apply that resolve and dedication to their own native land. Their British Loyalist father, Henry I and grandfather John, were without doubt great influences on Henry II and his brothers.

In 1719, twenty families of the Anabaptist/Pietism movement still in the Netherlands under the leadership of Peter Becker, emigrated to America and settled in the Germantown, Pennsylvania area. The remainder of their number remained in the Netherlands, among Mennonites and Collegiants. Fully 10 years went by before in 1729 another 120 members of the movement from the Netherlands emigrated to join them. Led by correspondence to join them in religious freedom, most of the rest of the movement emigrated in 1733.

By 1740 so many of the sect had moved to Pennsylvania in America the Schwarzenau Brethren ceased to exist in Europe. Given their name, it is not surprising they were known commonly and collectively as Pennsylvania Dutch, not because they had come from the Netherlands, but because in standard German, they were, Deutsch.

It is likely the families of Baltimore, Hardman and Powell were among this group.[173]

CHAPTER EIGHT

HENRY FOX II

The family names of those that intermarried in the family of Fox began with the children of Henry I and his wife Anne. Both the relationships and the surnames would carry forward better than 100 years; well past when most even remembered the origin of the names or relationships.

Henry II may have been married once before he married Mary Kendrick in about 1697. Like his father, Henry II married well. Mary was third generation American of the well-known and respected Kendrick family, with Scottish origins. Mary's father, John William Kendrick was born, lived and died in Glaucester County, Virginia between 1652 and 1681 and is considered the patriarch of the Kendrick family.

Following in the footsteps of his father, in 1724 Henry Fox II was appointed Sheriff of King William County and reappointed the following year. In 1730 he served at his parents church, St. John's Parish as vestryman, like his father. He and his wife moved the following year, in 1731, to newly created Brunswick County. The following year Gentleman Henry Fox II was appointed justice of the newly created county and held the position for two years. He was chosen the same year to represent the county in the House of Burgesses. By 1735, Gentleman Henry's health was failing and he disappeared from record of his duties.

Henry II and Mary had four sons; Colonel Henry Fox III, 1698-1770, Colonel Richard Fox, 1707-1771, William Fox, 1710-1764 and like his parents, had a son named John, who died young and no dates were recorded. The couple also had a single daughter named Unity, 1704-1778.[12; 78]

Henry II brother, Thomas Fox, 1680-1733, married Mary Polly Tunstall, whose father Edmund, mentioned previously donating property for a church, was a well-respected and connected colonial associate of the elder, Henry Fox I.

Henry II and Thomas's sister Anne Fox, 1684-1733, married Captain Thomas Claiborne, from the well-known and connected colonial family. Thomas Claiborne's grandfather was William Claiborne who served as secretary for the colony of Virginia. Thomas Claiborne lived in a stately manor called Sweet Hall, which still stands today, said to be quite quaint and interesting. Thomas and Anne had many children and their ancestors would continue to cross paths with the Fox family for many generations.[67; 33]

Despite the very respectable public persona of Henry II, recent DNA testing of a Black man has proven at some point Henry II sired a male child from a slave. Additionally, though he seems to have treated him the same as his siblings, Henry II's second son, Richard, born in 1707, was not his biological son. Tit for tat?

Thus far, it has not been determined who fathered Richard. He could have been a nephew of Henry II or an indentured servant that became like family.[216] It's easy to assume Henry Fox II's affair with a slave was kept secret, but we will never know if Henry II and Mary ever told their children that Richard was not one of their biological children. Of Richard's siblings, only older brother Henry III who would have been 9 years old when Richard was born, would have been old enough to know what was going on; but did he? Did Richard ever know?

Because indentured servitude of children and their subsequent adoption by their 'masters' was so common, it would not have carried the same social stigma it would generations later. There are a number of questions that this DNA proof give rise to, however one thing is indisputable, if Richard knew, it made no discernible difference in how he or his siblings dealt with each other, nor in the way that his adopted parents treated him. Richard's mother Mary Kendrick-Fox passed away in 1716 while his father Henry II lived 31 years longer, passing away in 1747 after remarrying Mary Claiborne, Thomas Claiborne's daughter. If couple Henry II and Mary Claiborne had children, they were never identified. Before he died, Henry II was given ten grandchildren by Richard alone; now we know, none of them were his blood kin. By his death, Henry II's remaining biological children had propagated a dozen more additional grandchildren.[20]

When Europeans began to explore their surroundings, they followed the trails made by Indians, who had simply improved game trails. It's unknown when the Great Indian Path was found. Used for commerce, trading and communication between the tribes, it was used when the same Indians were carrying weapons of war, so was also known as the War Path. A myriad of trails connected the coastline colonies of Virginia to New England and westward to the Ohio River. The first time the trail was mentioned was in November of 1728 when William Byrd II wrote of its unusually easy course, *"The Indians, who have no way of traveling except on the hoof, make nothing of going 25 miles a day and carrying their little necessities at their back, and sometimes a stout pack of skins into the bargain."* [333] Though the Indians would retreat westward faced with European settlers, the Great Indian Path, or War Path, or Great Indian Trail, would continue to be used until parts were paved with asphalt hundreds of years later.

The Ambrose Cobbs family was well established in America for 100 years by 1735. As was the custom of the era, as owner of vast amounts of land, they practiced slavery in a variety of ways. While bonded indentured slaves worked for a period of years other indentured slaves were owned outright, until death. Members of the Cobbs family took in children as bonded servants to pay the debts of the children's father. The agreements varied but usually always called for the child's own bed and that they be fed and clothed properly. The sale of a child for debt coupled with the benevolent treatment of their adoptive parents often led the children to take the name of their 'masters', who often had become loving and supportive parents.[178] This historical note would become of great importance to our story.

By the 1740's everything east of the Mississippi River was claimed by the British or the French, though the boundaries of these areas were largely arbitrary because when agreements for boundaries were made, no one knew really knew what was out there.

From the colony of Newfoundland, Nova Scotia in the north to the Province of Georgia to the south, British colonials now numbered 1.5 million. Sharply opposed, the French population in America only numbered 75,000 where they heavily occupied the St. Lawrence River Valley in present day New Brunswick and parts of Nova Scotia. Smaller French settlements were to the south in New Orleans, Biloxi, Mississippi, Alabama and some very small settlements in the Illinois Country, hugging the east side of the Mississippi River and its tributaries. From here French trappers traveled throughout the St. Lawrence and Mississippi watersheds doing business with the indigenous Indians. These transactions created relationships with the Indians and many trappers married Indian women. When the marriage involved a chiefs daughter, it was considered by them a high-ranking union and created a strong relationship between the trapper and the tribe.

Spain laid claim only to current day Florida, Cuba and other territories in the West Indes. Several companies of British troops occupied Virginia, but the remaining British colonies relied on local militia's to defend from Indian attacks. The French had no occupying forces and their colonies relied solely upon local militia's for defense against Indian hostilities.

After a French expedition in the summer and fall of 1749 throughout their claimed land, the British began to worry about French expansion and not without good reason. Every British merchant, trapper or settler they came upon was warned to get out because the land they were on was French.

In answer, the British government gave land to the Ohio Company of Virginia, for the purpose of developing trade routes and settlements in the Ohio Country. But the territory was already claimed by Pennsylvania, leading both colonies to action securing their claims.[341]

In 1750 medical Dr. Thomas Walker, also a surveyor, was employed by the Loyal Land Company of Virginia to explore Kentucky lands that had been granted to a man named John Lewis. The group traveled through the Cumberland Gap and down the Cumberland River to current day Barbourville, where the party split. Half remained to build a cabin and the other half continued on to survey more land. They never made it far enough west to find the great fertile valleys.

By July, 1750, the group was back in Virginia to report that the area was disagreeable and there was nothing there to see.[324] About a year later British explorer and surveyor Christopher Gist was employed by the Ohio Company of Virginia to travel down the Ohio River to survey and promote good relations with the Indians along the way, so to frustrate French efforts to vilify the Redcoats. Gist strengthened relations with Indian Chieftain "Old Briton" and went on with a Black servant into Kentucky, exiting out the Cumberland Gap, toward the Yadkin River. When he returned home, his family had fled in response to Indian attacks, but he soon rejoined them.

Gist is credited with making the first detailed description of the Ohio valley country (that included Kentucky) and making the information available to colonists, including a young 20 year old

George Washington who lived in North Carolina but was interested in making investments in property in the frontier.[67]

There was a temporary lull in hostilities between settlers and Indians when the Treaty of Logstown was signed in 1752 between representatives of the Ohio Company of Virginia and the Iroquois including terms to build a strong house at the mouth of the Monongahela River at the present-day site of Pittsburgh. However, that year the Governor General of New France died in March and he was temporarily replaced by Charles le Moyne de Longueuil. The interim commander took it upon himself to send another expedition with 300 men, including French-Canadians and warriors from the Ottawa tribe, to punish the Miami people of Pickawillany for not following the previous expedition leaders orders to cease trading with British merchants.[341]

The first attack of the French and Indian War is often credited as beginning on June 21, when the French attacked the trading center at Pickawillany. They captured 3 traders and killed 14 Miami Indians before some of the Indians in the expedition party ritually cannibalized the dead Miami Indian's Chieftain and ally of the Redcoats, Old Briton, who John Finley had dealt with only a year before.

The effect of these barbaric acts did nothing if not further the opinion of the Whites that the Indians were savages to be feared. In the spring of 1753 the French sent another expedition into the Ohio Country, this time with 2000 troops of regular militia as well as Indians. This time they established forts and as they moved south, they drove off or captured British traders, causing alarm among the Iroquois and the British.

A chief of the Mingo tribe, now part of the Iroquois, who hated the French because he said they killed and ate his father, threatened the French with military action. He was summarily dismissed by the French commander. The Iroquois sent runners to the British colonies asking them to honor their obligations and eject the French but they were rebuffed. The Iroquois answer was that the "Covenant Chain" had been broken between the British Crown and the Iroquois Confederacy.[341]

As matters intensified, the Ohio Company of Virginia realized their investment would be lost if the French held their claims. Twenty-two year old George Washington of the Virginia Regiment and brother of one of the Ohio Company of Virginia's investors, was tasked with warning the French to leave the Virginia territory.

After a civilized and stately supper, Washington gave the French commander a letter demanding his withdrawal from the area. His only response was that he felt he didn't have to withdraw. George Washington returned to Williamsburg in January and reported that the French were taking steps to secure their forts and claims. Before Washington even got back to Williamsburg, British troops under William Trent were sent to construct a fort.

When 500 French troops arrived at the construction site, they allowed the British to evacuate and even bought their tools, so they could finish the fort. Unaware of the change in ownership, Washington was on his way back to reinforce those building the fort, when he heard of Trent's retreat. Since the Mingo chief had committed to fighting alongside Washington's troops, he continued to the Indian camp.

While he was meeting with the Indians, Washington was told of a French scouting party nearby and so went in pursuit in partnership with Tanaghrisson, the chief of the Mingo Indians. When the French party was found they were destroyed, albeit barely. Washington lost any control of his Indian allies and many French-Canadians died including their commander, whose head was split open by Tanaghrisson who intended the move to ingratiate himself to the British and inspire his own people who leaned toward allegiance to France.

Known as the Battle of Jumonville Glen, it is seen as the opening battle in the French-Indian War.[341; 276]

Washington pulled some miles back and built Fort Necessity, but it was assaulted, led by the brother of the French leader whose head had been broken open with a tomahawk and Washington was forced to negotiate an armed withdrawal. As hostilities increased, knowing that negotiating agreements with the myriad of Indian tribes would be essential in defending their colonies, the Congress of Albany was convened to formalize a unified front. The format of the congress and specifics for organization would be a prototype for confederacy during the Revolutionary War.[341; 242]

Of all American military actions, perhaps the French-Indian War is the most difficult to understand, for a variety of reasons. It was actually the fourth hostility from 1688-1763 between the French and British and both sides had Indian allies. The war was known by different names by all those involved; the French called it the Fourth Intercolonial War, or the Great War for the Empire by French Canadians. The Brits called it the Seven Year War, because even though the fighting was over in colonial America, the French and British continued fighting for an additional two years. It was called the French-Indian War by the colonists, despite the long standing tendency of them to name wars after their ruling monarch. There had only recently been a King George's War that took place from 1740-48 mainly in the British provinces of New York, Massachusetts Bay (which included the area known today as Maine), New Hampshire (which included Vermont in that era).

The French colonists were supported by the Wabanaki Confederacy that included the Abanaki, Mi'kmag, Alonquin, Lenape, Ojibwa, Ottawa, Shawnee and Wyandot tribes while the British colonials were supported at times by the Iroquois, Catawba and Cherokee. Despite the complexities of understanding the changing combatants and titles, the series of wars were vital to the future boundaries of an emerging new country that would become known as The United States of America.[341]

CHAPTER NINE

DANIEL BOONE

By August 1754, the Crown got a report about the two battles and ordered Major General Edward Braddock to expel the French. But the French heard about the British response and so dispatched six regiments of soldiers to New France. In response, the British sent out their fleet in February 1755 intending to blockade French ports, but the French had already sailed. Admiral Ethan Hawke detached a fast squadron in an attempt to intercept them, but they never did. However, in June 1755 the British captured French naval ships sent to provide war materials to the militia's in Nova Scotia. In that month British naval commanders captured the French ship *Alcide* and two additional troop ships.[341]

On the frontier militias were raised, and unknown 21 year old Daniel Boone volunteered to be a wagoneer in the service of Gen. Braddock. Boone was a fairly large man; 5'10" and built burly with a ruddy cheeks and fair in complexion. His reddish-sandy colored hair was typically "bunned-up" in the back and he never liked fur caps, but all his life preferred wide brimmed felt hats that were most common on the frontier.[338]

It cannot be proven beyond all doubt that Daniel Boone was a member of the German Brethren, but his name appears on a membership roll of a Baptist Church at Boone, Ashe County, NC, which may have been the same Baptist Brethren Church that was banned in the 1798 Annual Meeting. This would have been before the English Baptists had come to the mountains of Pennsylvania and the Brethren were the only denomination of Baptist church in that part of the frontier.[296]

The British suffered a crushing defeat when Major General Braddock was killed along with 1000 British regulars and Indians.

While in his service with the militia, young Boone met fellow wagoneer John Finley of North Carolina who had been granted a license in 1744 to trade with Indians on the upper Ohio River. Finley had roamed present-day eastern Kentucky and southern Ohio for years until he joined with Shawnee, near the Falls of the Ohio. They took him to Indian villages in the fertile Kentucky low-lands where bluegrass grew in abundance. Initially he was essentially lost, but hunting with the Indians, was the first White man to see much of the area that would someday become Kentucky. He learned from wandering traders there was an accessible way back to North Carolina, through what is now eastern Tennessee, by way of a gap in the imposing Cumberland Mountains.

Boone and Finley were quick friends, but of course when their terms of service were over each went their own way. For the balance of the year the British fleet seized ships and captured seamen, leading to a formal declaration of war in the spring of 1756. The military action continued back and forth, drawing Indians from remote villages far away into the fray.[341; 338]

When smallpox swept through the ranks of French allied Indians, many died. Others returned sick hundreds of miles to their tribes where they infected their loved ones. The French suffered greatly in 1757 for the smallpox outbreak. In addition, the following year of 1758 was a poor year for crops. The French began the war outnumbered 20-1 and it was only getting worse.

One effective tactic they used was telling the Cherokee that the White American settlers on the Yadkin River wanted to kill them. In 1759 the Cherokee began a series of raids against the settlers thanks to the French rumors. Settlers were killed and burnt out, but for all their lives lost and suffering they endured, it did the French little good. By

1760 after a number of serious defeats, particularly the Battle of the Plains of Abraham, which claimed the life of both French commanders, the French government had lost its will to fight.

By 1760 the Crown was redistributing its forces to the West Indes and other theaters of battle. Fighting continued in the American colonies, though it was sporadic, until a capitulation was agreed to in September of that year. The British and French continued the war for two more years until the British won and a treaty was signed in Paris, 1763.

From the Mississippi east, the French ceded New France to the British, including an area largely not colonized that was set aside as an Indian Reserve that included all of modern day Florida and all the area between the thirteen colonies and the Mississippi, all the way north into Nova Scotia. The French secretly transferred the Louisiana territory to their ally Spain to pay them for debts they had incurred and retained only Saint Pierre and Miquelon. The French also ceded Canada to the Crown.

For their part in paying at least some of their debt they had incurred, the Brits offered military bounty lands to privates and officers who planned to remain in the colonies.[341]

CHAPTER TEN

RICHARD FOX, ADOPTED SON OF HENRY II

Before the 1760's, the western expanse of North Carolina was mostly undiscovered. During that decade men known as longhunters began following Indian and buffalo trails into the western frontier. For almost 20 years only the heartiest men explored the area that would someday become Kentucky and Tennessee.

Of those earliest explorer/settlers, were the grandsons of Richard Fox. And while DNA has discovered he is not the biological son of Henry II, the argument cannot be made that he was not part of Henry II's family. How Richard came to be raised by Henry II might never be known, but someday DNA advancements will likely identify who his real father was.

The science of DNA cannot be disputed, but it does not tell the entire story. Indisputable documentation proves that despite these relationships not beginning as biological, they were family. They might have been adopted and it is technically correct of DNA research to say, "they aren't related", but it's doing the dead a disservice to reject the relationships they shared. The proof will show, without any dispute or argument, that these children were treated so equally to their siblings that had it not been for DNA, no one would be the wiser. They were named after their mothers mother and fathers grandfather. They were not biological sons, but they were family.

The first mention of Richard Fox was when as a 10 year old he pulled some sort of shenanigans on the property of John Lett. One historic document asks, "*was he hunting the red fox, trampling the crops of John Lett? We may never know because the records were completely destroyed in the war between the states.*"[132[p.44]] The surviving document notes the charges were dropped against the boy before he was prosecuted.

Young Richard was educated because he knew how to read and write as an adult. The Williamson family were neighbors to the Fox family and when Richard was grown, at 21 years old, he married the families beautiful daughter, Johanna "Hannah" Williamson, in 1728 in Prince George County, Virginia.[78]

Like most youths during the era, Richard served in the local militia, as did his step-brothers. When he was 29, in 1736, he bought 550 acres in the county of Brunswick for 5 shilling Sterling, agreeing to pay an additional 26 pounds current money a year later. The property was on the cutting edge of the frontier and had not been settled. It was here that Richard built a home and he and his wife Hannah raised their family for the following 30 years. In total, Hannah would bear Richard 5 sons and 9 daughters.[49; 13[p.296]]

The children of Richard and Hannah were 5th generation British Colonials. Their lives were typically not impacted adversely on a daily basis by the British government. While their grandfather Henry II might have recalled the family had a crest, that information was slipping away in his grandchildren's lifetimes. Notes still existed in a few family bibles, but as they aged the slips of notes were misplaced or blurred; in any event, the information was slipping away.

It was when William Fox was just a toddler that his father Richard took title to the 550 acres in what was then Brunswick County, Virginia, close to the North Carolina border. Though records of his service no longer exist, Richard used the title Lt. Colonel, as did others who referred to him, no doubt denoting his participation in the local militia.

On the Roanoke River, Richard operated a busy ferry and also a mill. Richard was successful and eventually owned at least 2500 acres in the southern part of Virginia, near the North Carolina border. This land was in Brunswick, which became Lunenberg, that finally became Mecklenburg County, Virginia.

As the massive counties were settled and divided, the longhunters came in periodically from the Ohio, Missouri, Holton and Kentucky Rivers, telling tales of lush valleys and plenty of rivers and streams. The lure they created would begin to pull colonials, eventually including the Fox family, westward.[19; 49]

Many British systems were initially used by the colonials and this was the case with their militia, which was based on arrangements used in feudal times. In those days, the country was divided into 'Wapentake', meaning "hundred spears"; with a baron over the whole of the area, 10 knights under his command and in turn each knight had 10 men under him. These last 10 men made up of bow men and spear men, constituted an 'infantry'.

There being no standing army, in times of duress the king would send for his barons who would send for their knights who would call for their infantry. Knights were responsible for not only their own armor and weapons of war, but the weapons, clothing, food and supplies for their 10 men.

In the colonies the system was adapted with the important difference that titles of military rank were given to older men in communities that were proven leaders, had histories of bravery and made sound decisions. As older men became counterparts of barons in the colonies, so did young men become counterparts to spear men and bow men, becoming infantry.

Each plantation was independent as much as was possible. Wagons were made on plantations out of great trees to make wheels, beds, axles, tongues, hounds and reach, single and double trees. Plantation owners, called "planters", not farmers, if wealthy enough, had wheels of metal, if not it was "wood on wood on dirt". Patient, kind and hard working oxen were preferred to horses or mules for their consistent work in adverse conditions. Barrels were made from great hogsheads of strong hickory or oak to store and transport tobacco for shipment and trade. Due to the lack of coins, the monetary system was set up on a 100 weight of tobacco, with all other things regulated by this value.[132]

CHAPTER ELEVEN

WILLIAM FOX

The sons of Richard Fox were John, Jacob, Richard, William and Isham, born in that order. Of these William was born February 13, 1732. When he was 26 he married his cousin Mary, a descendant of his grandmothers brother (not biologically related, as DNA has proven), who had the same given and surname, Mary Kendrick.

William and Mary had nine children. Subsequently, Richard and Hannah's sixth child, Amy Fox, 19, married 24 year old debonair John Kendrick, also a cousin through a brother of her grandmother. Despite DNA proving Richard was not the biological son of Henry II, the subsequent relationships these two of his grandchildren shared with their grandmother's family, serve to prove the familial relationship that existed; but there is much more proof.[78; 12; 20]

In February 1761, William and Mary had their first child, named Arthur who would lead his father's children west. Later in the year in November the Cherokee War ended when the Treaty of Long-Island-on-the-Holston with the Colony of Virginia was signed by the Cherokee. The end of hostilities allowed the frontier to be pushed back to the foothills of the Blue Ridge Mountains. Three years later in 1763, William and Mary welcomed twins, William and Richard.[78]

Though rancor had been building for years, after 1765 discourse between the colonists and Great Britain became strained to its limit. In England when the Stamp Act of 1765 was passed, requiring many printed materials used in the colonies to have an embossed tax stamp them. Further, the products must be purchased with British currency, not colonial paper money, from England. The colonists were outraged and protested strongly.

The Act intended for the colonists to pay for British occupation after the French and Indian War, but the colonists didn't fear French invasion and saw this simply as taxation laid down in England without their representation. Colonists argued they had already paid for the war and this taxation was nothing more than required patronage to the crown. Local Committees of Correspondence sprang up from New England to Maryland, loosely organized to respond to British policies in the colonies. A clandestine group called The Sons of Liberty began and worked to organize the patriot response, including protests and boycotts. In response, the economic impact prompted British merchants and manufacturers to begin resistance to the Act as well[237]

On January 26, 1766 Richard Fox's 10th child, 19 year old daughter Polly Lucinda (called 'Lucy'), was married to 27 year old Luke Matthews, whose family had lived in Virginia for a number of generations. Though the exact date is unknown, Lucy's sister Mary, just one year older was also married that year, to Samuel Jones. The Jones name would appear throughout subsequent generations of their offspring as well as those of Mary's siblings in the Fox family.[49; 12]

The Crown responded to growing unrest in the colonies by repealing the Stamp Act in 1766 but passed the Declaratory Act, affirming their right to rule the colonists. A whole new series of regulations and taxes followed and patriots in America resisted them all.[237]

Meanwhile, concerns about settlers that lived outside the boundaries for White men set in the treaty following the French-Indian War led to two conflicting treaties in 1768, the first with the Cherokee and the second with the Iroquois.[319; 357]

In 1766, William and Mary Fox had a fourth son named Henry.[83] Meanwhile civilization had grown beyond his parents Richard and Hannah's home and the old man was aging. Richard Fox sold his plantation, downsizing to buy 106 acres on Smith's Creek and Reedy

Branch in a new county named Bute, North Carolina. Richard and Hannah didn't remain at the new home long, for within 5 years, they were living in Virginia again, in Mecklenburg.[227]

In 1769 trader John Finley rode out of the Shenandoah Mountains and up the Yadkin River to meet with Daniel Boone. Finley was keen on returning to the Kentucky country but he was unfamiliar with the trails beyond the Cumberland Gap because he had entered and left the country along the course of the Ohio River. Finley knew about an Indian trail that, translated to English, was ominously called Path of the Armed Ones, or The Warriors Path. He convinced Boone that if they could find that trail on the other side of the Gap, it would lead them into Kentucky. With Boone's brother Squire, their brother in law John Stewart and three camp keepers it was decided to make a business venture of the trip, returning with a fortune in pelts.

The party left from Boone's cabin May 1, 1769. Rebecca, Daniel Boone's wife, had six children and would realize after he left that she was pregnant with a seventh. Despite given the almost generic title of "Quaker", it is believed that Daniel's brothers Squire and George were Baptist Brethren preachers; Squire was allegedly an elder in the church. The Brethren believed keeping records of membership was prideful, so we may never know.[338; 296]

A month later, in June, after the party followed the Warriors Path until it turned many miles north to what would become known as the Red River, they climbed a prominence now known as Pilot knob, and beheld below them the 2400 acre expanse that would later become known as the Inner Blue Grass. Located in the northern portion of the present-day state of Kentucky, the area is dominated by 450,000 million year old ancient limestone, roughly separated from the Outer Bluegrass by a series of short steep hills called the Eden Shale Hills. The Inner Blue Grass was for the most part, a great lush flat valley, the Outer Blue Grass, while also largely made up of the same limestone, was much more rugged. The Inner Bluegrass made up of limestone, is dominated by subterranean water drainage, creating 1600 square miles of sinkhole topography and another 75 square miles of karst topography; sinkholes and caves; sinking springs and creeks created from the dissolution of rock.

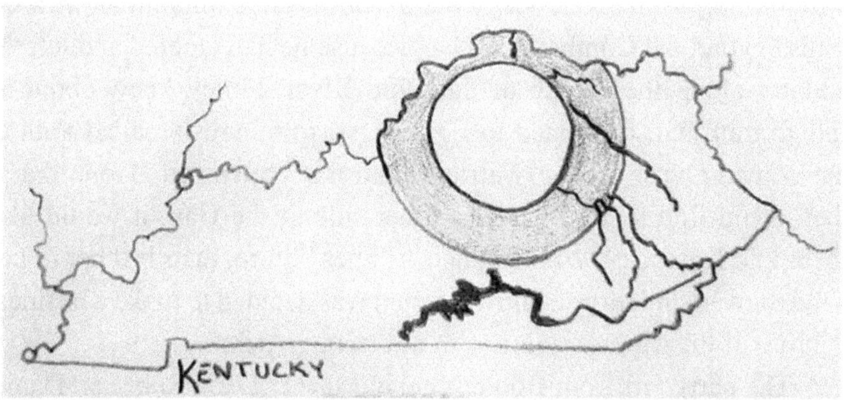

Kentucky: Center represents the Inner Bluegrass and shaded area, the Outer Bluegrass, a series of short steep hills called the Eden Shale Hills (4)

The Inner Bluegrass was drained by the Kentucky River, one of the oldest rivers on the continent.[338; 248]

One hundred million years of running water in the Kentucky River cut the largest fault in the limestone and created abrupt cliffs cut like palisades, dotted with caves. The hills were dotted with Sycamore, Cedar, Poplar, Dog Wood, White Oak and Red Bud but the Inner Bluegrass was not a forest when Boone found it; only along the rivers and creeks. The open canopy was so high among the trees that grass grew uninterrupted into broad natural meadows; some 20 and 50 miles in circumference. These savannah's were dotted with fire resistant Burr Oak, which had survived fires along with Blue Ash and Oak trees. The ash left in the expansive Inner Bluegrass contributed to grow a grass that was mainly known then as English or Meadow grass but was also known as Blue grass.

Surrounding these savanna's were massive canebreaks. The cane is a reed-like grass that grows 10'-16' tall, and back then, some canebreaks were 8 miles deep and 4 miles wide. Passing through was difficult if not impossible for a wagon and what made it dangerous was that it was so thick, people could disappear into it or appear from it, without warning. An abundance of buffalo, elk, deer, bear, gray squirrels, rabbits, otter, beaver, raccoon and game birds including wild turkeys filled the Inner Bluegrass.

The first time Boone saw the Inner Bluegrass he remarked about seeing buffalo by the hundreds, in fact larger than any herd of cattle he had ever seen, but that their fearlessness was only from ignorance of man's violent capabilities.

The buffalo followed fault lines that created great salt licks and those salt licks are what made life possible for the White man to live so far removed in the frontier. The salt was vital for their diet and as a preservative, as well as being an attractant to wildlife. The buffalo cut great paths between these licks, through the canebreaks and settlements would be created near them.[338; 248]

Along the ancient bison routes the licks took names as they became settlements. Places like Big Bone Lick, near where the buffalo entered Kentucky, by crossing the Ohio River south into present-day Kentucky. Then Drennon's Lick and Stamping Ground at the southernmost point of their circular route where the trail split and parallel, one side to Blue Licks, the other to Upper Licks. The side by side trails converged just before May's Lick, where their "trace" crossed the Ohio River again to finish their ancient circular routine.

These established traces were very wide and had been used by the Indians who in turn created trails to and from the traces, creating a network of roads, albeit populated by unfriendly hunting parties of Shawnee and Cherokee.

In fact, eventually Boone and his brother in law were captured by angry Shawnee that warned them to leave Kentucky or suffer the stings of wasps. The party did not heed the warning but became more cautious. Eventually John Stewart, the brother in law, disappeared and by 1770 all rest of the party but Boone had returned home to North Carolina. Squire Boone promised to return with supplies. What was believed to be Stewart's remains and his powder horn were found 5 years later in an old rotten hollowed out oak. Left alone Boone traveled using caves to camp in for concealment, though he could not remain in any one cave for more than a day or two, for fear of being set upon.

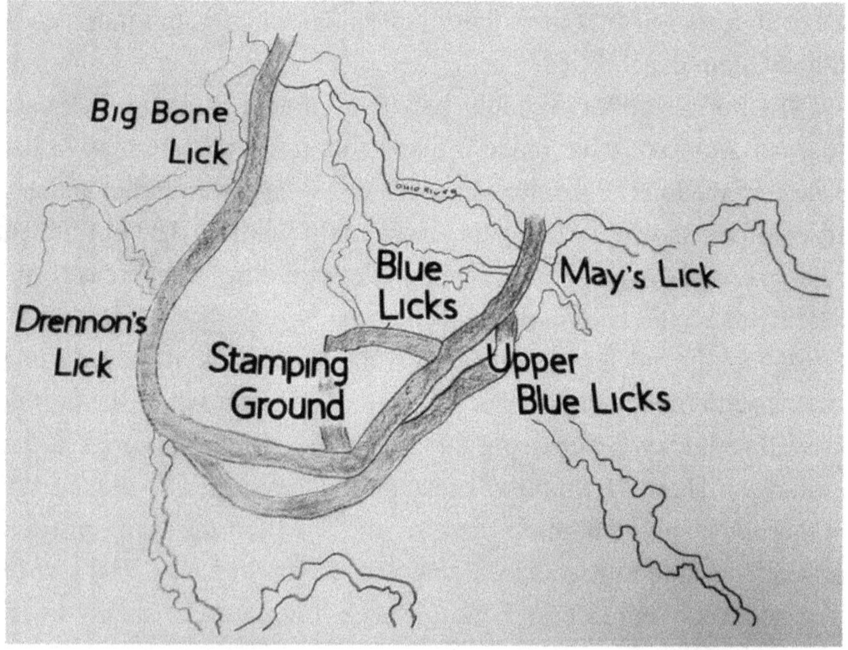

Buffalo paths called 'traces' cut a circular path through the frontier where settlements sprang up (5)

He went as far as central Kentucky and as far north as the Ohio River and dodged Indians, risking close death more than once. Eventually his brother returned and in March of 1771, Daniel Boone went home, but he was determined to settle Kentucky.[338; 248]

A third treaty in 1770 was reached with the Indians along the frontier that set the boundaries the same as the first treaty. The treaty ceded Cherokee and Iroquois land west of the Alleghenies and south of the Ohio River to the colonies, however other tribes, particularly the Shawnee and Mingo, continued to inhabit and claim their lands that the Cherokee and Iroquois had sold. [357]

In the spring of 1771, Richard Fox passed away at 64 years old, in Mecklenburg, Virginia. In his will was listed his personal inventory that included *"18 cows, 10 steers, 10 heifers and steers, 15 young heifers and steers, 24 sheep, 31 hogs, a parcel of young hogs, 2 roan horses, a black mare and foal, 1 black horse, 1 sorrel mare and colt, 1 bay horse, a parcel of old horses and oxen etc."*

Considering the lands, multiple business's and personal property that Richard left behind when he passed away, he was a wealthy man. His sons and daughters mostly lived nearby and his will showed no malice. Particularly, his son William was given the 400 acres that he already lived on. Richard's son Isham Fox died young before he had married, so as per his instructions his portion of his father's estate was divided by his surviving siblings.[227]

Am important note appears in the Virginia Genealogical Society Quarterly, vol 26, number 3, that states in the 1771 Louisa County (VA) list of tithables, that Spencer Norvell was living with John Fox, that year. Tithables were kept because people were taxed on how many "heads" lived under their roof. Spencer Norvell and John Fox must have been friends for some time, even before Spencer had been married the year before to Frances Hill.

The Norvell family had deep roots in Virginia, extending back to Jamestown. Spencer was second-born in 1750; his elder brother Thomas was born the year before.

While the families of Norvell and Fox lived in Virginia, it was only recently discovered the link went this far back. Thomas Norvell was married twice. His first wife, Mary Dawson, bore him four children before she died, likely trying to give birth to a fifth. The same year Spencer Norvell was living with John Fox, his brother Thomas's wife Mary gave birth to their second child, also a girl, named Martha, born August 24, 1771.[78]

Six months later, records indicate that William and Mary Fox had Benjamin Fox on May 12, 1772, in Mecklenburg, Virginia. When Benjamin Fox was 20 years old, he married Martha Norvell. These series of documented events proves the Fox and Norvell families were familiar and socialized together.

Records also impossibly indicate that in 1772 William and Mary had their second daughter, Sally Jones Fox. [78] As Benjamin was born in May, it is impossible that the couple had a daughter the same year. Or was it?

The only portrait of Daniel Boone painted in his lifetime, by Chester Harding in 1820. (6)

CHAPTER TWELVE

BENJAMIN KENDRICK FOX

Shortly after submitting to the FamilytreeDNA Big Y 700 test in 2017 it was confirmed that Benjamin Kendrick Fox is my fifth great grandfather. But shockingly it was also discovered that he was not the biological son of William Fox.[216] For some time it was believed he was fathered by Ambrose Cobbs Sr, born 1729; that theory has since been disproven.[286]

His father's identity remains unknown. Who were Benjamin's parents and why did he end up being raised by William and Mary Fox?

In colonial times the common practice of chattel slavery of taking children in for debt or trade might explain the why of it, but not the who. He might have been the product of an illicit affair as continued DNA testing indicates there was a lot of fooling around in the colonial era, despite the religious nature of people at the time.

Had it not been for DNA evidence, Benjamin's parentage would never have been questioned because historical documents indicate he was treated equally to his step-siblings and leave no clue that William was not his biological father.

Because of this, it is unknown what Benjamin's age was when he was taken in by the Fox's, but it must have been early in his life, for he carried his adopted mother's maiden name (Kendrick). It is fair to assume Benjamin was treated well by his adopted mother Mary (Kendrick) and William Fox, who mentioned him in his will as he did his biological sons. William and Mary had six children of their own by the time Benjamin was born and would have three more daughters in the next few years.[216]

Two days shy of Benjamin's first birthday, on May 10, 1773, the Sons of Liberty organized a tax protest in which they boarded ships in

Boston harbor and destroyed their cargo of tea. Though the Boston Tea Party temporarily raised patriot morale, British response was immediate; they closed Boston harbor and passed a series of punitive measures against the Massachusetts colony. A little over a year later on September 9, 1774 Massachusetts County leaders made a declaration of the Suffolk Resolves in which they demanded the punitive actions ceased or they would boycott all British goods.

A shadow government grew in power and began to wrest control of the countryside back from British control. It was becoming time for colonials to pick a side. If there was any Fox family member that was a British loyalist, they haven't been found. Instead, most are listed in local militia's, pledged to the Patriot cause. [115; 237]

In this turbulent time, as the fight began for American freedom, it could be said a Fox family was born.

As the population had grown, so had the desire to settle further inland. Restrictions that had been placed on settlement became a flash point in the coming American War for Independence as well as a source of financial gain.

Boundary restrictions were the focus when on July 5, 1773 well-known Virginian William Russell and a group of about fifty immigrants including obscure hunter and trapper Daniel Boone, who hadn't yet made a name for himself, made the first attempt at a settlement in Kentucky. The party had crossed Powell and Wallins Mountains and was nearing the Cumberland Mountains when on October 8, Russell and Boone's sons as well as some other young men, following the main party with flour and cattle some three miles behind, took camp along Wallins Creek. As darkness fell, the howl of wolves could be heard, but nothing was seen and the camp remained settled throughout the night.

Just before dawn a group of Delawares, Shawnees and Cherokees snuck up and opened fire on the small camp. Most of the young men were killed in the initial fire of muskets, but for a Black slave who escaped. James Boone, 16 years old, and young Henry Russell were shot in the hip and paralyzed. Unable to flee or fight, the boys became a bloody message sent to the colonials by the Indians as they set about to gruesomely torture them.

The leader of the group was Big Jim, who had been to Boone's house before and knew his family. The braves unsheathed their knives and set to work. Down the creek, the escaped slave heard the screams of the boys as the Indians worked, until their screams became pleas to be killed. But Big Jim and the war party were not done. The boys arms and hands were slashed to ribbons where they tried to deflect attacks that tore out their toe nails and finger nails. The cries of the boys finally stopped resounding off the walls of Wallins canyon when Big Jim broke their skulls open with multiple blows from his tomahawk. Boone buried his first born son, building a fire on top the grave, then covering it with stones to conceal it from predators.[338]

The grave and bloody message was received grimly up and down the colonies, causing panic. The settlement in Kentucky was abandoned in the aftermath, but the flood couldn't be held back for long. Meanwhile, violence escalated in Virginia where colonists were exploring and settling in lands south of the Ohio River, all in accordance with earlier treaties with the Cherokee and Iroquois, yet at odds with other tribes who had not made any such agreement. The Royal Governor of Virginia, John Murray, the 4th Earl of Dunmore, called on the Virginia House of Burgesses to declare a state of war with the hostile Indians and called for an elite volunteer militia to execute it.[347]

About this time, in 1774, investors including Richard Henderson of the Transylvania Company of North Carolina purchased a large tract of Cherokee land west of the Appalachian Mountains; most of which is mostly the current-day central and eastern half of Kentucky and a little of northern Tennessee, down to Nashville. This despite at the time, the land was claimed by both Virginia and North Carolina. In addition, neither the British Government nor the renegade Cherokee chief Dragging Canoe agreed with the sale, but it moved forward, regardless. During negotiations Cherokee Chief Dragging Canoe warned the White men about the capacity of the Shawnee north of the Ohio River for war.[360]

By this time, the "Great Road" or "Philadelphia Road" was established that led west from Philadelphia to Lancaster, across the Sisquehanna River to York and on to Chambersburg, Pennsylvania, then south into the Valley of Virginia. By using parts of the Great Indian Path, the colonists had connected their colonies.[297]

CHAPTER THIRTEEN

THE CUMBERLAND GAP

Offering "military bounty land" became popular by the end of the Revolutionary War, but using land as a lure for military service began with the British many years before. In fact in 1774, by order of John Murray, Fourth Earl of Dunmore and Royal Governor of Virginia, James Harrod led 37 men west to survey the boundary of lands promised by the British to veterans of the French-Indian War.

Traveling down the Monongahela and Ohio Rivers, to the mouth of the Kentucky River, the men crossed the Salt River into what today is known as Mercer County, near to center of Kentucky. There, June 16, 1774, they established the first pioneer settlement in Kentucky, naming it Harrod's Town. As White men so far removed from support and deep in heretofore Indian land, they lived in constant vigilance. Despite this, while they endeavored in their work a few weeks later, Shawnee and Mingo warriors bushwhacked a small party of the men on July 8; they killed two and the rest made a terrifying escape three miles back to camp.[347]

A short time later, about the time they had finished the first basic structures, Gov. Dunmore recalled Daniel Boone, who was to fetch the settlers back to serve in militia's he was raising for what was then becoming known as, Lord Dunmore's War. The settlement was abandoned as the men raced back to help defend the colonies. They arrived, however, too late to be involved in what turned out to be the single military action of the war, on October 10, 1774, called the Battle of Point Pleasant.

The Indians were forced to capitulate and lost the right to hunt in the area and agreed to recognize the Ohio River as the boundary between Indian and colonial land; as the treaty with the Cherokee and

Iroquois had set out. There was not full agreement, however, among the various aboriginal tribes, but their chieftains signed the Treaty of Camp Charlotte mostly out of fear another war would simply mean further losses of life and more land lost to the more powerful British.

With the brief war over and violence at least temporarily quelled, James Harrod and his men returned west to the remote village they had begun, establishing Harrod's Town as the first permanent White settlement in what would many years later become the state of Kentucky. Records indicate that a Baptist Brethren community attempted to become established nearby, but according to their beliefs refused to fortify. Subsequently they were all killed.[347; 296]

Boonesborough (7)

When the short Lord Dunmore's War was over, the Transylvania Company of North Carolina contracted frontier explorer, hunter and trapper Daniel Boone (by now becoming well known), to establish The Wilderness Road, going through the Cumberland Gap into southeastern Kentucky.

The company bought what today would be most of Kentucky and half of Tennessee for 2000 lbs of food, clothing, tools, rum and trinkets and signed the treaty March 17, 1775.

With 30 axe men, Boone began a course that would be repeated by about 300,000 emigrating west; cross the Clinch Mountain using Moccasin Gap, then Powell's Mountain using Kane's Gap, crossing Wallins Ridge, staying briefly at Martin's Station to ready for the Cumberland Gap, eight miles west along the Warrior's Path.

They were tasked with cutting a path for fifty miles to join the Hunter's Path leading them north and then continue to slash trail until they reached modern day Madison County. Here they were attacked and the captain of their party was mortally wounded as was his slave. Boone scribbled a note to Captain Richard Henderson, the leader of the expedition, and begged him to gather militia and men and come face the Indian threat. With fifteen miles left to clear, undeterred, Boone continued north with his axe men down Otter Creek, where it emptied into the mouth of the Kentucky River. On April 1, 1775, the party began to erect the fort of Boonesborough, near a salt like on the south side of the Kentucky River.[338; 360; 35]

CHAPTER FOURTEEN

REVOLUTION

To the east, along the coastline the colonies were a powder keg. Talk of war was everywhere and every family was drawn into it, whether Quaker, Baptist Brethren or not. Stark proof that in a time when communication were limited to how loud you could yell, or pass handwritten notes, the word spread fast enough that the entire sprawling boiling pot of colonials was about to explode.

Twelve colonies formed a Continental Congress. Only Georgia didn't sign on initially. They established committees and conventions of speaking engagements to rally fellow colonists. Militias were formed and in months the patriots had taken control of the land all around British occupied Boston. By February of 1775, the British declared the colony of Massachusetts was in an active state of rebellion. In March Patrick Henry gave his famous, "Give me Liberty" speech to the Continental Congress. All up and down the Atlantic coast, the disjointed communities of colonials were in revolt.[237; 348]

In April of 1775, from his stronghold in Boston, Lt. Col. Francis Smith with 700 British Army regulars were given secret orders to proceed to Concord and destroy a stockpile of patriot military supplies of the Massachusetts militia they believed was being stored in a barn. Unknown to the British, the patriots had already received advance word of the raid and had moved it.

On the evening of April 18, 1775, Paul Revere, who was in the employ of the Boston Committee of Correspondence and the Massachusetts Committee of Safety as an express rider as far away as Philadelphia and New York, was summoned by Dr. Joseph Warren. He was tasked with carrying word that British regulars were going northwest out of Boston in the morning to Lexington, intending to arrest Samuel Adams and John Hancock where they were hiding in a house. He was also to add the Redcoats would likely then proceed to Concord to destroy the patriot cache of military arms; not just rifles and powder, but many cannons.

Though unproven, Revere likely contacted Robert Newman, of the sexton of Christ's Church, and instructed him to put two lanterns in the tower of the church as a signal in case he was unable to leave town. The two-lantern signal to Revere's contemporaries meant that the British planned to row across the Charles River to Cambridge, rather than march out Boston Neck; it was NOT, one if by land, two if by sea.

Revere stopped at his house to gather his boots and coat, then proceeded the short distance to the waterfront where two friends waited to row him across the Charles River. Quietly and carefully the boatload of patriots crossed the river, slipping past a British war ship in the dark to the dock in Charlestown where Revere took to the shadows while his cloaked friends silently disappeared, floating back across the river. Slipping through the streets, Revere made it to Col. Conent and other Sons of Liberty where he informed them about the coming British hostility. After verifying they had seen his signal from the church tower, he received warning there were British in the area who might likely try to stop his midnight ride.[237]

By about 11pm Revere was off on a borrowed horse. Just outside of Charlestown he was nearly captured and so changed his planned route to ride through Medford to the home of Isaac Hall, the captain of the local militia. Once Hall had been woken from his sleep to the news, Revere continued to alarm almost all the houses from Medford, through Menotomy (current day Arlington), riding though the property of but careful to avoid, the Royall Mansion, whose owner Isaac Royall was a well-known loyalist.

He arrived in Lexington sometime after midnight where he had some difficulty gaining entry to the house Hancock and Adams were hiding in. After Hancock heard his voice, he was allowed entry and told his tale. Half past midnight, William Dawes arrived in Lexington, carrying the same message as Revere. The two men decided to ride on to Concord, Massachusetts and make sure the military cache was secure.

Dr. Samuel Prescott caught up to them just outside of Lexington and as he was deemed a fellow "high Son of Liberty" they allowed him to join their ride. A British patrol intercepted them a short time later and Prescott and Dawes were able to escape but Revere was held for some time and his horse confiscated to replace the tired mount of a British sergeant. Left alone, Revere walked back to Lexington in the dark, minus his borrowed mount. Despite this slowing him down, he still made it in time to witness the latter part of the battle on Lexington Green.[283]

April 19, 1775 there were 700 British troops just outside of Lexington when they saw a group of 77 militiamen. A British major yelled, "*Throw down your arms! Ye villains, ye rebels!*", the militiamen were badly outnumbered so a commander gave the order to disperse.[46[p.31]] Just as he gave the order, someone in the group popped off a musket at the assembled Redcoats, followed by their rapid response, unleashing several volleys into the running farmers.

When the acrid White smoke cleared, eight patriots were dead and nine wounded while only a single British soldier was wounded. Relatives, friends and neighbors of the dead and wounded farmers suddenly seethed for revenge. Emboldened, the British troops moved on to Concord, where they still believed there was a cache of rebel weaponry. By the time they got into town, hundreds of militiamen occupied the high ground and watched the Redcoats begin their search.

Frustrated by not finding a large cache, the British troops began to burn what few weapons they could find. The fires got a little out of control and from the distance they were at, the militiamen thought incorrectly that the British were going to burn the whole town. British troops tasked with guarding Concord's North Bridge suddenly had the mass of militiamen rushing into view. The British fired first but fell back immediately as the militiamen returned the volley, still coming dead on the run.[237; *273*]

After about four hours of searching Concord and burning what little they could find, the British decided to return 18 miles to Boston. By now 2000 militiamen who made the term "minute men" famous, had gathered outside Concord, with more arriving all the time. As the Crown's troops marched from town, they were surrounded by farmers with rifles who initially followed alongside the Redcoat column to intimidate, but soon started firing from hidden positions along the way.

This was unconventional fighting for British troops. Shots came from the trees, behind rocks, walls and ditch lines. As the Redcoats tried to begin an orderly retreat the shots just kept coming and they were soon shedding clothing, weapons and their equipment to run, faster and faster. They ran all the way to Lexington where they were met by a fresh brigade of Redcoats sent as reinforcement.

Perhaps the fleeing Brits might have thought they were saved but swelling their ranks did not slow the harassing fire from the pursuing patriots. The moving battle continued though Menotomy (Arlington) and Cambridge with the British doing their best with flanking parties and cannon fire to keep the rebels at bay.

A new contingent of minute men from Salem and Marblehead, Massachusetts arrived and that evening purportedly had a chance to head off the retreating British troops and perhaps finish them all off, but the overly cautious commander ordered them not to attack. The shot up British troops made it to Charlestown where they had naval support and so survived the day. But the fight was on now.[237; 273]

Though news of these events had not yet made it to Williamsburg, unconnected to these events, Virginia's Royal Governor, John Murray, the Lord of Dunmore had seen tensions rising, so even though unaware of other situations, he ordered the removal of gunpowder from the magazine in Williamsburg to a Royal Navy ship. The move was met with outrage and a small militia force led by Patrick Henry began to muster throughout the colony. When a payment was made to Patrick Henry for the cost of the powder, the matter was resolved without conflict, but Dunmore himself later moved to a naval vessel for fear of his safety onshore. It was the end of royal control of the colony of Virginia and Patrick Henry would become the first native Governor of the colony the following July 1776.

When the British lost control, they lost control everywhere and it didn't take instant communication for it to happen. Patriotic independent and armed men all over doing what they felt was right, in the moment created America. Sides had been chosen and neighborly relations became strained between patriot and loyalist sympathizers.[344; 348]

The conflict had a devastating effect on the Confederated Iroquois who had maintained a unified position on decisions for 200 years. When a consensus could not be agreed to about who to support, Redcoats or Americans, their league of tribes fractured. In the end, some fought for the Brits, some fought for the colonial Americans and some tried to stay neutral. The result was everyone was killing Iroquois and the confederated tribes never recovered.[299]

The summer of 1775 first saw Skenesboro, New York captured by patriot leader Lt. Samuel Herrick, May 9. Then Fort Ticonderoga was captured by Ethan Allen, Benedict Arnold and the Green Mountain Boys the following day on May 10, coincidentally the same day the

Second Continental Congress met. From that historic meeting came votes June 14, to create the Continental Army from the militia, with George Washington of Virginia as commanding general.

Three days later was the Battle at Bunker Hill. On July 2nd Washington arrived in Cambridge, Massachusetts to take command of the Continental Army. Back in Philadelphia, four days later, the Declaration of the Causes and Necessity of Taking Up Arms was issued on July 6. On July 8, an Olive Branch Petition was sent to King George III, but they were all well past any olive branches.

All up and down the coastline colonies were in open revolt. The countryside was already a lost cause but the rebels were taking cities as well. From offshore in Virginia, Lord Dunmore issued the Dunmore Proclamation that winter on November 7, offering freedom to slaves that abandoned their Patriot masters to fight for the Crown. Three days later in a tavern the Continental Marines were established by the Continental Congress.[233; 237]

Fighting continued albeit restrained for the winter weather. Fifty-nine cannons captured at Fort Ticonderoga and Fort Crown Point in New York were moved that winter to Boston. Meanwhile British forces repelled an attack by Continental Army generals Richard Montgomery and Benedict Arnold at the Battle of Quebec on New Years Eve, 1775. Battles continued through the winter and accelerated in the spring of 1776 as the weather allowed.

In March, the British abandoned Boston. On July 2nd the Second Continental Congress enacted a resolution declaring independence from the British Empire and on July 4, 1776, approved the written Declaration of Independence. By late summer, the British had so many patriot prisoners of war that they begin storing them on British prison ships in Wallabout Bay, New York where more men died miserable deaths than did on battlefields of the war.[233; 234]

Daniel Boone had fulfilled his contract with the Transylvania Company by 1776 and marked a path to the Kentucky River, where he had established Fort Boonesborough a year before, intended to be the capital of Transylvania. He had used the ancient 'buffalo traces' that traveled through the mountains in a great loop, from one salt lick to the next. These trails connected to the Warriors Trail and Great Indian Path in places to create the interstate of the day.

Though Boone was unaware of it, investor representative Richard Henderson was leading another expedition behind him widening the trail to accommodate wagon traffic. It was called Boone's Trace for some time before it became known as the Wilderness Trail. Known as a Yadkin-man, the trail blazer's route traveled from his home, up the Yadkin River in northwestern North Carolina to its headwaters in the Blue Ridge, crossed to the west side of the Ridge, where the headwaters of the Watauga River led down to where it joined the South Fork of the Holston River. The trail crossed ridge after river after ridge until it reached the only opening in the Cumberland Mountains, the famous Cumberland Gap.[360; 338; 35]

Henderson did his best to convince the Continental Congress to legally recognize Transylvania, but it was already claimed by North Carolina and Virginia and Congress declined to act without their consent. Additionally they prohibited the Transylvania Company from making any demands on settlers in the region. This allowed settlers to begin to pour in, to the chagrin of Cherokee Chief Dragging Canoe that then began war on the settlers.

At a point sometime in May of 1775, the first religious service was held at Boonesborough and though it is commonly described as being held by Quakers, it was held by the Baptist Brethren. May 23, 1775 Col. Richard Henderson of the Transylvania Company of North Carolina called for an assembly of the three settlements in Kentucky. Representatives from Boonesborough, Harrodsburg and St. Asaph's met at Boonesborough. Among other things, Daniel Boone suggested that the communities invest and promote the breeding of good horse flesh. Quite an omen given what was to come in the Bluegrass State. It looked like the Kentucky country would finally be settled, so in August of 1775, Boone rode out of Boonesborough to retrieve his wife Rebecca and their children.[296; 338]

As the War for Liberty raged, in order to pay the military, Congress promised Continental line soldiers acreage in Virginia, Connecticut, Massachusetts (including Maine), New York, Pennsylvania, Maryland, North Carolina, South Carolina and Georgia. Those who had lived there for untold generations were not consulted.

Captains were granted 300 acres, non-commissioned officers and privates 100 acres and other ranks received amounts that varied widely. As these men completed their terms of service, many took their claims and families to parts far-flung. The timing of the opening of the Cumberland Gap, and promised land claims, led families inland.

By this time, the Fox and Cobbs families were well established 5th generation Americans, spread throughout Virginia and the Carolina's, ready to take land claims and begin moving in combined family groups.

It was neither to the liking of the British nor the Shawnees that Kentucky was being settled by American colonials. Royal commanders took advantage of the shared goals and worked to get the Indians to fight their battles on the frontier. In a combined effort the Crown appealed to their old allies to drive the White men out of the Kentucky country. To the east Gen. Frederick Haldimand, the governor of the province of Quebec, solidified the relationship the Crown had with the Iroquois. In Detroit, Lt. Gov. Henry Hamilton, British Superintendent of Indian Affairs was able to negotiate agreements with the Shawnee, Delaware, Chippewa, Mingo, Miami, Ottowa and Wyandot, to form the coalition of Seven Nations. The British supplied the Indians with clothing, blankets, food, shelter, muskets, gunpowder, flints, lead, hatchets and tomahawk's. They also offered reward for colonial scalps, in fact, Henry Hamilton made the transaction so much he earned being known as The Hair Buyer. Life in Kentucky was about to get much more dangerous.[241; 299; 237]

In 1776, new settlements were begun in the Kentucky country, located mostly along the buffalo traces that lied north of the three established settlements. Directly north of the settlements, McClellan's Station began to be built with Leestown nearby. Just north of Boonesborough, Bryan's Station began to grow from a modest campsite. To the north of all of these, was Hinkston's Station. More settlements made the area safe.

On Sunday, July 14, 1776 Daniel Boone's daughter Jemima, and Betsy and Fannie Calloway got into a boat and paddled out into the River in front of Boonesborough. As the girls chatted and let the boat float near the canebreaks across the river, a band of Shawnee and a Cherokee Chief called Hanging Maw that were concealed in the reeds, snatched up their boat and drug the girls onto the bank, dragging them away. In an effort to help a rescue party, the girls broke branches and dropped bits of cloth.

Daniel Boone and eight others took in after the group, but did not follow through the canebreaks, but took a different route instead, chasing the kidnappers to the Blue Licks, quite some distance away. The White men startled the Indians who assumed their enemy was fighting their way through the reeds behind them. Black powder rifles roared and filled the forest with acrid smoke. The Indians took to fleeing and the girls were saved.

However the same day, another force of Indians separated to conduct raids on the new forts, recently constructed. Men were shot in their fields tending crops and all the cattle around the stations were snatched by the Indians. That winter, December 29, 1776 Shawnees led by Chief Pluggy attacked McClelland's Station (or fort, for all intents and purposes). Ironically, two days later as this attack was being perpetrated, on December 31, politicians in the state of Virginia designated everything west of the Appalachian Mountains as Kentucky County. Chief Pluggy had led an attack by that time for two days that did not recognize the edicts of White men. In fact, when the opportunity finally presented itself about the time the area was named Kentucky County, the settlers at McClelland' Station had to escape to Harrodsburg, January 30, 1777.[338; 296; 241]

To the east, throughout the last months of 1776 the Brits were pushed back mainly to New York, where a number of bloody battles took place. In a last parting shot, Danbury, Connecticut was burned and looted by British regulars under Major General William Tyron April 26, 1777.[237]

CHAPTER FIFTEEN

JAMES BUNCH, BORN 1750

By the spring of 1777 all the settlements in Kentucky that had been recently built were abandoned. The only three left were the original Forts of Harrodsburg, Boonesborough and St. Asaph's. Two to three hundred settlers retreated back through the Cumberland Gap, to civilization in the colonies. Behind them, separate attacks on Harrodsburg took place March 7, and April 18 and 19.

A few days later on April 24 the Shawnee attacked Boonesborough and when Daniel Boone tried to help a wounded settler get back in the fort, he was shot in the ankle and was saved only when frontiersman Simon Kenton ran from the fort to help him get back to its safety. The Shawnee withdrew but returned May 23, 24 and 25, launching more attacks. A few days later they attacked St. Asaph's Station but withdrew and reappeared at Boonesborough on July 4, having grown their numbers to about 200 warriors. Inside the wooden fort, 22 men stood against them for a siege that lasted 48 hours. St. Asaph's was then attacked by probably the same 200 Shawnee braves. By the middle summer in 1777, the situation in Kentucky was getting desperate.[35; 338]

James Bunch, born in 1750 to a man known by historians as Samuel Bunch, The Quaker,[116] was the great, great grandson of John Punch, who had been a Black slave. Samuel, his father, grandfather and great grandfather (all named John Bunch, not Punch) all married White women.[159] Considering all that had happened, these grandsons of John Punch whose great grandfathers had altered their names to Bunch, were not likely aware of 'uncomfortable' family information. Therefore, now four generations later, these people had no clue from where their line had begun in America, aside from a vague note in a few family bibles that the first Bunch to America was 17 years old.

At this point, some owned slaves themselves.

The Bunch family has roots as deep in America as nearly any. From the beginning the family had remained in Virginia, with many children having many children. Some of the sons of John Punch altered the last name differently, spreading the family even further and wider than can easily be found.[34] James had 10 siblings, one of which a brother named John J. Bunch, was two years younger. Both James, John and a couple siblings had been disciplined by their Quaker church by the mid-1770's and when they joined the militia, they were discharged from the church.[136]

The frontier erupted in violence and militias were formed, to which James and John joined, to protect settlements. Displaying their adept ability to move stealthily in the woods, the brothers became scouts; sometimes called spies, due to their sneaking around the woods keeping an eye on enemy movements.

When hostilities were taking place in the Kentucky country, James and John Bunch were serving the militia in Powell's Valley (named for longhunter Ambrose Powell family; not related to Cader or Joab Powell, whose families will be met later) that was a natural broad expanse through which led to the Cumberland Gap, along the Wilderness Trail. Though settled by White men by June 1777 the Powell Valley had to be evacuated because the Indian allies of the British threatened to kill them all.

In September of 1777 local militia led by Captain John Dunkin met James and John Bunch; spies who had been following the movements of the Indians. The militia were tasked with retrieving the settlers possessions, which they did, but on the way out they were attacked. James was badly wounded and two men were killed as men scattered in the underbrush, arriving haggard back at camp throughout the night and next day. James was the focus of a number of reports by officers who distinguished he and his brother and lamented his grievous injuries. To what degree he healed from his injuries is unknown.[35; 34]

The first Fox to leave Virginia was not a son of Richard Fox, but his daughter Mary, married to Samuel Jones ten years prior in 1766.[140]. In fact of Richard's 13 children, only two left North Carolina and Virginia; both of them daughters. By 1777 Samuel and Mary Jones were among some of the earliest settlers taking bounty lands in the frontier of the colony of Georgia. The Jones family was large and a name that would subsequently be used in the Fox family for generations, as the Kendrick name was. The couple may have settled in Georgia hoping to avoid Indian hostilities and they would, but only for a while. Plenty of settlers blood was yet to be spilled in the southern colony before the last Indian was killed or evicted.[227]

In Kentucky, Daniel Boone was captured by a Shawnee hunting party as he was hunting to feed a party of 20 men who were working at a salt lick. When he was taken to the Indian camp, led by Chief Blackfish, where he observed 100 warriors readying to attack Boonesborough.

In order to save the lives of the settlers, Boone agreed with Blackfish to go with his warriors and try to talk the workers at the salt lick into surrendering. The ploy saved their lives, but the Whites were all abducted and removed north to a Shawnee village, where some of them were sold as slaves to the British military. Boone was sent back to live with the Shawnee Chief Blackfish where he learned their language and customs.

There were those that never forgave Boone for what the Indians did to the settlers after he talked them into surrendering.[338]

CHAPTER SIXTEEN

THE WAR COMES TO KENTUCKY

As the British continued to lose the war, they abandoned their occupation of Philadelphia in June 1778. By this time Rebecca Boone had not seen her husband for a year and assumed he was dead. She loaded up the families belongings on horses and led them back through the mountains, to the colonies.

During the same month, Boone, still residing with the Shawnee, returned from a hunting trip where he observed over 400 Shawnee preparing to attack Boonesborough. The next morning on June 16, Boone slipped away from the Shawnee camp at dawn and in four days he ran 160 miles though the wilderness to warn the settlers an attack was imminent. He found Rebecca gone, but resolved to hold Boonesborough back from being destroyed by the Indians. He quickly drafted two letters requesting reinforcements.

The wait for an attack ended September 8, when 444 Shawnee warriors showed up at Boonesborough led by Chief Blackfish and commanded by a French Canadian Captain with eleven provincial soldiers. The White men inside Boonesborough knew that death was preferable to being taken captive, so resolved to fight to the end or save the last lead and powder for themselves, cheating their enemy the satisfaction.

The British Captain sent word he wanted surrender but Boone refused, in turn the Captain asked for a parlay in front of the fort and stalling for time, hoping for reinforcements, Boone agreed. Nothing was decided but it ended cordially. When the meeting was finished they stood to shake hands and at that point some Shawnee braves tried to seize Boone, but he escaped, running for the fort. The area around the fort blew up into gunfire as the Indians kept up a continuous fire and deadly assault that lasted for nine days.

In the last assault on the fort, Indians came from out of the surrounding wood, armed with torches, racing to light the wooden structure on fire. Persistent and steady rifle fire from inside the fort stopped their last violent effort. In the course of the attack, only two White men were killed and four were wounded.[338]

In retaliation for the attacks Col. John Bowman of the Kentucky militia conducted a raid across the Ohio and engaged the Shawnee in their villages including Old Chillacothe. After several desperate fights, Bowman backed off, retreating to Kentucky. The Indians had successfully defended their crops and their villages but this time it was they that felt the sting of the wasp.[338; 237]

As these battles were transpiring other events behind the scenes were taking place to defend Kentucky. George Rogers Clark with the approval of Virginia's governor, Patrick Henry, secretly organized 175 Kentuckians and left the fort at Corn Island near present-day Louisville, descending the Ohio River earlier in the summer of 1778. By July, the little army had crossed the Ohio River at Fort Massac across from present-day Paducah, Kentucky and marched to Kaskaskia.

On the night of July 4, 1778 Clark's Kentuckians took the British-led city without firing a shot. The next day Col. Bowman and his militia force took the village of Cahokia in the same way. They faced little resistance because the French-speaking and Indian inhabitants refused to take up arms on behalf of the British. Next to surrender was the garrison at Vincennes along the Wabash River, the British called Fort Sackville; then came several other villages and British forts. To counter these efforts, Gov Henry Hamilton left Detroit with a small British force and reseized Vincennes.[237; 348; 29]

During this summer of 1778's violent conflict, after years of political and financial wrangling, the Virginia's Assembly declared the Transylvania claim void, compensating them with a grant of 12 square miles on the Ohio River below the Green River. The enterprise was suddenly a memory that would fade in a matter of years. Those that invested did not make money, and that would include Daniel Boone, who never was compensated for his work. It would likely console him little today to know that his families suffering for his efforts to make money brought him fame. Though Transylvania is a place not on a map that few remember were directly responsible for opening up Kentucky, the man that made it possible by blazing the Wilderness Trail, Daniel Boone, lives on immortalized in every medium.[338; 360]

In February of 1779 Col. Clark once again organized a force of 170 men, this time somewhat funded from his pocket and those of some his friends, as his budget had run out. They endured melting snow and ice and cold rain and wind, but by February 23 the patriot force engaged British Gov. Hamilton's forces. In two days Hamilton surrendered and was subsequently taken prisoner. This stunning victory launched the career of George Rogers Clark and served to make the colonists feel finally as if the Indians and British were no longer in control of Kentucky.

In retaliation, some months later to the east, in the Battle of Fairfield, British General William Tyron destroyed 54 barns, 47 storehouses, burned 83 homes, 2 churches, the courthouse, local jail and schoolhouse on July 11, 1779.[29]

In October 1779, Daniel Boone took his family back to Kentucky and took a land claim in Fayette County on Boone Creek, where they built a fortified station and settlement. Around them Daniel and Rebecca's relatives settled and eventually the growing village became known as Boone's Station.

By the end of 1779 there were 25 new pioneer settlements in Kentucky, and by the end of 1780 there would be 57 more. A stockade for British prisoners of war was established on January 28, 1780, on the banks of the Cumberland River. Two years later the area around it developed into the frontier town of Nashville.[338; 165]

On March 14 after a two week siege, Spanish general, colonial governor of Louisiana, and Viceroy of New Spain, Bernardo de Galvez captured Fort Charlotte, taking the port of Mobile in present day Alabama, from British forces. The collapse of British control of the fort pushed their influence from the western shores of western Florida to its capital, Pensacola.[237]

In response, on April 1780 a British force left Detroit to invade Kentucky. In June, 500 Shawnee, Wyandot, Delaware and others joined the British troops; crossed the Ohio River and then began following Licking Creek, intending to take the northern settlements.

The British engaged Ruddle's Station first, keeping their Native American allies hid while they tried to intimidate the settlers with the two light cannons they had brought. The Indians refused to take orders from their masters and began to assault the fort. Capt. Ruddle surrendered the fort upon the condition no one in the fort would be harmed. Royal Col. Henry Bird gave his word and the inhabitants opened the fort, only to have the Indians pour in firing on men, women and children, killing them all.

The British commanded the Indians to stop, but were powerless against the blood lust. Ruddle's Station was put to the torch whereupon the British and Indian forces continued to Martin's Station and forced its surrender. These captives were marched to Detroit and those that had a hard time of it were executed.

In retaliation, George Rogers Clark was given promotion and field artillery to go north into Ohio and destroy the Shawnee villages of Old Chillacothe and Piqua. The Shawnee capitals were burnt to the ground and the inhabitants scattered to the forest. After the Shawnee were devastated in these attacks they would only resort to sneak attacks on the Kentuckians.[338; 295]

The War for Liberty continued and by May 12, 1780 after a month long battle known as, the Siege of Charleston, the city fell to British troops under General Henry Clinton and naval forces under Admiral Mariot Arbuthnot. The British lost 255 men, but captured a large American garrison. It was considered the worst defeat the Patriots had sustained. Later that month on May 29 at the Battle of Waxhaws, the Continental Army was dealt another crushing defeat.[237]

On June 30, 1780, the state of Virginia abolished the vast Kentucky County and divided it into Fayette, Jefferson and Lincoln counties, which were still immense in size. Each remote county had a county-seat with one way in and out. Louisville in Jefferson County was accessible by the terminus of the Ohio River; Boone's branch of the Wilderness Trail led to Lexington and Harrodsburg in Lincoln County was accessed by the Crab Orchard branch of the Wilderness Trail.

A resident of the new Fayette County, Daniel Boone was named Lt. Col. of the county militia. Coincidentally the same year, James Bunch, having healed from his wounds, as well as his brother John; both still single men; moved northwest to North Carolina, closer to the frontier. They had each finished their terms of service and looked toward to the frontier for their futures.[184]

At the Battle of Camden on August 16, 1780, British General Cornwallis conducted a humiliating victory in South Carolina over General Horatio Lloyd Gates, a retired British officer who had come out of retirement to serve the Continental Army.

To add to the bitter defeats the Americans endured, on September 23, the treason of Benedict Arnold was exposed when John Andre, a British Army officer was arrested as a spy who attempted to aid

Arnold, who was then commander of West Point that controlled the Hudson River, in surrendering to the British forces for L20,000.

The coward Arnold found out that his incriminating letters had been confiscated as he was heading in a boat to breakfast with George Washington. He also found out that another courier had been dispatched to give Washington the letters he had written, that were confiscated the night before from Andre. He quickly went to shore and hired bargemen that took him downriver to where the fittingly named *HMS Vulture* was awaiting to spirit the traitor away. He sent a letter to Washington requesting his wife was given safe passage, which the American General granted. Though he didn't show his emotions at the time, the treason of Benedict Arnold was a deep wound to General George Washington.[237; 234; 232]

In Kentucky, the Shawnee continued their tactics of sneak attacks on unsuspecting White settlers. In October of 1780 Daniel Boone was hunting with his brother Edward when the two were separated. Though Daniel had heard the shot and his response was far too late, he heard the Indian's who thought they had killed Daniel Boone so summarily cut Edwards head off to show their tribe, working the corpse over with knives and axes. Boone escaped, killing one Indian in the effort, returning later to retrieve Edward's mutilated body to bury on Boone's Creek in Fayette County.[338]

Benedict Arnold was tasked with razing Richmond, Virginia specifically because he was an American and the British hoped his presence would inspire Loyalists. Beginning the first of January 1781 Arnold commenced moving, sailing his fleet up the James River, burning and laying waste to settlements and plantations. By January 4, the turncoat had reached Westover Plantation where he readied for the assault on Richmond. The following day Arnold sent his "green coats", Loyalists troops consisting of infantry, dragoons and artillery, to meet the patriots guarding the city. There were only about 200 militia guarding the city because most of the locals had already served their time in service and felt they had already met their duty.

As the enemy approached, the patriots fired a weak volley and retreated into the woods. Thomas Jefferson, the governor of Virginia at the time, saw his defenses fail and immediately called for an emergency evacuation of the city, including most military supplies, then he promptly took a carriage quickly from the city. It was a decision that would haunt him politically for years.[232; 356]

Arnold rode into town triumphant at noon without a shot being fired. He wrote a patronizing letter to Jefferson that day, claiming if he could move all of the cities tobacco stores and military supplies to his ships, he would leave the city untouched. The letter angered Jefferson who wrote back the next day sharply informing Arnold that he refused a turncoat do anything with the cities stores.

When Arnold read the response he ordered the city be set to the torch. British soldiers roamed the streets setting fires and ransacking government buildings and private residences. Strong winds fed the flames so by afternoon, Arnold was moving from the wreckage of the day, toward the Westham cannon foundry, which his troops then sacked and torched. When the foundry was destroyed Arnold moved across the James River to the port town of Warwick where his troops again sacked and set fire to every building they encountered.

When Jefferson heard Richmond was mostly gone, he was outraged and called on Virginia militia Col. Sampson Mathews to confront the traitor and his troops. Though slowed by sickness, bad weather and mutiny Mathews managed a surprise attack on Arnold with 200 militiamen. Using tactics made famous by Nathaniel Greene, the militia managed to inflict significant damage on Arnold's troops over the course of a few days.

When Arnold felt like the damage was serious enough, he raced down the James River, setting fire and looting his way to Portsmouth where he planned to set up defenses and wait for reinforcements. Along the way he assaulted the plantation of founding father Benjamin Harrison, who was inside his home and saw the British coming. Harrison quickly gathered his family and fled in a carriage, saving their lives. Arnold knew it was Harrison's mansion, who he disliked and felt was a traitor to Britain. He ordered all the belonging's inside Harrison's home be brought out of the house to the lawn and burned.

The purpose of destroying Harrison's possessions was due to Arnold's feeling that the war would soon be won and he wanted a nice home. He arrogantly did not destroy the mansion or buildings and took 40 slaves with him when he moved on. Arnold eventually made it to Portsmouth, where he was welcomed as the conquering hero. The month of January 1781 saw some of Benedict Arnold's finest hours, while ironically securing his identity as a traitor at the same time.[232]

While the war raged, the government organized. Positions were named and filled and Articles of Confederation were ratified by March 1, 1781. Later in the year on October 19 of that year, the combined forces of the Continental Army and French troops led by Comte de Rochambeau won the Yorktown campaign, which proved to be the last major battle of the American Revolutionary War. British rockstar General Cornwallis surrendered, and he and his army were captured. The success served to boost American morale and revive French enthusiasm for the war while deflating British support in England. The war was almost finished on February 1782, when the British House of Commons voted against further war, informally recognizing American independence. It wasn't over, but it was close.[237]

However in the summer of 1782, out of the Shawnee capital of Old Chillicothe, came the combined forces of seven different tribes;

500 warriors strong, joined by British Butlers Rangers led by William Caldwell, sent to the frontier from Fort Niagara.

Joining this military force was the notorious Capt. Alexander McKee and Simon Girty, who worked as liaison between the Crown and the Seven Nations. Daniel Boone had served on a jury two years before when McKee was stripped of his land claim in Kentucky for being a British Torie, or sympathizer.

On August 15, the invasion force came into sight of Bryan's Station. From a tall cornfield a smaller force began firing on the forts southern wall while the main force organized in the canebreaks along the river. Amazingly cool, many of the women in the fort single filed out with pales and buckets and walked to the river for much needed water. Their concealed enemies watched but did not fire upon them and allowed them to return to the fort. Then the firing commenced and it was a blood bath.

All the animals around the fort were riddled as smoke from rifles drifted in waves around the beleaguered fort. Outbuildings were set on fire and destroyed, as the attacks kept up for 2 days before the Brits and Indians broke off and headed north, up a buffalo trace.

In response Daniel Boone led a group of militia from Boone's Station to Bryan's Station. There he was joined by the founder of Lexington, Col. Robert Patterson, leading their militia. In addition, militia leaders Col. John Todd and Col. Stephen Trigg joined the troupe for a total of 175 well-armed Kentuckians; the militia from Lexington wore red leggings.

They pursued the British and Indians back past the destroyed Ruddle's Station to the Blue Licks River, where the Indians purposely left an easy trail to follow. Here the enemy lay in hiding along the river. Boone was suspicious and counseled against pursuit, but when Major Hugh McGary from the Lincoln County contingent was implicated a coward, he impulsively led a charge across the river.

As the bold Kentuckians went to cross the river along the buffalo trace, the woods opened up in gunfire. An overwhelming force of Indians drove the Kentuckians back after about 15 minutes of ferocious fighting.[338; 161]

More than 67 Kentuckians died as the Indians chased them down with knives, tomahawks and axes. Of those killed was colonels Patterson and Todd, Daniel Boone's son Israel Boone was killed next to his father, as well as Thomas Boone, Daniel's nephew. The bloody fight became immediately known as the Battle of Blue Licks.

Though online lists do not include their names, an unsourced notation found at the Brownsville Historical Museum claims David and Solomon Hardman were with Daniel Boone at the siege of Blue Lick and Boonesborough. These were German Baptist Brethren, not a people given to violence, but could have been drawn in. Solomon Hardman was the father of Benjamin Hardman, who would become related to the Fox family through the Baltimore's, about ninety years hence.

Incidentally, before the end of 1782, the German Baptist Brethren forbade their members to practice slavery, 70 years before the subject brought the country to a civil war.[338; 296; 128]

Sometime later, Boone returned to the site of the battle with a burial detail. In a mass grave were lain the mutilated bodies of dozens of men. Daniel could only identify his son Israel from the blood soaked shirt he had been wearing the day of the battle.

There were yet battles in 1782 but support for the war was gone in England and by November 30, preliminary Articles of Peace were signed by British negotiator Richard Oswald and representatives of the Unites States of America. Two weeks later on December 14, the British evacuated Charleston, South Carolina. The American Indian had lost a valuable ally when the Redcoats sailed away.[338; 241]

In the following months, the Tates Creek Baptist Church was established in a stone building near Boonesborough. The first church in the Kentucky country was German Brethren Baptist affiliated. The founding pastor of the church was a friend with Thomas Jefferson and it is said their relationship helped shape some of Jefferson's ideals.[296]

About a year after the war, privy to an anonymous letter being circulated by his officers, on March 15, 1783, George Washington showed up unannounced at a clandestine assembly. The letter addressed to the Continental Congress complained of promises broken for payment of duty and reimbursement for their personal costs in their service.

Washington plead to their sense of history and asked them not to sully the accomplishments they had achieved. The aging general pulled a pair of reading glasses out after he had addressed the men, in order to read a letter from the Continental Congress. Before he began, he offered in an almost apologetic tone, *"Gentlemen, you must pardon me. I have grown old in the service of my country and now find that I am growing blind."*[335[p.8]]

As tears welled in the eyes of his men, the promises made in the letter became irrelevant. The assembled officers realized that Washington had given as much or more in sacrifice. Within minutes the officers capitulated and voted unanimously to express confidence in the Congress and their country.[335]

The truth though, was that it was Washington. It was always Washington. He was the perfect man, at the perfect time to bind the fledgling country with ideals he epitomized. He was not a politician.

However, despite the best efforts of patriots, 'government' is a place a certain type of individual is drawn to. Politicians historically, generally love to spend other people's money, and they don't like to pay their bills.

Three months after Washington talked down his officers who had not been paid, on June 17, 1783, congress received a letter from soldiers stationed at Philadelphia demanding payment for their service during the war. Payment for their service, like many, had never been prompt and now they demanded paid.

While the Treaty of Paris in 1783 decided international borders, no one consulted Native Americans, who still laid claim to the lands. (8)

On June 20, as many as 400 soldiers mobbed the State House where the federal government did its business. Alexander Hamilton talked the soldiers into letting the congress meet their concerns, then promptly drafted a request of the Philadelphia Executive Council to protect them from the soldiers.

The council was uninterested in providing them security so the founding feds hightailed it for Princeton, New Jersey. George Washington heard about the mutiny 4 days after it began and sent 1500 troops to quell the protesters, only a few of which were arrested.

Named the Pennsylvania Mutiny of 1783, it is the primary reason the framers of the Constitution decided to create a federal district, distinct from the states; where Congress could provide for its own security. The government of the United States has historically neglected it's veterans from the very beginning. Every war, every era.

That fall, September 3, 1783, the 1783 Treaty of Paris ended the American War for Independence. On November 25 the British evacuated New York, ending British rule and General George Washington triumphantly returned with the (unpaid) Continental Army. About a month later, with his duty accomplished, George Washington resigned as commander-in-chief of the Continental Army.[234; 284]

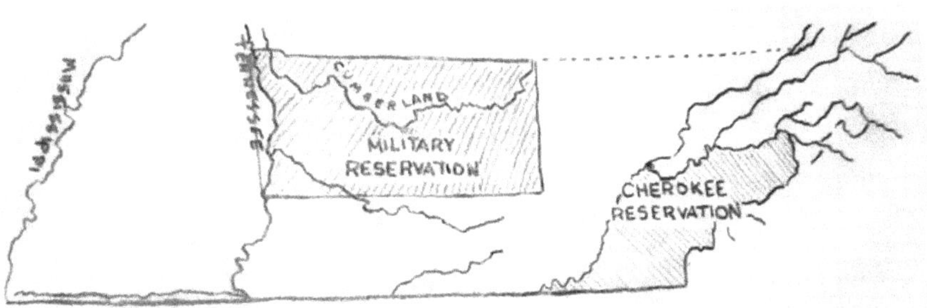

Post Revolutionary War Indian reservation land (9)

CHAPTER SEVENTEEN

DEATH OF WILLIAM FOX

In the last months of the American War for Liberty William Fox, 51, knew his time was close and wrote his will on September 4, 1783. Accent to lines has been added as well as ages of his children in parenthesis, for reason of comparison.

Will of WILLIAM FOX, 1783 – Mecklenburg County, Virginia In the name of God, Amen, I William Fox, of the County of Mecklenburg County and State of Virginia being sick and weak of body but of sound and perfect Sence and Memory blessed be Almighty God for the same and calling to mind the uncertainty of life and that it is appointed for all men once to die do make and ordain this my last will and Testament in manner and form following, that is to say first and principally I recommend my soul to Almighty God the giver thereof in full hopes of my Resurrection through the Merits of Jesus Christ my Saviour.

First I wish my body to be buried in a Christian like and decent manner at the Discretion of my Executors hereafter mentioned and as for what worldly Estate it hath pleased Almighty God to bless me with in this life, I give and dispose in manner and form following.

Item: I give and devise to my son Arthur Fox (22), *my Bay colt called Liberty and my Sorell Filley to him and his Heirs forever.*

Item: I give and devise to my son Richard Fox (19-one of twins), *my Filley named Betty Fine and my Pocotate Filley to him and his Heirs forever.*

Item: I give and devise to my son William Fox (19-one of twins), *my great bay mare and her future increase to him and his Heirs forever.*

Item: I give and devise to my son Henry Fox (17), *my Sorell Colt to him and his Heirs forever.*

Item: I give and devise to my daughter Mary Kendrick Fox (15)*, one Good Feather bed and Furniture to her and her Heirs forever.*

Item: I give and devise to my son Benjamin Fox (11*), 20 pounds specie to him and his Heirs forever.*

Item: I give and devise to my daughter Sally Jones Fox (coincidentally, also 11 years old) *one good Feather bed and Furniture to her and her Heirs forever.*

Item: I give and devise to my daughter Johanna Fox (5), *one good Feather bed and Furniture to her and her Heirs forever.*

Item: I give and devise to my daughter Priscilla Fox (6), *one good Feather bed and Furniture to her and her Heirs forever.*

Item: I give and devise to my daughter Betsey Fox (younger than 4)*, one good Feather bed and Furniture to her and her Heirs forever.*

Item: I give and bequeath to my beloved wife Mary Fox (45) *the use of my plantation and land also the use of Jack, Sucka, and Chainey and all the rest of my estate both real and personal during her life except she marries and in case she marries then for her to have only her thirds and my desire and will is that after my wife's death except as aforesaid all that part that I give my wife the use of during her life to be equally divided amongst my Surviving children.*

My will and desire further is that if any of my Surviving children should die before they come of age or without Lawful Issue that his or their part to be equally divided amongst all my surviving children and lastly my desire and will is that my beloved wife Mary Fox and my Friend John Kindrick be my soul Executors of this my last will and Testament hereby revoking and Disannuling all other former wills and Testaments by me heretofore made and Declaring this and this only to be my last as witness my hand and seal this 4th day of September in the year of our Lord one Thousand Seven Hundred and Eighty Three.

Signed and Sealed in presence of us John Kindrick, James Blanton, Lucas Sullivant s/ William Fox (L.S.)

P.S. I desire that all my children that has not Sufficient learning be Taught out of that part that I leave my wife – of and that my estate be not appraised.

s/ William Fox

J.K.; J.B.; L.S.[226](Mecklenburg County (Va.) Will Books, 1782-1798. Will Book 2, page 36)

John Kendrick mentioned in the document was married to Amy Fox, William's daughter, and James Blanton and Lucas Sullivant probably just friends at this point. But James Blanton, born in 1764 in Cross Creek, North Carolina, a militia veteran that served in both the infantry and cavalry in the militia from 1780-81 had a son named Thomas who would wed William's granddaughter by his son Richard. Lucas Sullivant, too, had been a private in the militia. It is interesting that William was more than a little concerned his widowed wife would remarry.[12; 157]

William lived his entire life in Mecklenburg County, Virginia. He died on November 10, 1783 and his will was proven in court nine days later. There doesn't seem to be any record of him serving with the militia in defense of the colonies against Indians or during the War for Liberty.

In his Will, Benjamin is cited similarly to his step-brothers and sisters, but there is quite a disparity in what the sons received. Each of William's sons but Benjamin received two horses or a horse and colt. By this point, William's sons Arthur, Richard and William were grown men; Arthur, 22, was in fact a veteran of the war.[36]

The fact William and Mary Fox had twins Richard and William may have been the reason that researchers never became suspicious that he identified Benjamin and Sally as being the same age. Even so, Benjamin's exact birth date is of record, and his stepsister Sally's is not. Were people at the time generally unaware Benjamin was adopted?

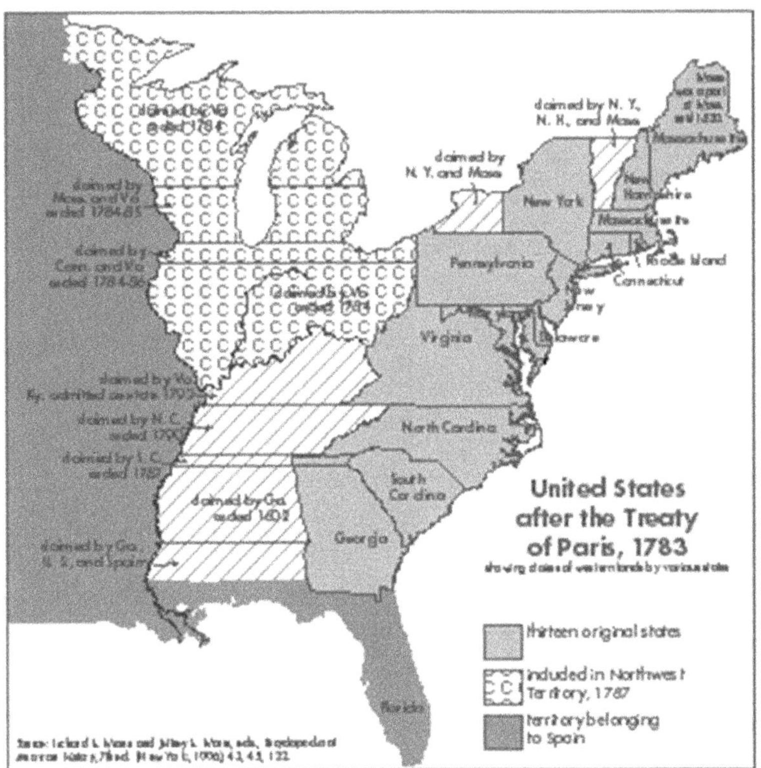

The result of border changes due to the American War for Liberty (10)

There are interesting items of note in this document, but it leaves just as much for conjecture. Why Benjamin did not receive valuable horseflesh as his step-brothers did, might be attributed to his youth or something deeper. At 11 years old he was too young to have spent his inheritance prior; nor are there documentation to support that theory.

Though William listed Benjamin as his child we know now through DNA that he was not. Is this final treatment of Benjamin by William upon his death a statement reflecting the subtle difference he felt about the boy? Though the Will does not list birth dates, the 10 children of William Fox are named correctly in order of birth.

Map of the original 13 colonies in the year William Fox, adoptive father of Benjamin, passed away in Virginia. The map illustrates the massive size of some colonies and disputes they had over territories as well as the vague nature of maps given much of the area was yet unexplored. (11)

The obvious difference in inheritance William left for Benjamin could lead to the belief that some if not most of the family, were aware Benjamin was not a biological son.

Benjamin had nine elder siblings; at least some of them must have been old enough to know he was adopted. If this difference in treatment by his adoptive father among his siblings is as stark as it appears, how must that have felt for the very young man?

If his adoptive father treated him this way in death, how was he treated in life? Did his siblings know Benjamin was adopted? Who his father was? No documents indicate if Benjamin was close to his mother, who lived many years after William passed away.

Sometimes what can be read is what is not there to read.

Daniel Boone Escorts Settlers Through The Cumberland Gap. (12)

In any event, the Fox family had nearly all remained in the Virginia colonies for 5 generations, or about 135 years. That changed after 1783 when William passed away.

Benjamin's eldest brother Arthur, the Revolutionary War veteran, now also a surveyor, soon left his family and the comforts of Virginia's settled eastern counties, for the frontier of the Kentucky country. Arthur Fox became distinguished as one of the earliest pioneers in what would become Mason County, Kentucky, where he began friendships with both Daniel Boone and Simon Kenton that lasted until he died.

Twins Richard and William Fox, both 19 soon followed their older brother Arthur, migrating west.[60]

Only the youngest brothers; Henry and Benjamin, remained in Virginia. But around them their neighbors and friends were moving west as well.

CHAPTER EIGHTEEN

LEAVING VIRGINIA

The year William Fox died, in 1783, James and John Bunch, distinguished war veterans, moved from North Carolina to settle eventually in Tennessee, with James's new bride Elizabeth Ann Asher, her parents and sister Mary Francis. John, in turn married Mary Francis Asher.

Soon after the group settled in Knox County, Tennessee, that some years later became Grainger County.[34] James soon moved to Knox County, Kentucky, which was mostly unsettled. In southern Kentucky, James and Elizabeth Ann (Asher) Bunch began a family.[146] At the same time in 1783, Capt. James Kendrick, the eldest brother of William Fox's wife, Mary (Kendrick), who had distinguished himself in the French-Indian War as well as the War for Liberty, took up 150 acres of bounty land in Georgia. A year later, in 1784, his brother, Jones Kendrick followed.[322]

Additionally in 1783, John Filson approached Daniel Boone, who he subsequently interviewed in order to author a pamphlet entitled, *"The Discovery, Settlement and Present State of Kentucky"*. The narrative was immediately popular in the United States and around the world, thus making Daniel Boone a legend in his own time.[338; 135]

By May 12, 1784 ratified treaties were exchanged between the United States of America and Great Britain, in Paris. The end of the war and the subsequent offering of military bounty lands made large the migration west in 1784. The Old Dominion State, Virginia, was extremely generous offering bounty lands. At the time it was the largest of the 13 colonies and the most populated. Primarily the lands offered were in the lands that would become Kentucky and Ohio.

The rush west began almost immediately, by only the most intrepid settlers, for the land was still anything but safe. That summer in August, the state of Frankland, later known as Franklin, seceded from North Carolina, but the following year Congress refused to allow Franklin to join the Union.

During the decade of the 1780's colonial longhunters traveling inland had developed hunting and trapping camps that sometimes became trading stations and as time went on some of the trading stations became surrounded by communities. As the war ended, there was a flood of movement to the western frontier and these modest camps and trapping stations began to grow.[188]

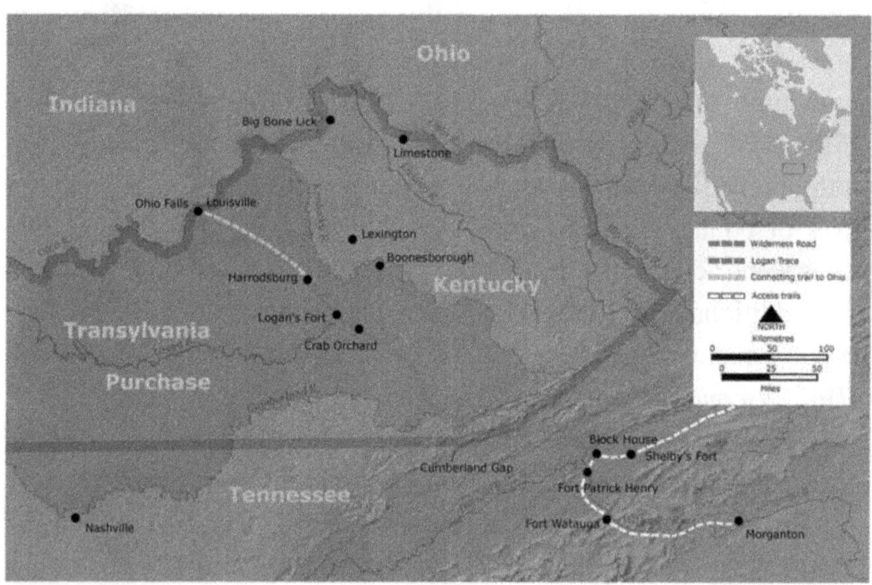

The Wilderness Road that Arthur, Richard and possibly William Fox used to lead the family through the Cumberland Gap (13)

Single men Arthur Fox and brother Richard became the first of William's children to move from Virginia when they joined a group led west in the summer of 1784. It is entirely possible their mother Mary Kendrick-Fox relocated with them, or certainly followed shortly after. It's likely Richard's twin William was with the group as well; his death is not of record; only that he died young and unmarried.

Also traveling with them were William's sister; their Aunt Lucy (Polly Lucinda) who was married to Luke Matthews. The couple had been wed for 18 years and had seven children. Lucy was pregnant with their eighth child the year the family walked west through the Cumberland Gap. Of the children of Richard Fox, only two daughters went west, Lucy (Matthews) and Mary (Jones). In that year of heavy migration west, were also many of the Bunch family.[56]

Henry Lee soon established a stockade settlement, appropriately called Lee's Station, two miles south of Maysville, it was later the site of his home, first called Clover Hill, renamed Leewood. Arthur Fox established Fox's Station, later named Washington(14)

Experienced in the route, Col. Richard Young led his father and family as well as a host of others, up the Wilderness Road, through the Cumberland Gap to settle in what at the time was Fayette County, VA, but would become Kentucky.[40]

Among those in the group was the family of surveyor Henry Lee (later to achieve the title of General in the Kentucky militia). Filled with hope, the pioneers rolled away from their families' homes.

Now 14 years old, Benjamin watched his elder brothers ride off into what must have seemed like a great adventure. Surrounded north, south and west by Shawnee, it was more than an adventure; it could likely prove fatal.

By the time the families reached their destinations young Arthur Fox and Col. Young's daughter, Mary, had fallen in love. The couple were wed and settled in what at the time was immense Fayette County. The settlement population grew enough that county borders were re-established by the end of the year, so the area Arthur and Mary lived became Bourbon County. Nearby, the county of Nelson, was cut from Jefferson County, Virginia.

Richard lived some distance away but remained inside the county of Fayette. For a while Richard taught in the fort at Lexington, but he moved and subsequently, with his brother Arthur and Col. Richard Young, founded the town of Versailles, Kentucky.[60; 56]

In 1786 Arthur Fox and William Wood (whose family had also been among those led west by Col. Young) bought 700 acres from Simon Kenton and laid out the town of Washington in what remained the state of Virginia. It was initially known as Fox's Station. The deed survives as the oldest deed in the county clerk's office of Mason County, Kentucky.[60]

That year, because county militia's in the vast state of Virginia were so fiercely loyal only to each other and refused to take orders from anyone else, the governor at the time, Patrick Henry, made specific appointments meant to bring the militia's under central control. Initially his appointments were met with huge protest that threatened revolt, but after some adjustments the positions were filled without further drama. Among those was surveyor Henry Lee, who was appointed captain of newly organized Bourbon County.[60; 348; 56]

The following year in 1787 a Constitutional Convention was held in Philadelphia. In addition, a state convention was held in Danbury, Kentucky, where Gen. Henry Lee served as commissioner, taking vital part of establishing Frankfort as the state capital of the proposed state of Kentucky.[56] There were many Baptist Brethren listed among the participants of the state convention.[296]

Richard Fox who still resided in Fayette county, married Mary Blanton, in 1788.[139] She was the granddaughter of James Blanton, who had signed as witness on Richard's father William's Will. The couple were well regarded, raising their family in a stone home on an elevation on the Frankfort-Versaille pike.[12] The area they lived was still Fayette County, Virginia, but became Woodford County at the end of the year.

Additionally, at the same time the area Arthur and his wife Mary lived in Bourbon County, became Mason County. Meanwhile next door, in the neighboring state of North Carolina, the legislature reasserted its claim to its Overmountain region, at which time the private investors government and very existence of Franklin ceased. Deeds from the land sold by the speculators who created Franklin were voided and the settlers who lost their money were never compensated.[188]

At the end of the year the first presidential election was held December 15, 1788 – January 10, 1789, to allow folks time to get where they needed, in order to vote. It was mostly ceremonial considering the popularity of the candidate. By April 30, 1789, George Washington was inaugurated first president of the foundling nation, at

Federal Hall in New York City. Celebrations were immense.[60; 296; 104; 351]

Counties recently created along the frontier really had no clue where boundaries were, thus by 1789, newly formed Mason County hired Capt. Henry Lee as its surveyor. During the same spring, Lee became a member of the Virginia legislature from the District of Kentucky.

Sadly, right from those first fledgling beginnings, the federal government of the United States, has only once operated in the black. It was a sham from the beginning created by bankers in other countries; As a new country needing credit, the newly formed United States federal government borrowed money to pay for the war, encouraged by countries willing to gain favors. And also in order to pay veterans of the War for Independence they gave Indian land away allowing them to do two things government loves; not paying their own bills and growing the government by creating an office of administration. The ones losing initially in the transaction were the Indians; the White settlers would begin to get theirs when the population reached the Pacific Ocean and their usefulness dwindled.

The emigration west was spurred when on December 18, 1789 the state of Virginia gave its consent for Kentucky to become its own state. The Indians of course, were not consulted.[56; 159; 184]

The only sons of William's remaining in Mecklenburg, Virginia by the late 1780's were Benjamin and his brother Henry, six years the elder.

In 1789 Henry married Sarah Kendrick, whose great aunt had wed Henry's grandfather; providing further proof of the relationship between the Fox's and Kendrick's. The couple had a daughter almost immediately and seemed content to remain in Virginia.[12]

To the west, between 1787 and 1794 Arthur Fox and his wife Mary had five children in Mason County, Kentucky along the Ohio

River. Some miles distant Arthur's brother Richard and his wife Mary made their home in Woodford County.[60]

William's children continued to age and move west, when his youngest daughter Sally Jones Fox married Thomas Norvell in 1790.[114] Almost immediately after the couple was wed in Mecklenburg, they left for the Kentucky country where they settled in Nelson County, a little over 100 miles southwest of Sally's brothers Arthur and Richard. The same year, in 1790 James Bunch was named Captain of Militia in Hawkins County, Tennessee. A well respected Revolutionary War veteran, James was a 40 year old father of three.[34]

By that year in Pennsylvania, the German speaking congregation of Brethren had grown to 1500 members. Many had spread west prolifically in Kentucky. Several churches were located near Maysville, including the Concord Church, Log Union Church, Shannon Church and Beech Creek Church, where the Hardman family as well as George Boone attended service. The largest congregation was north of Boonesborough on Hinkston Creek; more of the Hardman family is listed among its members. Many of these churches became Church of Christ, Christian church or Baptist church in 1826, as a result of The Second Great Awakening.[297]

CHAPTER NINETEEN

BENJAMIN FOX, MARRIED WITH CHILDREN

A month before Kentucky was made the 15th state, carved from the state of Virginia, on June 1, 1792, Benjamin was married May 9 to Martha Norvell whose generational family roots in America and relationship to the Fox family has been established.[9] Both the groom and bride were 20 years old.[114]

Many of the Norvell family were Quakers, but no documents indicate that the Fox family followed that religion. Settlers had been pouring into the Kentucky country for years, but little had been done to the Wilderness Road or the branches that accessed the county seats. The far flung communities devised a private enterprise plan to improve the roads, led by John Logan and James Knox. Over 70 men signed on for the work; one of them was Arthur Fox. Later in the year, Isaac Shelby, the Governor of Kentucky commissioned Capt. Henry Lee of the state militia as a Lieutenant Colonel, a title he had previously earned in Virginia during the Revolutionary War.[114; 149; 60; 56]

In Kentucky on September 1, 1792 Logan County was created from Lincoln County and in December Clark County was formed from Bourbon and Fayette counties. Logan county was named after Benjamin Logan, the 2nd in command of the Kentucky militia during the Revolution and a leader for the people in gaining statehood. John Logan who led the effort to improve the Wilderness Road was the younger brother of Benjamin Logan and served under his brother during the Revolutionary War.[184; 343]

The second presidential election was held that fall between November 2 and December 5, 1792. George Washington won reelection unanimously, as was expected. Such a victory is historical proof of the man's terrific public popularity and sway with politicians at that time.

Washington did not like the two party system but unfortunately also had an ear for federalists a lot. Despite that influence, he was honest and true to the ideals of breaking away from a monarchy. In the beginning the federalists wanted the office of president to be much like that of a king. It was absolutely Divine Providence that Washington was there, because he was not like most men who would gleefully eat up all the adulation, welcoming the title of His Majesty.

George Washington was a man politicians feared for his honesty and many waited silently for him to age. He could not be bought and he would not disrespect the lives that had been spent in the war by playing politics. By the time he left office because he was too old to serve, the shills were lurking in wait to grease palms. They had dared not ever make such feelings public considering his popularity.[234; 352]

Benjamin and Martha were still living in Mecklenburg, Virginia,  when a daughter was born they named Nancy Norvell Fox, on July 29, 1793.[205]

The following year, Benjamin's eldest adopted brother Arthur Fox passed away April 11, 1794, as a result of a small pox inoculation, which were a hideous and horrible experience in those days that killed many. It entailed cutting a healthy person open and shoving puss from the boils of those who had died from the horrible disease into the open wound. It made people sick but if they lived, they would were immune, if not, they died.

Arthur and his wife had three sons, two daughters and claimed ownership to 55,000 acres at his death, indicating he had accumulated great wealth. Mary was a cultured and educated woman and would see to it that her children attended schools and received educations. When Arthur died he and Mary's youngest child Matilda was only about three months old and their eldest only seven years, so most of his children would not remember their pioneer father. Any secrets he may have held in regard to lineage discrepancies with his 'brother' Benjamin, likely went with him to the grave. When Arthur's children grew and some did great things, they each remained in Mason county, Kentucky. His daughters married well and Arthur Jr. led a particularly exemplary life of accomplishments.[60; 181]

Gravestone of Arthur Fox, Mason Co, KY. (15)

In August of 1794, the Shawnee were defeated at Fallen Timbers, making the trek through the Cumberland Gap much safer, setting off a wave of families moving west. Fifth generation American Ambrose Samuel Cobbs, Sr the great, great grandson of Ambrose the Planter, was born in 1729 and married Sarah Howell. Documentation is contrary, but claims the couple began having children in 1749 and by 1770 they had about a dozen. DNA results made about 2017 resulted temporarily in the belief Benjamin Fox might be the youngest son of Ambrose Samuel Cobbs, Sr. because researchers assumed the paper trail on Ambrose Samuel Cobb Jr was correct. This would have been easy to believe considering records indicate when Benjamin and his brother Henry moved west out of Virginia into Kentucky, the sons of Ambrose Samuel Cobbs Sr. moved west as well. One of these sons, Ambrose Samuel Cobb, Jr., born 1761, settled in Knox County where Benjamin Fox and his family did also. Coincidentally, Ambrose Samuel Cobb Jr. had a son named Samuel born 1792. While documentation does not prove these Cobb and Fox families moved west together, they certainly left the same place and ended up in the same place in the same time frame.[177] Both families continued to grow and prosper in Knox County, but it was said that Ambrose Samuel Cobb Jr remained homesick for North Carolina until the day he died.[177]

It's important to note James Bunch and his wife had their 4th child, a second son, they named George, in Knox County, Kentucky in 1794. If James Bunch and Benjamin Fox did not know each other in Virginia, they certainly did in Knox County, as documents will show. That same year in Tennessee his brother John was made a Captain of the local and similarly named Knox County militia.[82; 34] Still in Virginia the following year, in Mecklenberg 1795, Henry Fox and his wife Sarah, had a second daughter they named Sarah Sallie Kendrick Fox, just as his mother Mary Kendrick-Fox passed away November 9 of that year.[147] A month later in Kentucky, Arthur's widow, Mary Young-Fox, remarried Lt Col Henry Lee on December 10, 1795.[111] Besides five very young children she had with Arthur before he passed, Mary gave Henry Lee ten additional children.[56]

CHAPTER TWENTY

NICHOLAS FOX, BORN 1796

Benjamin and Martha had their second child, a son named Nicholas born in Virginia in 1796, though the exact date and location is unknown.[117] Of all men in this Fox family, Nicholas has the least amount of documentation detailing his life, in fact for many years, the genealogical trail ended with him and little hope to ever know more. Were it not for the advent of DNA, it would have never been proven which Fox family Nicholas originated from, nor that his grandfather William Fox wasn't really his biological grandfather.

The following year, the state of Tennessee was created on June 1, 1796 from North Carolina, with some deviations to the Mississippi River, the states western boundary. Andrew Jackson was elected as Congressman of the new state.

There were a number of established counties that were absorbed from North Carolina but much was yet frontier. Almost immediately the counties began to divide into smaller jurisdictions of counties. Grainger County, where the well-respected Bunch family was concentrated, was cut out of Knox and Hawkins counties, Tennessee.[355] It was here that same year that John Bunch built a double walled tavern house in the town of Rutledge and since he was one of the new county grand jurors, his tap house became the de facto seat of government, besides a place to gather for political discussion.[294]

When Tennessee became the 16th state of the Union there was great feelings of national pride. Capt. Bunch as he was known by then, was well respected and documents still exist of the matters dealt with while the county government operated in his tavern. One such partial entry is the following;

"On September 12, 1796, according to early records, the county squires met at Bunch's Tavern and it temporarily became the first Grainger County courthouse. Several notable pieces of business were handled that day, including the licensing of a public house to David Shelton, and fixing fees for ferry crossings at 6 1/2 cents at the Powell crossing and 8 cents at either the Clinch or the Holston Rivers. The sale of a Negro slave girl named Suky was also recorded."[239; 294; 53]

The tavern remained in operation as a popular inn from 1796 through the early decades of the 20th century. It was finally torn down about 1950.[239]

When James and John Bunch left their American ancestral home of Virginia, they had left behind many sibling, the youngest of which was their little brother Charles. The youngest Bunch son was favored by his father and remained with his parents until his father, Samuel the Quaker, passed away in 1782. Just as his elder siblings had fell afoul of edicts of the strict Quaker faith, so did their little brother. Though Charles remained living with his widowed mother, by 1784 the Quaker church recorded in their minutes that Charles Bunch of Camp Creek was "in the practice of gaming and neglects attendance of our religious meetings."[142]

On 26 February 1785, a meeting recorded that Charles had "gone out into several disorderly practices such as gaming, cursing & swearing, we therefore disown him."[143] His mother remained with the faith and was no doubt let down by her son, but he remained living with her.

Charles didn't move from his mother's estate until 1788 and in 1792, when she had died, he married Mary Bellamy in Louisa County, where both had lived their entire lives.[144] The couple sold 150 acres to Henry Martin and Morris (would marry into the Bunch family). Charles and Mary left Virginia with his young bride and moved to Tennessee, where the Mary died after just a few years at only 24 years old. Despite tragedy, the families of Charles and his brothers James and John grew vastly and quickly, mainly in Grainger, Tennessee. Of the Bunch brothers, only James lived and became well established in Kentucky, though some of his nephews and nieces married and moved there as well.[292]

In the fall of 1796, from November 4, until December 7, presidential elections were held. It marked the end of the moderating influence that George Washington had on the new American government.

Despite general agreement beforehand that two party systems bred division, when Washington refused a third term that is exactly what was created.

The Federalists generally believed in many British policies; taxes, a central bank, standing army and monarchical hierarchy held by members of a strong federal government. Republican policies were sharply at odds with all of that, believing in political equality among the people and expansionism of those ideals. John Adams, Federalist, won the race against Thomas Jefferson, Republican. Caught up in the times and the system they were working and creating, even the men who warned against the two party system, created just that.

Later in the month of December 1796 in Kentucky, the county of Montgomery was carved out of Clark County and Warren County was created from Logan County as the frontier state continued settlement.[353]

By the latter part of the 1700's, most of the Cobbs dropped the 'S' from the name. Ambrose Cobb, born 1729, passed away in North Carolina, in 1797. Many of his seven known children were grown. When the elder Ambrose died, his son Ambrose, born in 1761 and living in Knox County, KY, was married to Rachael Black and the couple already had seven children, one of which, a daughter, did not live long enough to be named.[177] The death of newborns was a common, tragic occurrence in the era.

Sometime that year, in 1797, Benjamin's brother Henry and his wife Sarah (Kendrick) had their third healthy daughter. They named her Martha C. Fox.[78] The same year to the west, in Clay County, Kentucky, James Bunch and Elizabeth Ann (Asher) welcomed their third son, they named Stokely, an old Bunch family name.[100] The following year Henry Fox and his wife Sarah had their fourth child in 1738; finally a boy, that they named after his brother Arthur,[78] who had passed five years previously.

During 1798, at some point, Kentucky Governor James Garrard appointed Lt. Col. Henry Lee as Brigadier General of the state, whereupon he earned the title history has come to know him as. The influential Gen. Lee served as president of the Branch Bank of Kentucky, as well.[56]

In Virginia, Benjamin's wife Martha (Norvell) passed away in about 1799, when she was only 27 years old.[1] The reason why or how is lost, as is her resting place. The young widower Benjamin Fox was left fathering six year old Nancy and three year old Nicholas. Ironically, the same year Henry's wife Sarah Kendrick-Fox died, leaving Henry a 33 year old widower with eight children.

Toward the end of the year, on December 19, in Kentucky, Knox County was carved from Lincoln County, generally in the southeast hills of Kentucky.[191]

Now 28 years old, widow Benjamin Fox soon remarried in Botetourt county, Virginia during the summer of 1800 to Elizabeth Anderson, the 22 year old daughter of Bartlett Anderson, another old colonial family.[145] Throughout many generations both first and last names of Bartlett Anderson would be carried by his Fox ancestors, just as Kendrick, Jones and Norvell names had been.

The election of 1800 for the president of the United States began on October 31 and ended December 3, once again pitting Federalist John Adams and Republican Thomas Jefferson against one another. When the dust cleared from the contentious election Jefferson had prevailed and for the first time since it had been created in war, the hands of power were given from one political party to another.

Jefferson called it a Republican revolution and swore to govern as he felt the Founders intended. His policies based on decentralized government and trust in the people to make the right decisions for themselves soon became known as Jeffersonian principals.[340] His intentions were good but by virtue of the type of human character drawn to the vocation, no government will ever maintain its own rational boundaries of power.

All hopes and dreams aside, soon after the two party system was created, the idea of lobbyists was born too.

CHAPTER TWENTY-ONE

MOVING TO KENTUCKY... AND TENNESSEE

Not long after Benjamin and Elizabeth married, they left Virginia accompanied by his elder widowed brother Henry and his many children. Records indicate they must have emigrated in about 1800, but what the impetus was, or why they chose finally to follow their brothers west, is not of record.

Both brothers' wives had passed away and one had remarried; it might be the last sons of William Fox in Virginia were at a turning point. Surely family and friends were involved in the decision. For whatever reason, the bold move forever altered the future of this single Fox family. What promising future they hoped, planned or dreamed for is unknown, but it was no small feat to move away from family and the comforts of an inhabited civilization.

One thing that came with them was the practice of slavery, though it is unknown if the brothers owned or brought slaves with them. Likely a variety of factors contributed to their decision to leave Virginia, but escaping slavery was not a goal.

As was the custom with all emigrants, they joined with neighbors for mutual support. Generally speaking, it was the practice that some slaves were taken and others sold. Of the neighbors that likely accompanied them, some were family already or would be in the near future. These would include but not be limited to the families of Daniel Hammack, Mary Sara's father and her many siblings, as well as possibly the families of Ephraim Moore and Joseph Chaffin, whose sons would wed two of Benjamin Fox's daughters in the following years.

Joseph Chaffin, like Benjamin Fox, was listed as one of the earliest pioneers to the untamed land of Jackson County, Tennessee.

Ephraim Moore might have followed a couple years behind the Fox, Chaffin and Hammack families.[17; 81]

By the time the brothers decided to go to the Kentucky country, Benjamin was married with toddlers and Henry had quite a few half grown children. Other than their cousins and some sisters, they were the last men of their family in the Old Dominion State. Ultimately, life in the Kentucky or Tennessee wilderness promised to not be easy on any of them, but evidently struggles they faced in the west were preferable to those in Virginia.

The wilderness of Kentucky and Tennessee offered opportunity they could no longer find in Virginia. Their brothers had certainly done well for themselves. Like all those hearty pioneers to leave civilization in Virginia for the frontier, they saw Kentucky as the promised land. While the west was safer than it had been, that was only because all-out war had not been declared, but Indians were still killing settlers and settlers were still killing Indians. It was far from a safe and settled land and treaties meant next to nothing for either side. Even so, the promise on the west side of the Cumberland Gap was promise enough.

The last two sons of William Fox rolled out of Virginia-proper, and west, on the same Wilderness Road their brothers had traveled almost 20 years before. Much of it was unchanged in that time. They knew when they left they would never go back and it was goodbye to aunts, uncles and cousins, forever.

Henry may have gone in advance in order to secure land and build a cabin or two, as was common practice. Further, it's likely he met his second wife along the Cumberland Trail. Henry was 34 and Sarah Parke just 17 when they were married in Kentucky.[106] The connection this marriage made between the Fox and Parke/s family pre-dates their more documented relation to the Bunch family written about extensively in by Alice Crandall Park, appropriately titled, Park/e/s and Bunch on the Trail West.[65]

Later in the year 1800, Henry and Sarah had their first child, a son they named Benjamin, after his brother. There are no other documents referring to this child; he probably didn't live long.[2]

Whether Benjamin joined or accompanied his brother Henry, into the Kentucky country, it is likely he was in the company of the sons of Abner Chaffin, who settled in what was to become Jackson County about a year later in 1801.[17]

None of the Fox brothers settled near each other, but miles apart in different counties. Nor did they settle near the family of their deceased brother Arthur, both of which lived in the northern part of the state of Kentucky and were very well-to-do. Henry settled in western Warren County, in the southernmost part of the state.[88]

It is unclear when Benjamin and Elizabeth settled in Knox County, Kentucky, which had only become its own government entity a year earlier. But it was here, Benjamin made somewhat of a name for himself exploring; perhaps employed as a hunter. Benjamin shows a peculiar dual residency in Knox County, Kentucky and in what was yet to become Jackson County, Tennessee. These locations are about 150 miles apart. The frontier at this point in Kentucky was precisely the line of settlements Benjamin and Henry relocated to. It was little populated by White men and still inhabited by Indians.

By 1800, there were 18 heads of Bunch families in Kentucky, among which were the sons of James Bunch, born 1750; the wounded Revolutionary War veteran. Generally speaking, these Bunch families were all related. In sharp opposition, there were 14 heads of Fox families and of those, none were related to the Fox's detailed here, though perhaps they are distant cousins.

Interestingly, Benjamin nor his brother Henry are listed in the federal census of 1800. Given the nature of emigration and communication at the time and destructive fires since, it's not hardly surprising. Many Tennessee census records for 1790 and 1800 were

consumed in fires that occurred many years later during the Civil War.[78]

In 1801 Jackson County, Tennessee was created from Smith County, named after local popular politician Andrew Jackson.[291] Benjamin was among the first to secure land in the newly incorporated county, though census records maintain he yet kept residence in Knox County, Kentucky. Fellow emigrant from Virginia, Joseph Chaffin was also of these earliest land owners.[168] When Benjamin claimed land rights in Tennessee, Chaffin claimed neighboring land.[17; 81]

When John Kendrick Fox was born in to Benjamin and Elizabeth Fox in 1802, his birth placed them in Jackson County, Tennessee.[199] The newborn carried the Kendrick name, the same as his father Benjamin and in turn, his grandmother Mary Kendrick's maiden name.

When the 1802 Compact of Georgia was agreed upon by the United States federal government and the state of Georgia, the complete and utter destruction of Indian culture began in earnest. The verbiage used in the agreement promotes the genocide of a people;

"...the United States shall, at their own expense, extinguish, for the use of Georgia, as early as the same can be peaceably obtained, on reasonable terms, the Indian title to the country of Tallahassee, to the lands left out by the line drawn with the Creeks, in the year 1798, which had been previously granted by the State of Georgia, both which tracts had formally been yielded by the Indians; and to the lands within the forks of Oconee and Ocmulgee rivers; for which several objects the President of the United States has directed that a treaty should be immediately held with the Creeks; and that the United States shall, in the same manner, also extinguish the Indian title to all the other lands within the State of Georgia."[318] The feds paid Georgia $1.25 million for current day Alabama and Mississippi. In turn promises were made to extinguish all American Indian title to the lands. Indians were seen as savages without intelligence and so, were not consulted.[18]

CHAPTER TWENTY-TWO

LEWIS AND CLARK

Eager to acquire the important Mississippi river port of New Orleans as well as spread the influence and stature of the United States, President Thomas Jefferson acquired the broad area of Louisiana in 1803 from Napoleon Bonaparte for 15 million dollars, or a little less than 3 cents an acre.

That year, the wars between Napoleon of France and the English Crown began and the French conqueror well needed the cash. The United States made every effort to remain neutral in the European conflict, so to maintain trade, however the European conflicts played greatly in negotiations for the sale.

The broad area of the Louisiana Territory spread from the Gulf of Mexico west to the Arkansas, Red and Sabine rivers, to the parallel of 42 north, generally speaking. The truth was that no one really knew what the sale entailed because no one really knew what was out there.

American negotiators, James Monroe and Robert R. Livingston, knew that and didn't care. The purchase nearly doubled the size of the United States, greatly enhancing it materially and militarily; spurring westward expansion.[186] Immediately a number of parties were approved by congress to explore, map and chart the area. Of these, Thomas Jefferson gave this directive to army Captain Meriwether Lewis;

"The object of your mission is to explore the Missouri river, & such principal stream of it, as, by its course & communication with the waters of the Pacific Ocean, may offer the most direct and practicable water communication across this continent, for the purposes of commerce."[186]

Meriwether's close friend and second Lieutenant William Clark accompanied him. The Corp of Discovery was commissioned in Jefferson's second year in office. At the time the Hudson Bay Company controlled the borderless region known generally as the Oregon territory. Jefferson's directive sent Meriwether up the Missouri and led them north across the Rockies trying to find a connection to the Columbia. It would be an ironic failure that was a historic success.[186]

Benjamin and Elizabeth (Anderson) had their first child together, a son they named William "Bill" Fox, born 1804, likely named after Benjamin's adoptive father.[210] Whether this indicates Benjamin was unaware he had been taken in and completely identified as William's son; was an homage to an adoptive father; or simple coincidence is unknown.

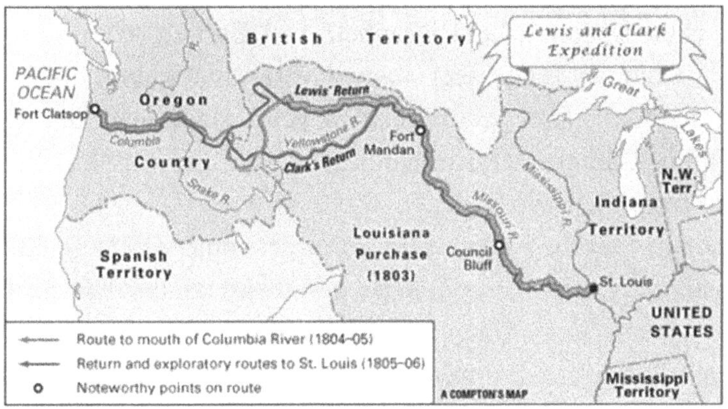

The Louisiana Purchase and route of Lewis & Clark expedition, far north of what decades later, became the Oregon Trail. Initial failure turned into an epic success. (16)

On the 4th of July in 1805, James and Elizabeth (Asher) Bunch had their sixth and last son, named Nathaniel, or Nat.[206] Considering they had been married for over 20 years and the death rate of infants in their time, it's entirely possible there were more children.

The federal government began lotteries in 1805, to sell the lands vacated by the Cherokee and Creeks who had lost their rights to live in Georgia, prompting settlement.[221]

By the dawn of the 19th century both the Fox and Cobb families were established among the earliest settlers across the entire front of the frontier. They had all used the Wilderness Trail that made Daniel Boone a household name. Specifically, Samuel Cobb remained in Knox County, Kentucky, while the balance of the Cobb families remained concentrated south in Tennessee and Georgia, also taking part in settling Alabama.[19] The fact Ambrose Samuel Jr. remained in Knox, Kentucky near the Fox's, lends further proof these particular families shared a close relationship. As things turned out, maybe too close.

In 1806 Benjamin and Elizabeth had Bartlett Anderson Fox in Jackson County, Tennessee; named after his grandfather on his mother's side.[192] That year, over two years since they had departed civilization, Captain Meriwether Lewis and 2nd Lt. William Clark returned from their trip.

Though they had taken a more direct route on their return, the consensus was that there was no easy way to the Pacific Ocean. Furious rivers, unyielding geographic formations and dozens of different tribes of Indians were sometimes dangerous. It was unknown and untamed.

However in the Oregon country they spoke of an idyllic valley named after the Willamette River that flowed through it. It was miles wide, from the coastal mountains to the Cascades and it went on for hundreds of miles, north to south. There were plenty of streams and rivers with scores of salmon and elk and deer in abundance. The Indians in the valley were said to be friendly and enjoyed trading with

Whites.[162] The thought in many men's minds was that they could raise a family there far from great populations and sickness, if you could reach it. Though the Willamette Valley was seen as a sort of Garden of Eden, it lay 2000 impossible miles across an unknown wilderness. No serious thought was given to the distant frontier by family men, who left it to the trappers.

In 1806, yet-to-be-legendary Andrew Jackson had the honor of his wife brought into question by a fellow, who then accused Jackson of cowardice. Demanding his accuser meet him in a duel, the two combatants met on the Red River in Tennessee at Harrison's Mills.

Jackson was intent for the duel, but knew his opponent was a better marksman, so enacted a plan to turn sideways exposing only his profile and allow the better shot to fire first. When Jackson's opponent fired his pistol at Jackson, the ball struck him in the chest and though it staggered the iron-willed yet-to-be war hero, he kept his feet, placing his left hand over his heart to stop blood from spilling.

Momentarily dazed, Jackson took careful aim and squeezed the trigger. The hammer fell but resulted only in a loud "CLICK" that did not ignite the powder. The two opponents stared at each other for a moment before Jackson thumbed back the pistol's hammer again and still staring at each other, settled into careful aim. The second time the hammer fell it resulted in a cloud of blackened smoke followed right away by the pistols discharge and finally as the gentle winds cleared the air, Jackson's opponent was lying dead for his slander, thirty paces away. Jackson carried the ball in his chest until he died many years later, as it could not be removed. The Tennessee congressman's legend began to grow.[229]

The Restoration Movement began in the beginning of the nineteenth century in a period of religious enthusiasm just as Benjamin and Henry Fox were getting established in Tennessee and Kentucky.

The first leaders deplored the many divisions in the church and called upon them to unite through a restoration of New Testament Christianity. They felt the Protestant Reformation had gone astray and the various denominations should be directed back to primitive Christianity. They felt everyone should use the name "Christian" and return to the biblical pattern of the New Testament. They called their movement, the "Restoration Movement" or the "Current Reformation". They felt they were participants in a movement within many different existing churches and wanted to eliminate all sectarian divisions. The Christians accepted the Bible as the absolute and final authority on religion and studying it would result in the discovery of truth.[70]

There were two streams of this movement, one led by Kentucky preachers Barton Warren Stone and John Mulkey, and the other by Thomas and Alexander Campbell; father and son preachers in Bethany, Virginia. In the summer of 1804 at the Cane Ridge Meetinghouse outside Lexington, Kentucky, Barton Warren Stone and four colleagues left the Presbyterian Church to become part of an independent movement of "Christian" churches. They renounced the name Presbyterian as being sectarian. These churches agreed and began to call themselves "Christians" only.

In the summer of 1807 they rejected the practice of sprinkling infants and restored traditional submersion. The Cane Ridge Meetinghouse became the center of the movement.[70] At least some of those in the Fox family became part of this movement.

The same year, in 1807, Explorer David Thompson of the North West Company became the first White settler in Oregon. Mostly forgotten now, Thompson was an accomplished trapper and explorer. In his life he traveled some 56, 000 miles across North America, mapping out nearly 2 million square miles.[301]

In 1809, Baptist preacher John Mulkey led his Mill Creek Baptist Church out of the Stockton Valley Baptist Association in southern Kentucky. In the next two years more than half the preachers in the Association followed, including Thomas Crawford McBride.

The Campbell's were unaware of the Stone movement but severed their ties with the Presbyterians the same year, calling themselves, "Reformers" or "Disciples". They established their first congregation at Brush Run, Virginia, in 1811. The following year the Campbell's rejected sprinkling for submersion. Both groups evolved from a reaction to Calvinism and its doctrines of total depravity, unconditional election and limited atonement. It would be many years before the two similar streams of belief met.[70]

CHAPTER TWENTY-THREE

THE 'OREGON' POWELL FAMILY

Cader Powell was born 1750 in what was called Virginia,[123] though after boundaries were established became Kentucky. After first taking bounty land in Georgia for his service during the Revolution, he emigrated between 1800 and 1805 again, settling in Floyd County, Kentucky.[78] The family originated in Wales, but had moved to England before they came to the American colonies many generations before, likely before 1650. This Powell family should not be confused with the Ambrose Powell family that Powell Valley and River were named for along the Wilderness Trail.

In 1773 Cader's father Moses Powell had taken his family to 'the Ceded Lands of Georgia',[78] that became Wilkes County, Georgia in 1777. Cader and his brothers were Revolutionary War veterans like their father. Cader was married June 3, 1782, in Warren County, North Carolina to Francis Foote. The following year in 1783 the couple began their family with a son named Allen.

After the war, in 1784, Moses Powell and all his sons but Cader took bounty lands of 287 acre parcels in Georgia. Cader remained in North Carolina for most of the rest of his life where he and his wife raised 11 children.[78] Shortly after the turn of the century, but before 1810, Cader sold his property in North Carolina and purchased 50 acres in Floyd County, Kentucky.

By the time Cader brought his family to the frontier state, most if not all of his sons were of sufficient age to be working, including their eldest, seventeen year old Allen. Most of Cader's sons did not remain in Kentucky but instead joined their father's family in Georgia as they grew of age. Cader's eldest son though; Allen Powell; remained in Kentucky and came to be familiar with Benjamin Fox and his sons, particularly Nicholas. Allen was married in 1806 to Mary Polly Johnson in Floyd County, Kentucky and soon began a family.[78; 228]

In November of 1810, Benjamin and Elizabeth had their first daughter, they named Elizabeth Ann. Like her brothers, she was born in Jackson County, Tennessee, despite the fact that Benjamin appears not in Jackson County in the 1810 federal census, but as a resident of Knox County, Kentucky.[87] Another land deed document, however, claims Benjamin was living on Flynn Creek in Tennessee in 1808.[134]

This unexplained dual residency would continue throughout Benjamin and Elizabeth's lives. About 1810, Benjamin's Aunt Polly Lucinda, who was married to Luke Matthews five years before Benjamin was born, moved to Tennessee with some of her children. She was a widow; her husband Luke had passed away some about 20 years before, in Virginia where she had remained since. With little else left but her children, when they chose to move west, Polly too, went along.[49]

Zebulon Pike journeyed to Colorado in 1806 and in 1810 he published his report: The plains were utterly worthless. From the Missouri River for 600 miles to the foothills of the Stony (Rocky) Mountains, there was nothing but scrub brush and buffalo.[79] The lack of forestation was repeatedly reported by people that had explored the vast plains. United States Army explorer and topographical guide, Stephen Long referred to it as a great desert, leading to the term, "The Great American Desert".[166]

Despite these reports and common beliefs, across the un-mapped frontier in Oregon the Hudson Bay Company was firmly entrenched and doing brisk business. The first house built by a White man that was meant to be permanent, was built on the south shore of the Columbia River in 1810; Nathan Winship of Boston sailed his ship the *Albatross* about 40 miles up the Columbia near present day Clatskanie and set his crew about to build a cabin.

SARAH ANN FOX

By June, the walls on the cabin were 10’ high. The post was doomed by floods and disgruntled Indians, but it was the first White home in the northwest. From this earliest contact the Indians in Oregon began to refer to White Americans as “Bostons”.[220]

On December 17, 1811 there was an earthquake whose epicenter was New Madrid, Missouri. For the next two months aftershocks continued and increased in ferocity. Current-day estimates for the aftershock that occurred in February of 1812 rated it up to 8.8 on the Richter Scale; fully 20 times stronger than the San Francisco earthquake. The broad Mississippi River stretched over a mile across at New Madrid and the back surge of the quake ran water upstream for two hours. Church bells in Philadelphia, Pennsylvania were rung by the quake and it was felt along the Atlantic coastline in Boston.[290]

Given the religious nature of American society at the time, it should be no surprise that many felt it was the end of the world and as the aftershocks kept up a steady dangerous rumble, more were convinced the end was near.

By the end of 1811, Benjamin and Elizabeth had a second daughter named Sarah Ann, who like the rest of the couple’s children, was born in Jackson County, Tennessee.[99] In fact, if not for genetic proof, documentation alone would not support the fact Benjamin was the father of these children while simultaneously living in Knox County, Kentucky. Little wonder many years of research could not prove the relationship. The distance between Knox County, Kentucky and Jackson County, Tennessee would have taken perhaps a week or more to travel by wagon.

Though his interest was in money and its attendant power, not colonization, John Jacob Astor was the next to contribute to finding a way to Oregon. The fur trade was high business in the early 1800's and though the Hudson Bay Company and its fellow British North West Company were legally in control of the northwest, Astor had a plan.

He sent two groups, one by land and one by sea to the mouth of the Columbia. The barque *Tonquin* was to round the Horn and head for the bar of the Columbia to resupply Wilson Price Hunt and a hearty bunch of men calling themselves "Astorians", who had gone overland.

The *Tonquin* stayed for the initial construction of Fort Astoria and by the end of June it was off to trade on Vancouver Island. Between when the *Tonquin* departed and the fort was complete, explorer and Oregon settler David Thompson of the British owned fur company happened upon it. Thompson was on his way south after having laid claim to land at the future Fort Nez Perce site and the confluence of the Snake River.[266] If Astor was just one month later in landing the *Tonquin* Thompson might have claimed that area as well.[151]

The captain of the *Tonquin* insulted a Native along the way to Vancouver Island while trading with Indians and in turn the natives destroyed the *Tonquin*; killing the entire crew, sinking the boat. Resupply never came to the fort, but it didn't matter, Wilson Hunt and the Astorians had already established Astoria near the mouth of the Columbia. In the ensuing years Astor worked on organizing trading posts along the upper Missouri.[266] Having left the year before on June 29, 1812, on April 30, 1813 Robert Stuart returned with a company of Astorians to St. Louis, to report on what had become of the *Tonquin*.

In the process they inadvertently found the Oregon Trail, in reverse, arriving in St. Louis 10 months later. While trying to avoid Indians, the return expedition took trails to the south and came out of the Rocky Mountains on the Platte, having crossed over South Pass without realizing what they had done.

Over 20 miles wide, South Pass was an expansive meadow, like Mother Nature's gateway to the west. But the desperate mountain men, following Indian trails and running from hostile Indians never knew it. Only later when the route was discovered again, by someone else, did they realize what they had done.[185]

CHAPTER TWENTY-FOUR

WAR OF 1812, SECOND AMERICAN WAR FOR LIBERTY

In Europe, the Napoleonic Wars continued as the massive armies of France, Great Britain, Austria and Russia clashed on the continent. But it was Great Britain that ruled the seas and so began to enforce an embargo against their French enemy. Despite initial attempts to remain neutral while maintaining trade with both sides, the very young United States began to find itself more and more the victim of British blockading efforts. In addition, the Brits were kidnapping the crews of the ships they waylaid and forcing them into service against the French.

As could only be expected, there was plenty of latent hostile feelings felt between the English and their American cousins that fought to be independent. In 1812 the American government issued an ultimatum to England – Leave our ships alone or we will declare war.

The dire warning gave the British government little worry and they paid little attention to it, however to the north, in Canada the furthest away and largest outpost of the Crown, military generals were already expecting war. And they were nervous, because most of England's resources were being used in the war against the French on their mainland. Fewer than 9000 British regulars were garrisoned in Canada to defend over 600,000 square miles of land. In fact, along the border with the United States, only 1700 British troops held the 1000 mile boundary line.

The total motley population of Canada was about 80,000 people; a collection of the First Nations Indian tribes, European settlers, French trappers and exiles from the American War for Independence. As hostilities became imminent, no one knew who they would fight for or against. To the south, the United States population had grown to 7 ½ million.

At the time it was believed by many; almost a general consensus; that American destiny was to lay claim to the entire continent. In the south Spain still laid claim to the Florida area and to the north the British held control of Canada's vast farmlands and stands of timber. Efforts were currently being undertaken to settle the area around The Great Lakes, considered to be the northwest territory of the United States. For those who felt the annexation of Canada was imminent, the war was a natural first step toward the inevitable. The war was argued heavily in the American congress, supported by Republicans and opposed by Democrats who argued against any goal of expansionism, calling it immoral.[61]

The Crown's defender was General Isaac Brock, a well-bred and schooled gentleman whose letters written at the time lamented his waiting for the war to begin. When his repeated requests for men and equipment were refused, he turned to the tribes that the British had allied with against the Americans before, but the remaining tribes, the First Nations, held distrust of the Redcoats as fair-weather friends. Just when British General Brock began to think he would not be able to broker an alliance, he was approached by a Shawnee war chief called Tecumseh, who envisioned an independent Indian nation east of the Mississippi under British protection.

Tecumseh was a boy when the Kentucky militia destroyed the village of Chief Blackfish's tribe, whom his widowed mother and family had recently joined. Though in his father's lifetime, his tribe had been forced south by the Iroquois, in his lifetime the White men moved in and forced the Indians north; it was the latter that he saw as the real threat, to all Indians.

Tecumseh was an exceptional leader and soon, with Mohawk war chief John Norton, brought together the fractured Indian tribes to form an alliance with Brock, believing him to have the full proxy of the Crown. But Brock was brash and he had obtained no prior approval for an independent Indian nation.[61; *315; 320*]

In the spring before all hell broke loose, Andrew Jackson, a rising star in Tennessee politics delivered a speech to that states militia that summed up the goals of America in the looming conflict,

"*We are going to fight for the re-establishment of our national character, misunderstood and vilified at home and abroad; for the protection of our maritime citizens, impressed on board British ships of war and compelled to fight the battles of our enemies against ourselves; to vindicate our right to a free trade and open market for the productions of our soil...*"[259; 219]

Even as rhetoric and threats for war increased in pitch, there were still those whose focus remained interested in stories about "way out west". In the May 15, 1813 *Missouri Gazette* from St. Louis, it was reported, "*By information received from these gentlemen, it appears that a journey across the continent of North America might be performed with a wagon, there being no obstruction on the whole route that any person would dare call a mountain in addition to its being much the most direct and short one to go from this place to the mouth of the Columbia River.*

"Any future party who may undertake this journey, and are tolerably acquainted with the different places, where it would be necessary to lay up a small stock of provisions, would not be impeded, as in all probability they would not meet with an Indian to interrupt their progress; although on the other route more north, there are almost insurmountable barriers."[264]

Sure they had exaggerated the ease of travel a little, perhaps overcome with excitement for the task, but this news now began serious discussion. The dreamers had begun to dream.

A combined militia of 450,000 men were called up in the War of 1812. It was in this first major conflict that it became evident to the fledgling new country they needed a well-trained standing army, despite concerns about doing so. As America was settled, a militia of the common man was proven to be necessary, sometimes deadly and more than not, incompetent of any military discipline. These men historically followed the man, not a military rank.[61]

Before 18 year old George Bunch, the son of James, the Revolutionary War scout, was to enlist,[112] he married Martha Elizabeth Morris in Knox County, Kentucky on May 23, 1812.[115] In addition, Joseph Chaffin (Jr.), whose father of the same name that had emigrated with Benjamin Fox across the Cumberland Road and settled in Jackson County, Tennessee, married Benjamin's sister Nancy Norvell Fox that fall, before he too joined the militia.[17; 81] Anxious young love combined with the tenuous return of southern suitors led to a number of marriages as the war broke out.

About three weeks after George and Martha were wed, that summer war with Britain was declared June 12. Two weeks later the news reached the Commander in Chief of British Canada, Sir George Prevost, who as a cautious leader, dispatched orders to General Brock to specifically not provoke the Americans. Most of all, Prevost did not want to provoke uniting the armed American settlers. General Brock was shocked and sent his commander his dissent, desiring immediate attack.[61]

General William Hull, the appointed governor of the Michigan territory, was given command of the American forces, though he accepted the responsibility reluctantly. The Revolutionary War hero had sustained a stroke and was left in a weakened state. On the morning of July 12, 1812 General William Hull, 61 year old commander of American forces, invaded Canada and issued a proclamation that read, in part,[61; 288]

"The army under my command, has invaded your country and the Standard of the Union now waves over the Territory of Canada. To the peaceable unoffending inhabitant, it brings neither danger nor difficulty. I come to find enemies, not to make them. I come to protect, not injure you.

"The United States offer you peace, liberty and security. Your choice lies between these and war, slavery, and destruction. Choose then, but choose wisely; and may he who knows the justice of our cause; and who holds in his hands the fate of nations, guide you to a result the most compatible with your rights and interest, you peace and prosperity.

"If the barbarous and savage policy of Great Britain be pursued, and the savages are let loose to murder our citizens and butcher our women and children, the war will be a war of extermination. The first stroke of a tomahawk, the first attempt with a scalping knife, will be the signal for one indiscriminate scene of desolation. No white man found fighting by the side of an Indian will be taken prisoner. Instant destruction will be his lot."[288]

Hull was convinced he would find little resistance. The 4th Infantry Regiment joined by common Ohio, Indiana and Kentucky militia, some from as far away as the Carolina's, were the vanguard of the invasion force. On the first day, they crossed from Detroit across the river of the same name, to Upper Canada at the far west end of Lake Erie, where they took the town of Sandwich, almost without opposition.[261]

Directly against his orders, Canadian General Brock, knowing that communication was horribly slow, organized an offensive in which he sent a British officer and a handful of voyageurs, to paddle in canoes 750 miles in a week from Fort George, across Lake Ontario to York, then up the Humber River, both paddling and packing their crafts, to Georgian Bay and north to Lake Huron, leading to Lake

Michigan. Their goal was the key American Fort Mackinac, which held a commanding view of the strait between lakes Huron and Michigan below.

Lined with heavy cannons, the fort took a large part in commanding the Great Lakes. The British officer and voyagers gathered at British Fort Joseph, 40 miles from their target, where they picked up arms and were joined by 500 Indian warriors and an armed schooner. Under cover of night, the British led attack force paddled across Lake Huron and surrounded the fort.

Brock was right and the commanders at the American fort were taken completely by surprise and immediately surrendered. Emboldened by his victory, Brock took an armada to face the American threat at the west end of Lake Erie, where American forces had stalled. Though his officers wanted to take the British Fort Malden, General Hull, citing concerns about long supply lines, seemed plagued by indecision.

News of the surprise surrender of the American Fort Mackinac had shaken the old man's confidence, wondering how many hundreds of Indians lied for him in wait. Instead of pressing forward, Hull retreated with his army to Detroit where he sent private letters to the Secretary of War confiding that he was afraid of the scale of attacks the Indians could unleash. In Hull's mind, he felt the country must prepare for a blood bath. As if in answer, 50 Indians led by Tecumseh staged two daring attacks on the American supply lines in August. Outnumbered 4-1, the Indians killed and wounded dozens; then took their scalps. The practice sent horror through the White population who were terrified of the bloody act.[61; 261]

General Hull suffered another self-imposed setback when he sent a trunk with all of his secret military correspondence to Washington D.C. on board a schooner across Lake Erie, that British forces controlled. The schooner; not a military craft; was easily boarded and taken by British ships, who then helped themselves to all the knowledge Hull had foolishly allowed them to take.

Hull's fears were now what emboldened British Gen. Brock, who now realized the Americans were under the impression the British commanded a larger force than they really did and what they feared most was the savagery of Indians. These of course, were Hull's observations and paranoia but Brock seized upon the information and prepared an invasion force to cross the Detroit River to take the American fort there.

Armed with full knowledge of the fear in his enemies mind, Brock issued the American General Hull an ultimatum to surrender or he would be forced to attack. Brock wrote,[231; 61] "*It is far from my inclination to join in a war of extermination, but you must be aware that the numerous body of Indians who have attached themselves to my troops will be beyond my control the moment the contest commences*."[231]

The whole thing was a bluff, but the veiled threat of hideous death at the hands of savages hit on the basest of Hull's fears. Brock knew he was outnumbered 2-1 and that Hull's cannons were more powerful, but the threat had the desired effect. When Brock opened up cannon fire on the fort, Hull refused to fire back. Inside the fort, Hull feared for the lives of his daughter and two grandchildren. Meanwhile, his officers were circulating a petition to get him removed from office. Intimidated and fearful Hull ordered 2500 men, carrying as many muskets, 39 cannon and a long supply train to surrender to a force half its size.

Americans were outraged. Hull was the most unpopular man in America. Other military leaders derided his lack of courage and bravery, indeed any military prowess in the least. For several months Gov. Hull was imprisoned in Canada, then sent back to Washington

D.C. There he was tried and convicted of cowardice and sentenced to be hanged, but President Madison commuted the sentence.

To this day, General William Hull is the author of one of America's greatest military failures. But there would soon be others who would give him stiff competition. Brock, on the other hand, was the toast of the British Empire, having brokered an alliance with the First Nations and defeated the bulk of the American army in 19 days. In lower Canada, his commander, Sir George Prevost, knew he had disobeyed orders, but under the circumstances made grudging approval of the winning strategy. Privately, Brock confided to friends that if the war lasted long, he had a premonition he would do something foolish.[231; 61]

Immediately Brock proclaimed the entire Michigan Territory under British sovereignty. It was here that Tecumseh and Brock began to imagine an individual Indian nation. But just as British Commander Prevost had feared, the sting of defeat had lit a fire in America, now out for revenge.

The Americans regrouped on the New York side of the Niagara River, near the falls while on the other side, Brock began massing troops. The British general knew he would be outgunned and outnumbered and any hopes of a bluff were gone. He was convinced his only defense was to know in advance what the Americans had planned and where and when they planned to cross the river. As he watched the American troops swell on the other side of the Niagara, Brock sent word to England that he expected a decisive action within a fortnight and if he were defeated, the province would be lost.[61]

Meanwhile in Washington D.C. in August of 1812 the first anti-war rally was held, and it was massive. Speakers warned the war was not only wrong, but it would raise taxes and force compulsory enlistment. President James Madison argued to congress that the war was the only way to get enough respect from Great Britain that they would quit kidnapping Americans lawfully at work on merchant vessels. Madison was well-enough convinced of this fact that he hung his entire political career on it.[160; 61]

In the early morning of October 13, 1812 the Americans crossed the Niagara River just above the falls at Queenston Heights. Artillery above sent down steady fire as oarsman pulled against the great current of the raging river. The cannon fire sent alarm to Brock some distance away, and Tecumseh, who saw Brock racing on horseback toward Queenston Heights. All ran to the sounds of battle where the Americans, despite the heavy fire, had reached the banks and mounted the hill, taking its cannon. One of the next generation of military leaders, Winfield Scott, was in the battle and remarked that after the humiliation of the loss of Fort Detroit, American fighting men were ready to sustain the shock of the enemy.

Regiments had arranged themselves behind Brock as he approached the battlefield, intent on taking Queenston Heights back. As the general had always said he would never send men where he would not go, Brock led the charge.

Among the Americans bracing for their impact, a rifleman spotted the generals scarlet tunic and shot him down. Hearing that Brock is down, the Mohawk's burst from the woods with terrifying war cries that the American militia could hear, across the roaring river as they prepared to cross it in boats, advancing to the battle. The sounds of Indians shrieking over rifle and cannon fire rattled them, however, and they came up with a Constitutional reason they shouldn't cross the river. When they would not cross the river, the first wave of Americans on the other side were stranded on the Canadian side.

Now the main body of British troops arrived and swept into the battle with withering fire and fixed bayonets. For a moment as the fighting came in close, there was a flurry of swords as the Americans retreated to the river. But there were no boats when they got there and before they all died, they were forced to surrender. British celebrations were dampened by the fall of their cherished General Brock; Tecumseh and the Indians had lost their advocate in Britain for a sovereign Indian nation. In both England and Canada, Brock is seen as a hero to this day.[328; 61; 187]

For his part, Tecumseh was unwavering and said the Indians would enjoy a great cry of victory or end the fight in the grave. Both his allies and enemies saw Tecumseh, a Shawnee, as a great orator and military leader. For many years he had worked to make alliances between the Seven Nations who were killing each other. Tecumseh was a visionary who knew the only way the Indians and their culture would survive would be to stop the Americans, who he saw as never getting enough land.

The painful and inconvenient truth is that the Shawnee were for the most part, a nation without a permanent home. They had been chased out of Virginia into Georgia by the Iroquois and by the Cherokee into Missouri where they were taken in by a tribe that feared the Iroquois and thought the Shawnee could be useful. In their history it is clear that they were a nation of mercenaries who fought battles for others and for at least a 100 years had not had a home but were nomadic. Nonetheless, Tecumseh had a great narrative and he was a great Indian and military leader.[315; 61]

Beaten and battered, the American forces were given to General William Henry Harrison who would someday become president. Harrison had great respect for his adversary and said in fact of Tecumseh, he was one of those uncommon geniuses that spring up followed by revolution.

Harrison and Tecumseh had private negotiations wherein Tecumseh claimed the Indian's right to land and disputed treaties. Harrison promised to relay the message to Washington, but admitted to the Indian leader that he was sure the land would be defended by the sword.

In one of these meetings Tecumseh, perhaps believing it was a threat, admitted to Harrison that he was going on a long trip to visit Indians throughout the southern United States. If it was a veiled threat, Harrison ignored it, in fact seizing upon it. Soon with Tecumseh absent, under the command of General Harrison, American troops began razing Indian villages throughout Indiana and the Ohio River, burning them to the ground. Destroyed in one of these raids was Tecumseh's own village, known as Prophet's town. With his home lying in ruins, the Indian leader called on all Red Men, to unite against the White Men. From Mohawk's in the north to Creek's in the south in Georgia, the Indian's responded to the call to arms.[315; 61; 154]

In the autumn of 1812 General Harrison organized a new American army to recapture the Michigan Territory, vowing to lead it himself. In answer hundreds of volunteers poured into Indiana, including many from Kentucky. When all were combined those with experience and military training were far and away outnumbered by those who were just willing to fight. Commanders knew that the bulk of the fighting would be borne by these untrained settlers and the prospect concerned Gen. Harrison.[326; 61]

Late in the year of 1812, beginning in Vincennes, in the Indiana Territory, the newly organized army traveled at great hardship into the north. Here they found the Canadian winters brutal and the conditions in camps deplored. Typhoid and exposure took many in the course of the journey and then in camp when they finally arrived. Despite conditions, the assault to retake Michigan began in January 1813.

Harrison divided his forces, leading one column himself, to Upper Sandusky, the other further west, led by Gen. James Winchester, yet close enough for support. Overly confident, Gen. Winchester pushed past Sandusky and into Michigan, to Frenchtown on the Raisin River.

The Brits, having watched the Americans movements, marched over the frozen Detroit River, hoping to ambush them unaware. Early in the morning January 21, 1813 British and Canadian troops marched on Frenchtown. The Americans were overwhelmed and 290 brutally died in bloody fighting before the remaining 600 troops surrendered. The mission to recapture Michigan was a disaster and Gen. Harrison had no problem laying the blame at Gen. Winchester's feet. The worst was yet to come.[326; 61]

Fearing that Americans led by Harrison would be coming, the British and Canadian troops moved back across the Detroit River, leaving the wounded American's that were unable to travel behind in Frenchtown. Left alone to be guarded by Indians that had suffered greatly at the hands of White men, the fate of the wounded Americans was grim. In their last hours, the Indians enjoyed letting the White men know they were soon to die. Officers plead for their lives and offered gold to be taken away before the bloody act ensued, but the Indians were not to be bought; but instead let them know they were all soon to die.

When they felt the time was right, the Indians set upon the wounded White men, slaying, scalping and mutilating over 50 men. Damn few were able to escape the melee. Gen. Harrison dripped sarcasm to say this was the way of fine British Gentlemen who leave their fighting to savages while enjoying the finer things in life. The Brits had no compunction about the outcome of the battle but relied on the prepubescent excuse that they hadn't started the war.[61; 326]

In the spring of 1813 the United States Army was weak, but strengthening itself at Fort Meigs, in northern Ohio, on Lake Erie. Of those to support Gen. Harrison, was the 13th Regiment of Kentucky Volunteers commanded by Col. William Dudley. The company was formed in Barbourville, Kentucky as early as March 1812 and marched during the spring of 1813.[330]

By this time all of our main characters were living near each other in Kentucky. The sons of Ambrose Samuel Cobb, Jr.; Ambrose and Samuel Cobb lived in Barbourville, as well as the families of Benjamin and Elizabeth Fox, and brothers George and William Bunch.

Samuel Cobb was born in 1794 and Ambrose was his younger brother by just a year. Samuel enlisted with Col. Dudley's regiment and was made a private in 8th Company, under Capt. Ambrose Arthur. George Bunch, born in 1794 was seven years younger than his brother William; both of whom joined this troop as well. In addition, Cornelious Taylor, the patriarch of the Stinking Creek Taylors, was among the volunteer company.[72]

The regiment gathered at Cincinnati; was one of four such units commanded by Gen. Green Clay that marched on to northern Ohio to relieve Gen. William Henry Harrison on the Maumee River.[326]

Fortunately for Arthur Fox Jr, he enlisted in Col. William Williams Regiment, Kentucky Volunteers, mustering on July 31, 1813.[107] The 4th Regiment were well experienced soldiers; the militia as usual, not so much.

The British and First Nations knew they dared not allow the American army to get back on its feet. Across the lake, at Fort Malden controlled by the Canadian Alliance, the tribes of the First Nations gathered to strike at Harrison's new troops across Lake Erie through use of ships. With preparations in place and ships in dock waiting, Indians and British Canadians stalled for the arrival of the Indian general, Tecumseh, whom the Indians would not fight without, and the British could not fight without. Finally on April 16, 1813, fashionably late but healed from battle, Tecumseh arrived to lead his warriors.[61]

CHAPTER TWENTY-FIVE

DUDLEY'S DEFEAT

Fort Meigs was a masterpiece of fort design. The walls were built high on rolling hills facing the enemy, which deflected cannon fire. Great mounds of earth around the battlements did the same thing. Inside, underground bunkers were extensively used to remain safe while the Army went about restoring itself.[325]

Harrison was ready for an attack and welcomed his enemy to come take their bitter pill, while Tecumseh vowed to take Harrison himself to have revenge for what he had done to Prophet Town. The Brits promised Tecumseh that their cannons would lay waste to the walls of Fort Meigs and so they commenced to firing.

After five days and 1649 cannon shot, the fortifications of Fort Meigs were unbroken. Downriver, 1400 reinforcements in the form of Kentucky militia, including Col Dudley's troops, worked their way toward the fort to lift the siege.[326]

Attacking the rear of the British troops, the militia caused the First Nation warriors to fall back, as well as the Brits. Devising a plan quickly, Tecumseh led his warriors back into the woods, luring as best they could, the attacking Kentucky militia, who took the bait.[330] Before Harrison could stop them they set off two miles at a dead run into the forest.

Ahead of them Tecumseh set an ambush that Dudley's men walked right into. Suddenly the woods erupted in gunfire and bloody hand to hand fighting. Over half the Kentucky militia were killed; 600 men. More were wounded or taken prisoner, including Cornelius Taylor.[72] What was left of the regiment managed to escape across the river to join the 10th Kentucky Regiment under Col. William Boswell.

Most accounts do not relate the last moments of Colonel William Dudley, but they were gruesome. Historian Lewis Collins put it succinctly – "Colonel Dudley was shot in the body and thigh, and thus disabled. When last seen, he was sitting in the swamp, defending himself against the Indians, who swarmed around him in great numbers. He was finally killed, and his corpse mutilated in a most shocking manner."[72p.294] Newspapers dubbed it Dudley's Defeat.

By the end of the War of 1812, though Kentucky provided just 5% of the troops, it sustained 64% of all combat dead.[61]

Once again the Indians set about killing their prisoners. First sniping the column of prisoners from the cover of the woods; soon they were butchering the screaming prisoners with tomahawks. British Colonel Henry Proctor stood some distance away watching the butchery, but said nothing to stop it.

This time however, Tecumseh had heard the massacre was imminent and rode full speed into the gathering crowd with his tomahawk raised threateningly. Gravely intimidating the Indians, the remaining lives of the Kentucky militia prisoners of war, including Cornelious Taylor, were spared. Turning to Proctor, Tecumseh was said to curse him for being a woman, "You are unfit to command, go and put on petticoats!"[327]

Even interrupted, an additional 30 men died before the bloody chaos ended. Later in public discourse the British were quick to cluck praises about the Indian general's mercy; infuriating Americans who blamed the British for unleashing such savagery in the first place. The battle for Fort Meigs ended after nine days when the Brits and Canadians marched back across the border.[325]

It is worth mentioning and interesting to note that 200 years after the War of 1812, Canadian and British intellectual material about the conflict continue to glide over the partnership between the British and Native American and make little or no mention of these massacres,

Nor do they focus on Brock ignoring orders.[61] It is clear the conflict dubbed 'forgotten', isn't over yet.

In the frontier where these battles took place, there were no roads and most movement of troops and supplies had to be done on the Great Lakes, which was dominated by the British Royal Navy. As this fact was absorbed, it became the task of 27 year old unknown naval officer Oliver Perry to construct a powerful new naval force on the lakes. He was told money was no object.

Perry's adversary was British naval hero Captain Robert Barclay who had little money and up until then, little to fear on the water of the Great Lakes. In early September Barclay, with 6 ships and 63 guns came out on Lake Erie to meet the American fleet. Facing him, was the American fleet of 7 ships with double the firepower Barclay had; he was up against poor odds.

On September 10, the first naval battle to ever happen on a lake broke out in the morning hours. It was also one of the most important battles of the War of 1812.[278] In the beginning moments of the battle, the superior experience of the British captain Barclay came into play as he dis-masted the flagship of the American fleet, killing or wounding 85% of the crew.

Yet alive and unwilling to let his fleet go without his command, American naval Captain Perry ordered himself rowed in a small boat to another ship where he could re-take command of the battle. Bringing all the American firepower upon the enemy, in a few minutes the British fleet was destroyed and surrendered.

Gen. William Henry Harrison received the famous dispatch from Capt. Oliver Perry, *"We have met the enemy and he is ours. Two ships, 2 brigs, 1 schooner and 1 sloop."*[61]

The destruction on Lake Erie of British naval power sent panic throughout Canada. Across Lake Erie in Fort Malden, British troops were ordered to retreat by Gen. Henry Proctor who had failed to crack

Fort Meigs. Tecumseh was disgusted and furious by the instant capitulation of the British commander and saw it as simple cowardice. A few days later American ships reported seeing Tecumseh riding alone along the shore, in defiance of their power. Some days later, however the Indian general made agreements with the British to move inland and set up defenses away from possible cannon fire from American ships on the lake.[61]

Now back in control of Detroit and the town of Sandwich across the strait of Lake St. Clair, Harrison saw the British retreating northeast and decided to pursue them. Troops were able to be moved on ships to within three miles of the British and Indian troops, without opposition. As the British began moving up the Thames River, Harrison was right behind him.[278] By October 4, the British reached Moravian Town, where they bent to Tecumseh's demands and decided to turn and fight. The night before the engagement the Indians seemed to feel as if the coming battle were part of a great destiny.[61]

The following morning Gen. Harrison led his 3000 troops onto the battlefield, just outside Moravian Town. Facing him on the right flank, were 500 Indians led by Tecumseh and 450 British regulars under the command of Gen. Proctor. Col. Richard Johnson and his 1000 Kentucky cavalry regiment led the charge but only after Harrison issued him a deadly serious order.

Knowing well how the Kentucky militia operated, Harrison warned Col. Johnson to tell his men that if any of them hollered back and forth with the enemy or fired a gun before they were told, officers had been ordered to shoot and kill the offender.

Moments before the trumpets sounded the beginning of the battle, Tecumseh rode the British lines and shook hands with many of the British officers before he rode back to lead his warriors. The battle was a short one.

In the face of 1000 Kentuckians on horseback at full charge, the British line faltered and their officers screamed to shame them back in line, but it was too late.[251] As the British broke to run, the First Nations held their line, taking the full force of the onslaught in one terrific crash of humans, horses, lead balls and tomahawks. Over the din of battle the voice of Tecumseh could be heard by those in the battle that survived. The Indians were overwhelmed and pushed back as Tecumseh was killed in the brief deadly battle. With him died the dream of an independent Indian Nation.[61]

Gen. Harrison sent a dispatch to Washington proclaiming his victory and the complete annihilation of British and Indian forces, adding, *"General Proctor has escaped by the fleetness of his horse."*.[326]

Indeed Proctor did flee the battlefield and was widely criticized in Britain, leading to his being court martialed, found guilty and reprimanded, before he was forced to resign his office in disgrace. Ironically for his service, Gen. Henry Harrison was the victim of politics being played within the American military and was replaced by the infamous, but well connected, Gen. James Wilkinson.[61]

Early in 1813 American forces were gathering a great force at Sackets Harbour, where they had built a naval yard, in preparation for an attack on British controlled Kingston, across the river in Upper Canada. Due to a shortage of British and Canadian regular troops in the area, the only soldiers left to support Kingston, were 1000 miles to the northeast, in Fredericton, New Brunswick. The Crown ordered a regiment from the fort in Fredericton to march in the dead of winter to the defense of Kingston, hundreds of miles away.

There were not even trails to travel on and snow covered the landscape with temperatures minus 18-20 degrees. Such a task had never been done. By April 12, the British and Canadian regulars reached Kingston, delaying any attack that might have been planned by their enemies.

The Americans across the frozen lake worked feverishly to finish a frigate meant to be the jewel of their fleet on the Great Lakes. Knowing the extent to which the ship would dominate the lakes, the Royal Navy decided to sink the frigate before it was launched.[61]

On May 26, the British expedition departed Kingston and sailed across the Lake Ontario, to arrive in the morning of the following day, at Sackets Harbour.[250] While it appeared to the British that they had caught the Americans unaware, they faltered in confidence for the remainder of the day. If indeed they had surprised their enemy, they lost any hope of capitalizing on it.

When finally a day and a half later, Gov. Prevost ordered the British troops to land, they were met by ready American militia at the shore. The fury of the British attack was of such intensity that military commanders feared the naval yard would be lost to the British, so they set it ablaze, then retreated to the fort. From their battlements, American sharpshooters began deadly lethal fire upon the British line until the Redcoats lost so many men they called a retreat.[61]

In Washington, President Madison was in such need of a victory, that the battle at Sackets Harbour was eagerly celebrated as a win. The ceremonial fence around the White House was sent to surround and honor the cemetery of war dead buried there. The truth, however, was that the American's prize frigate was destroyed along with their naval yard and any hope of dominating Lake Ontario had gone up in the fire.

In New England, where trade with England was a large part of their economy, opposition to the war intensified. As Washington banned trade and business came to a standstill, the New England states refused to call out their militia to support the war. In the northeast United States, the president had little support for the war and what he needed was a real victory. With the naval yard destroyed on Lake

Ontario, the Americans looked to the fort at Montreal near the mouth of the St. Lawrence River. To control Montreal, was to control all the Lakes.

When the British tried to enlist French-Canadians there was a revolt and resulting riot in which the British troops were called out to quell the violence and make arrests. Commander Prevost, immediately ended forced enlistment, instead creating French speaking regiments to make enlistment more appealing.[61]

President Madison named Gen. James Wilkinson to lead the United States in the war, despite his reputation for being neither a leader or courageous, but for drinking and intrigue. He was a Revolutionary War veteran and close personal friends with many well connected people in the nation's capital. His appointment shocked the next generation of military officers.

Winfield Scott was moved to say, *"If a booby be at once made a commissioned officer the odds are great that he will live and die a booby. How infinitely unwise then in a republic to trust its honor and safety in battle in a critical war to imbeciles and ignoramus's".*[61] Truer words could not be spoken, as was soon proven.

Wilkinson's plan involved a troop of 7000 men marching from Sackets Harbour, up the St. Lawrence River, to join another 5000 men from the fort at Plattsburg. From here the forces would combine to take Montreal before another Canadian winter moved in. The British forces numbered hundreds in opposition to the terrific amount of Americans.

Of those facing the Americans were units of Catholic Scots called the Glen Gary light infantry. These units were sent to a forest near Chateauguay, where the American invasion force was expected and British commanders were constructing defenses. At 2pm in the afternoon of the 22nd of October, 1813, the American troop force of 5000 marched in a column to face the British defenses built in the woods. With odds in their favor 7-1, an American officer was dispatched with a demand for surrender from the much smaller British defenders.

Upon hollering the demand, the officer was shot by Charles de Salaberry, commander of the Canadian regulars. Together with a union of French voyageurs, Glen Gary infantry and Mohawk warriors the lines of fire commenced.[45] The shrill screams of the Indians cut through the forest as black powder smoke filled the woods to the canopy above. The response by the smaller force was of such ferocity that to the Americans, it appeared they were in greater numbers, leading the American commander in charge to lose his nerve and order his troops to retreat back across the border.[61]

While this exchange was happening, U.S. Commander General James Wilkinson was leading the second invasion force. Using the St. Lawrence River, the Americans traveled north to land on the Canadian side of the river near Prescott, Ontario. With the Americans in place Nov 10, 1813, Gen. Wilkinson would not leave his bunk aboard ship, though a battle was imminent. His staff reported he had been drinking heavily and had dosed himself with opium.[61]

The next morning by 11am any chance of shocking the enemy was lost, in fact the larger invasion force faced a similar union of British enemies, who though outnumbered, now stretched in a complete line across a vast farmers field along the river, preventing them landing. When fighting commenced the larger American force dominated the field, but with their general missing, lost cohesive structure. Instead of throwing their overwhelming weight at the British and their allies, they attacked piecemeal, bogged down in soft banks and the rain soaked field. After a number of American cavalry charges were made and cut to ribbons, the much larger force retreated from the field in defeat.[61]

Gen. James Wilkinson was called to Washington to account for his actions but his friends in high places managed to keep the philandering alcoholic and drug addict from being censured.[243]

The war was toxic. Massachusetts and Connecticut threatened to leave the Union if the conflict was not stopped. Those who supported the war were disgusted with its management and found it hard to defend.

There was a house-cleaning in the U.S. military command and Winfield Scott was named as Wilkinson's replacement, ushering in a new generation of military leaders into the field. Immediately Gen. Scott began rigorous 10 hour a day drill training, employing regulations drawn up for the Napoleonic army. As their training made them better soldiers, the men began to take more pride in their service.[328]

When they were ready, from Fort Buffalo in northwestern New York state, the U.S. forces crossed the Niagara River, to Fort Erie on the other side, where they received a quick surrender. From there, moving up the river toward the falls, the Americans were confident they had taken upper Canada.

At Chippewa, the British made their stand, in a farmers field, not far from the river. As 1300 American troops advanced, the British believed they were facing the same rag-tag bunch of undisciplined militia men they had been, and their force of 1500 would easily defeat them. Instead, the lines were straight and when men fell, the lines did not break. A few minutes after the contest had begun a British general watching, said, *"Those are regulars, by God!"*[61] The battle was fierce, lasting a half hour and leaving 456 dead or wounded British soldiers in the field. The Americans lost 295 lives but had finally won a battle. It was the first time American regulars won in a face-off with British regulars. Around the country optimism lifted.[61]

Far south in the spring of 1814, on March 27, federal troops and Indian allies under the command of Gen. Andrew Jackson, defeated the Red Sticks, part of the Creek Indian tribe, at the Battle of Horseshoe Bend. The defeat was essentially the end of what was called

The Creek War, and the tribe itself. Their defeat allowed the settlement of current day Alabama.[54]

"The Dying Tecumseh", by German-born, Italian-trained sculptor Frederick Pettrich took twenty years of intermittent work to complete in 1856. There were numerous paintings of the famous Native leader as well, but the truth is, there are no authentic images of the Native American warrior, because no artists ever met him and he was disfigured by his enemy after death. About a decade after his death the national feeling in regard to Tecumseh was editorialized in the Vincennes, Indiana **Centinel, "Every schoolboy in the Union now knows that Tecumseh was a great man. His greatness was his own, unassisted by science or education.**

"As a statesman, warrior and patriot, we shall not look on his like again." (17)

CHAPTER TWENTY-SIX

ARTHUR FOX, JR.

With war raging not far to the north, Arthur Fox, Jr. married Lucretia Taylor of the Stinking Creek Taylors, in Mason County, Kentucky where his father had settled as one of the first White men in the area. The event took place June 14, 1814[109] at Cedar Hills plantation and was said to be of such style that people were guaranteed to not soon forget.

When his father died, Arthur Jr. received $22,000 inheritance, equating to $454,457 in 2020[321]; as well as property and a log home, in which he took his young wife. On the many acres he cultivated were also bred a fine line of horses. All said, Arthur Jr., just one of Arthur Fox's children, received well over a half million dollars value in his inheritance alone.[60]

Arthur Sr's estate had been well managed by his widow Mary Young-Fox and her subsequent husband Gen. Henry Lee.[56] Arthur Fox's heirs supped at one fine table, the old pioneer had set for them. One has to wonder how much the success of his line of horses was affected by those given to Arthur Sr. by his father William Fox, in his Will.

Throughout the winter and early spring Gen. Scott methodically worked his way up the Niagara River to a place of high ground within earshot of the falls, near Lundys Lane, in late July of 1814. The British formed defenses and prepared to face their invading enemy in a cemetery nearby. Across Canada almost 3000 troops were streaming in as well as a band of Indian warriors, to the coming field of battle.

The Battle of Niagara Falls began in the evening of July 25, 1814 at 9pm. The evening was warm, as 2000 Americans moved into position at dusk, inadvertently so close to the British position that Gen.

Scott could see British cannons and hear their whispered voices in preparation. The American general knew his men were in harm's way, but there was no going back.

In the growing dark, officers on both sides began to bark orders and troops began to move in unison though they could not be clearly seen. An eerie silence was punctuated by the clear sounds of both sides' officers hollering orders and unseen troops shuffling to meet the enemy.

Finally the Brits opened up with grapeshot from their cannons, flashing brightly, shattering the silence and lighting up the American line. Gen. Scott could see the fight enough to see his men were being destroyed and so made a desperate decision; instead of turn to retreat, Scott encouraged his men to stand their ground.

When the Americans didn't flee as was expected, the British officers became concerned that a larger force of Americans was coming. While the battle raged, another American officer was tasked with taking the enemy cannons at all cost. Leading his men through an orchard to attack on a flank, the officer and his men were spotted by Mohawk war chief, John Norton. Before the Indian could raise any alarm, the Americans began a blistering fire upon the flank of the enemy.

British officers who survived the battle and had served in the bloodiest battles with Napoleon in Europe said nothing they had seen matched the fight for the guns at Lundys that night.

By 10pm, Americans had seized the cannon but the British mustered three terrific assaults trying to retake them. At midnight Gen. Scott began marching the troops he yet had, north to finish off the British, when in the dark, an American column mistook them for being British and opened fire. At the same time, the British opened up on Scott and his men and they were cut to ribbons for the second time that night.

For his hubris in each of case, Scott had lost much of what he had gained. He was wounded by a musket ball in the battle and sat the rest of the war out.[61] The Americans still held the cannons, but fearing British attack, they retreated and gave up the bloody hill and cemetery of death. When dawn came the dead and wounded British numbered 878 dead, wounded or missing and the Americans, 860. The strategic defeat forced the army of America back inside their borders.[328]

By spring of 1814, the British won the war with Napoleon with substantial military aid from Russia and Austria, now turning their full attention to the war with America. It couldn't be better timing for Gen. Prevost in Quebec City, who wrote a series of letters bemoaning the five failed attempts by the Americans to take Canada, and his need for military aid.

In the summer of 1814 tens of thousands of British troops were stationed at Quebec City at the discretion of the British commander. While now Prevost had troops, he was still known as a hesitant leader. Nevertheless, it was now the British general's turn to invade America.

His plan was to move his main troops south from Montreal into the United States, taking the fort at Plattsburg, though both sides knew that the crown jewel would be Sackets Harbour, at the mouth of the St, Lawrence River, guarding the entrance to the Great Lakes. Once Prevost had eliminated the American control of Sackets Harbour, he planned to re-take the Michigan Territory, that the British yet planned to give to the Indians. The Americans knew their naval base at Sackets Harbour was pivotal in controlling the lakes and President Madison remained concerned about its security.[61]

As it would turn out, the president might better have concerned himself more with matters closer to home. In the late summer of 1814, a British fleet sailed into Chesapeake Bay to make a diversionary attack on Washington and Baltimore.

In August when ships sailing British flags sailed up the river there was dismay and shock. As people wondered where and what they were doing, the ships began unloading 5000 crack troops in great long boats, fresh from the Napoleonic War. In Washington there was a curious disbelief that the capital of the federal government could be in danger.

At the President's Palace as it was then called, there was no concern because the secretary of war had assured the president there was no need to be concerned. Gen. John Armstrong admitted the British might attack Baltimore, but they most assuredly would not attack the capital city.

The president's wife Dolly Madison, well connected to Washington society had received numerous correspondences relating to the imminent threat, but her husband had full faith in his military.[287]

CHAPTER TWENTY-SEVEN

WASHINGTON BURNS

The British marched relentlessly to Washington, knowing full well the significance of attacking a nation's capital. Only a volunteer militia was present in the city to defend the capital and the Brits knew that too. Finally, when it was obvious the enemy was coming, Madison had to search out his Secretary of War, Gen. Armstrong and question him on his plan. The general replied he had none, and that since it was volunteer militia defending the city, the battle was lost.

On the 25th of August, 1814, the British column marched down Constitution Avenue into the heart of Washington, bearing a flag of truce and a demand for surrender. Suddenly someone fired, somewhat distant, from an upstairs window in a house. The troops descended on the brick home and slaughtered those inside, then set it ablaze. From there they moved to destroy every building associated with the government.

The president and cabinet escaped across the Potomac and into the hills of Virginia as Washington D.C. was set to fire. Dolly Madison said she would have stayed at the palace with cannons out every window, but those responsible for putting them there had already fled.[287]

When finally President Madison returned to the city he took up residence in the French ambassadors home, called the Octagon House. His first matter of business was with his secretary of war, Gen John Armstrong, who after the meeting, tendered his resignation the following day.

Meanwhile the British were marching overland to Baltimore where they found the city was defended by Fort McHenry with heavy cannon and thousands of regular troops. The Brits took up a naval bombardment of the fort in the early morning hours of 5am on September 13, 1814.

Francis Scott Key watched the red glare of British rockets fired from Royal war ships and bombs bursting in the air over the city and harbor, inspiring him to draft a poem about the red, white and blue American flag that still waved after the three day siege, which would become our national anthem. The poem at the time served to galvanize the American people.[287]

While the British retreated without defeating the Americans in the fort, they were satisfied with the destruction they caused, including the razing of Washington. Next, British Gen. Prevost planned an even bigger invasion to begin in Montreal, moving south into the United States. At least 10,000 British regulars moved south under the personal command of Gen. Prevost, across the border into the United States, ignoring small arms fire from hidden militia.

As Redcoat troops moved down the shore of Lake Champlain, American troops fell back to Plattsburg to make a stand. At the same time, ships of the Royal Navy sailed down Lake Champlain, in search of the Unites States troops to engage them. Aboard their flagship, carpenters were still at work finishing the building of the craft, but Prevost now in position, was in no mood for any delay.

Outside Plattsburg Bay, American naval commander Capt. Thomas MacDonough waited with his fleet, knowing the British ships inside the bay had long range artillery. The American naval officer commanded many powerful short range cannon and predicted that the Brits would try to sneak out of Plattsburg Bay around the point of the peninsula, allowing him to shred them. Under extreme pressure from Prevost, the British navy set sail before it was ready and true to prediction, sailed into the guns of Capt. MacDonough.[61]

At first blast from each side, the American flagship lost one fifth its crew. Fifteen minutes into the broad side firing, the commander of the British fleet was killed by a cannon ball. Regardless, for the next two hours the ships jockeyed for position and blasted each other until at a critical moment, MacDonough was able to winch around his flagship ship and deliver a devastating broadside against the British fleet.

The battle was finished and for the Americans, ended a hard fought victory. British Gen. Prevost, rattled by the destruction of his navy, retreated back to Montreal, despite the protestations of his officers. The moment victory might have been in his grasp, Prevost was again plagued by indecision; and that indecision led to the British losing the war.[61]

At the climax of the War of 1812, on November 10, 1814, young Nicholas Fox married the beautiful neighbor girl, Mary Sara Hammack,[117] the daughter of Daniel Hammack and his wife Agnes (maiden name, Pruitt).[3] The newlyweds were both 18 years old.[97] Despite the war raging around them, records have never been found by the author to indicate Benjamin or Nicholas served in the militia.

Peace negotiations had been ongoing in Europe for some time, but when the defeat of the British navy reached the treaty table, it changed the mood of the negotiators. By December, in Ghent, the combatants worked out their differences as each country was ready to put the violence behind them. The British people and its government were tired of endless wars and the American people had already voiced their dislike of the calamity.

On Christmas Eve a peace treaty was signed by the two parties. However it took six weeks for the news to reach combatants on the frontier engaged in deadly battle. The battle that occurred during the War of 1812 that history most remembers, took place after peace treaties had been signed. The loss of life was needless, numerous and immaterial, but it would have broad implications.[61]

Earlier in the month, after being involved in the burning of Washington, a British fleet was sent on a punitive mission against the territory of the southern United States, with the secret mission to seize the port city of New Orleans at the mouth of the Mississippi River. They had not received the dispatch about the treaty.

United States Army commander Gen. Andrew Jackson had not heard about the treaty either and was yet engaged with the enemy and complaining to Washington about the nearly non-existent supply chain. The letters he wrote were scathing, they were public, and they were truly well deserved admonishments to the bureaucrats in Washington. He gave voice to Americans who were fed up with the quid pro quo that creeps into the foundations of every government.[61]

CHAPTER TWENTY-EIGHT

GEN. ANDREW JACKSON, LIVING LEGEND

Andrew Jackson, born 1767, was five years older than Benjamin Fox, and was already well on his way to becoming a living legend. His parents were Scots-Irish from Northern Ireland, bringing two sons with them when they landed, likely in Philadelphia, before traveling overland through the Appalachian Mountains to a remote area along the border of North and South Carolina, where he later claimed to be born.

His father died in a logging accident and his eldest brother died in the War for Independence, before he and another brother joined the militia at young ages, acting as fast riding couriers. He and his brother were taken prisoner, and at some point a British officer ordered the boy to clean his boots, to which Andrew refused. The officer slashed his sword at the youth who swung his hand up to deflect the blow, leaving him alive, but with scars on his head and hands for life.

The actions of that British officer who on that day held such disregard for an American boy he would haphazardly swing a sword at him, created a hatred that would run deeper than his blade ever could have. The boys contracted small pox in captivity and were nearly starved by the time their mother succeeded in petitioning for their release.

On the 40 mile walk home Andrew's brother rode their only horse, as his health was most dire. In fact, within two days of reaching home, his brother died. When his mother had nursed Andrew back to health, she volunteered on a prisoner-of-war ship where there had been an outbreak of cholera. She contracted the disease and subsequently passed away.

At odds with extended family, young Andrew moved around, sporadically getting education when and where he was able. He worked for a saddle maker and even taught school, but distinguished himself in neither profession. In his youth, Jackson was said to be a bit of a bully, but was also protective of weaker children who were in his circle of friends. Moving to Salisbury, North Carolina he studied law and September 1787, Andrew Jackson was accepted to the North Carolina bar.[230]

The following year he was involved in his first duel, but as cooler heads had prevailed, he and his adversary agreed beforehand to shoot their guns in the air. In that same year Jackson moved to the growing settlement of Nashville and bought his first slave.

He became a boarder with a widow, whose daughter was in an unhappy marriage with a man given to fits of rage. In 1790 the couple was separated and Jackson later said he believed they were divorced, before he and the young "widow" were married.

In fact, there had been no formal divorce, it was instead a frontier divorce; a separation that is wholly accepted by the peer community, but without benefit of legal documentation. After the couples divorce was legally completed, he and Rachel were married again.

Personable in character, Jackson became the protege of a powerful man in the area who was a friend of his in-laws, and by 1791 was the Attorney General of the Tennessee country. In 1796 he served as a delegate to the Tennessee constitutional convention where he began to associate with a slightly radical pro-French, anti-British element, that many accused Thomas Jefferson of being part of as well.

He was elected by the state legislature in 1797 as a Senator representing the state, but seldom joined in debate and was admittedly dissatisfied. He resigned the following year, proclaiming he was *"disgusted with the administration"*[313] of John Adams, who clung to many tenants of British aristocracy and did his best to steer George Washington that way as well.[230]

By the time Andrew Jackson returned to Tennessee he had a strong following and was soon elected to the states Supreme Court where he served until 1804, when he returned to private life. His term on the court was viewed favorably and he earned a reputation as an honest man. While he was serving in that position he applied for Commander of the Tennessee militia, upon election tying with the former governor John Sevier. Acting Governor Archibald Roane broke the tie in Jackson's favor, in return receiving incriminating evidence on John Sevier whom Roane feared running against, the following year. When indeed Sevier announced his bid for governor, Roane released the information and Jackson followed up with a letter in the newspaper accusing Sevier of fraud and bribery. Sevier responded by insulting Jackson in public and the episode nearly resulted in a duel, but it did not and in the end Sevier won the governorship.[313]

In 1803 Jackson built the first store in Gallatin, Tennessee and the following year acquired a 640 acre estate called, The Hermitage, that he continued to annex land to, until his estate totaled over 1000 acres. Slaves were quartered in various cabins made of brick or logs of 400 sq. feet; enough for individual family units. Though the conditions were better than average, he believed in beatings if they helped production of the crops.

When illness and injury threatened Jackson's troops during the war he ordered his and his officers mounts given to his men. This story illustrated to impressionable young men the sacrifice that an honorable man made to those he led. The manner in which Jackson showed honor and defended American principles while being argumentative and physically violent with adversaries; fond of solving problems lethally, led his troops began to call him Ol' Hickory. An homage to a man they saw, of impeccable honor and an iron will that was willing to sacrifice for them.[61; 230; 313]

The city he was tasked to defend, New Orleans, presented a geologically difficult location to defend, as it was accessible from every side. Gen. Jackson predicted the Brits would come up the Mississippi River to attack from the south, or they would attack from the north, where the city was close to the sea.

Instead, the British came from the east, marching across land across Lake Borgne. Due to the shallow nature of the lake, their troops loaded into shallow boats to ferry 6000 regulars and marines to shore. When the wind died, the ships full of men relentlessly approached the American ships guarding the eastern approach to New Orleans. The Americans were overwhelmed and retreated into the bogs and marshes around the city. The cold weather of December in the bayou did not suit many of the British troops, especially the Black regiments serving from the Caribbean's, but they pursued the Americans into the swamps.

The following day the British continued to a plantation a few miles outside of New Orleans, along the Mississippi River. Two nights before Christmas Gen. Jackson brought all he had to bear in a surprise attack on the British troops, in order to buy him time to get supplies into New Orleans. The bold move worked and New Orleans was able to get arms and supplies, before both sides settled in for a showdown.[61]

At the plantation, military engineers placed cannons behind earthen defenses that lay behind an old canal that was deepened by Black slaves. It was called the Jackson Line, and stretched 1000 yards from the Mississippi to an impassable bayou at its eastern edge.

In early January 1815, the British launched the final assault of the war. In the ranks of the British troops, morale was unusually high when at dawn on January 8, the British planned to advance on the Americans in the heavy fog. As fate would have it, there was a delay in their movement and the fog lifted.

Exposed to the enemy, 5000 British soldiers were ordered into the battle field, facing 3000 militia behind earthen embattlements. On horseback, Gen. Jackson directed the fire and movements of his troops, as cannon fire rained into the British ranks. Fire directed at the Americans was mostly ineffective, but the fact the British didn't falter either, despite withering artillery, impressed American Gen. Andrew Jackson.

British soldiers on the left flank using ladders to get across the deep canal had some success but in the fog of war, ladders for the main force were left behind, leaving the British troops struggling in and out of the canals, being shot up by American marksmen in crossfires. Twice they were repelled and twice they reformed their ranks and came back for more before they began to die; first in clumps then in whole regiments and companies, spilling bodies and blood in great waves.

The Brits lost 2036 men in the battle that day and the Americans lost 7 men with 6 men wounded. The size and breadth of the one-sided battle was, by any accounting, a complete disaster for the Crown.

Ironically, word of the American victory arrived in Washington at the same time word came about a successful treaty at Ghent. The war was no less than a world-wide referendum on the resiliency of the new American government and it had proven itself willing and able to defend itself. The values it took to win the war were taught to the grandsons of the fathers of the Revolution. The successful end to the war led to a resurgence in patriotism and made Andrew Jackson a national hero.[61; 229]

After all of that, the combatants basically agreed to go back to what things were before the war broke out. Borders were restored to what they were before hostilities. In congress some complained that nothing had been accomplished in the war, but most were just happy it was over. One thing that never happened again, was Britain kidnapping Americans to be used on their war ships. In Canada, Gen. Prevost was called back to England to face a trial for his retreating at Plattsburg. His health failed and Prevost died before the trial began.[61]

The result of the War of 1812, in the Oregon country, was that considering how isolated Fort Astoria was, it had been accepted that instead of losing it to the British anyway, it was sold to the North West Fur Company. With the signing of the Treaty of Ghent, American claims to Fort Astor were restored.[28]

The Jackson Line separating the combatants. (18)

CHAPTER TWENTY-NINE

KENTUCKY!

When the War of 1812 was over, Samuel Cobb (born 1794, a son of Ambrose Samuel, Jr.), George and William Bunch and Cornelius Taylor were lucky enough to be among those left alive to return home to their families in Knox County, Kentucky. In the next few years, most of Samuel and his brother Ambrose Cobb's siblings left their lives behind in Virginia and joined their brothers, settling in Knox County, Kentucky. George and brother William Bunch returned home to Kentucky as well, where their siblings remained near their Revolutionary War veteran father, James.[4]

During the summer after the war ended, in 1815, Nicholas and Mary Sara, both nineteen years old, had their first child; a baby girl that never lived long enough to have a recorded name.[5] Unfortunately, it was just the first infant for the couple that wouldn't survive.

Chances were in 1800 that over 46% of children would not survive to 5 years old, and a mother's chance of dying while giving birth was 1-2%, multiplied each time they had a child, whether the child lived or died. By the time some of these women had 10-14 children, their chances of not surviving the next birth were pretty high. There were no anesthetics other than whiskey and few had the benefit of even a mid-wife, let alone a doctor. Most children were delivered into the hands of their father, alive or dead, alone in a log cabin.[279]

The following year, in 1816 Mary Sara gave birth to a healthy daughter, that she and Nicholas named, Susan.[101] In the same year, on April 30, Nicholas's father and step-mother continued having children, when Elizabeth gave birth to a daughter in Barboursville, Knox County, Kentucky they named Marinda.

Of all the children Benjamin and Elizabeth had, Marinda was the only one to show documentation of birth in Kentucky.[201] Stories written about Benjamin, Elizabeth and their children make no issue of their residence anomaly.

About three weeks later in north-adjoining Clay County, May 21, 1816, after four years of marriage, records indicate George and Elizabeth Bunch had their first child, George William Bunch, in Clay County, Kentucky.[197] They called him John. Given the time it took the couple to have a documented child, its likely they lost one or more children before George William (John) was born.

A year later in 1817, Benjamin and Elizabeth had another son, they named Richard O. Fox.[98]

On July 8, 1817, another agreement called the Treaty of Cherokee Agency was signed in Tennessee by representatives of the U.S. government and the Cherokee Nation.[172] This document ceded lands in northwest Georgia and southwest North Carolina to Whites for settlement, but maybe more importantly it created a fissure among the Cherokee people, because only the negotiators wanted to sign the treaty. The Cherokee Indians did not agree with it. In fact, delegation of Cherokee people went to Washington and protested the treaty, stalling its passage. The act was endorsed as a means to education and other services for the Indians, but the majority of Cherokee didn't care, they wanted to stay on their lands. In the following decade, in a bid to defend themselves against the feds, the Cherokee Nation put together a government, based on the American model.[26]

In 1818, Arthur Fox Jr took part in laying out the town of Dover, in Mason County, Kentucky where his father had settled the family decades before.[60] Like his father and his Uncle Richard, who had prospered very well, Arthur Jr. saw the advantage of creating town lots and making money from platting towns.

In the same year, Elizabeth Bunch, wife of George Bunch the elder, passed away at only 24 years old.[6] There is no indication of what took her life. But considering the lapse of four years between when she and George were married and when she gave birth to George William Bunch, known as 'John', she might have had difficulties with pregnancy that ultimately took her life.

Her death left George with a year and a half old baby boy, but only for about a year and a half, before he remarried, to Nancy Maupin, on March 11, 1818.[110] Records indicate it was a decade before the couple had a child but again, it is more likely they had a number of them, but all were buried without documentation.

Also passing away in Knox County, KY that year was Mary Sara's father, Daniel Hammack, leaving his widow Agnes and a number of half grown children.[3]

By that year in 1818, joint occupancy agreements were beginning to be made in the northwest between British and American governments, for control of the Oregon country.[167]

Charles Wakefield and his sons with the families of three other men and the widow Petties and her children settled near Cold Creek in the frontier of Illinois in 1818. The land was inhabited by Indians but they were not hostile. A year later in 1819 Thomas Pugh relocated there from Christian County, Kentucky and soon wed one of Wakefield's daughters. These settlers formed the Cold Creek congregation of Christians and though they didn't know it, those modest few pioneers had begun something of great historical significance.[180; 27]

As their elder children began to grow families, around 1819 Benjamin and Elizabeth Fox had their eighth and final child, a son named Henry, born in Jackson County, Tennessee as six of his seven siblings had been.[95] The newborn might have been named after

Benjamin's brother Henry, as he passed away that year in Bowling Green, Warren County, KY where he was buried.[94]

Additionally that year, as part of the Adams-Onis Treaty, also known as the Florida Purchase with Spain in 1819, the land north of the 42nd parallel was relinquished to the Unites States.[158]

Despite having stalled in Washington for two years, through the efforts of the Cherokee Nation, the Treaty of Cherokee Agency was passed by congress and signed without change in 1819. While the act had been sold as a means to provide for the Indians, the result was that it gave the president nearly unlimited power over the Indians.

The act was signed by Major General Andrew Jackson, governor of Tennessee, Joseph McMinn and David Meriwether, commissioners plenipotentiary of the United States. Their counterparts, Cherokee chiefs, head men and warriors of the Cherokee Nation, east of the Mississippi River, and the chiefs, head men and warriors of the Cherokees on the Arkansas River and their deputies, John D. Chisolm and James Rogers, duly authorized by the chiefs of the Cherokee on the Arkansas River, in open council, *by written power of attorney, duly executed, in presence of Joseph Sevier and William Ware* (italics added for emphasis).[172]

The deck was stacked from the beginning and signed in part, on behalf of those affected, by those that stacked the deck. The stage was set for more of the same as White settlers took up these lands and were left wanting more. By 1820 any pretense of cohabitation was gone and the general belief was that whether they were civilized or not, the presence of Indians would not be tolerated.

But the fact is, the Cherokee people were unlike any tribe that had encountered White civilization before. They had adapted in ways other tribes had not and showed great intelligence. The Indian nation continued to adopt White ways; wearing White men's clothes, living in stick built homes, establishing plantations where they owned slaves.

Those Cherokee that adapted to White ways that felt they were safe from eviction because of the similarity, soon found they were wrong.

Daniel Boone lived long enough to be a living legend. He was an early pioneer of Missouri, where he passed away September 26, 1820. He was buried next to his wife Rebecca, and both their graves remained unmarked until the mid-1830's. In 1845 the state of Kentucky exhumed Daniel and Rebecca and took them back to the Bluegrass State. Rumor persists that the wrong graves were dug up and moved to Kentucky; that Boone's family knew of the mistake but disliked him being moved, so didn't correct the error as they saw it being made. A forensic anthropologist examined a crude plaster cast of Boone's skull in 1983, made before it was re-interred in Kentucky and claimed it could be the skull of an African American slave woman.

The true site of Daniel Boone and Rebecca's bones are subject to rumor and local legend.[338]

According to the federal census of 1820 both Benjamin and Nicholas Fox were living in Knox County, Kentucky and most of the same people who were their neighbors ten years before were still their neighbors. Nicholas's nearest neighbor was his mother-in-law, Agnes Hammack, who was raising a sizable family. Her husband Daniel, dead for two years, was not listed. Curiously, there is a James Fox listed as their neighbor but despite exhaustive efforts, he has never been identified.

The 1820 census indicates Benjamin claimed a 26 year old female slave, two teenage male slaves and two teenage female slaves. It is reasonable to assume that at least some of these people were a family unit.[89] Given what we know now, we may wonder just how close of a relationship Benjamin had with the women and her children.

Sometime during 1820 another daughter was born to Nicholas and wife Mary Sara, though she too, died without a documented name.[5] Common or not, the loss and grief surely caused Sara to hold five year old Susan just that much closer. Nicholas placed another simple cross marking her grave behind their cabin, in a sad, crude graveyard, which was becoming entirely too full.

In 1820, patriarch James Bunch passed away at 70 years old.[146] Soon after, his married children began to leave Kentucky. Initially, the deceased veteran's daughter Dentian, married to Isham Boling, moved to Tennessee, but in the years to come, most of the rest moved on as well.[113] The decision on the part of the adult children of James Bunch to move to Tennessee from Kentucky, was a pivotal turning point in the future of not only their families, but those they would meet there.

The 1820 federal census shows most of the Bunch family remained in Clay County, Kentucky, at least for the meantime. In addition many neighbors with names like Morris and Maupin are listed as well. The children of these families would inter-marry with the grandchildren of the deceased James Bunch, whose children would in turn inter-marry with the Fox family. Together, this small clan would leave all those they loved and all they had ever known, in search of a better life and in doing so, contribute to western expansion.

In August of 1821, Missouri became a slave state in what was an ongoing contentious issue.[263]

Additionally, one of the greatest proponents of settling Oregon, Thomas Hart Benton was seated as one of Missouri's first Senators in December of that year. His interventions would become pivotal to the expansion West.[309]

During the same year, the North West Fur Company and the Hudson's Bay Company merged. When they did, Fort Astor became their headquarters, and renamed, Fort George.[301]

CHAPTER THIRTY

EPHRAIM FOX & JOHN R. COBB

William Henry Ashley was a Virginian who had enjoyed varied careers as a surveyor, land speculator, merchant and manufacturer of gunpowder. On February 13, 1822, in the *Missouri Gazette* he ran a celebrated help wanted ad,

"To enterprising Young Men: The Subscriber wishes to engage ONE HUNDRED MEN to ascend the river Missouri to its source, there to be employed for one, two, or three years. For particulars, inquire of Major Andrew Henry, near the Lead Mines, in the county of Washington (who will ascend with and command the party) or to the subscriber in St Louis."[265]

On the west side of town, someone read the ad to a gangly, good natured boy named Jim Bridger, and he signed up for his first trip into the mountains where his legend began. The fur trade really launched in earnest in 1822 with this expedition. With the fur trade, began the discovery of the West.

The timing of this advert and what it portended is ironic, given just a month later, on March 14, 1822, Ephraim Fox was born.[125] Born and raised in Barboursville, Knox County, Kentucky, to Nicholas and Mary Sara Fox, their first son Ephraim might have been named after Mary Sara's little brother by the same name, or after the biblical figure.

The name Ephraim means fruitful and productive in Hebrew,[270] and while it might have seemed at times as it does to all fathers, the name was misplaced, it was indeed a fitting name. The infant boy's name embodied the hope his parents had for the future of their family; for in the Bible, God chose Ephraim to lead his people to the promised land.[262] They couldn't have guessed how he would someday do just that.

Also born in 1822 in Knox Co. KY, was John R. Cobb who until fairly recently was believed to be the son of Samuel and Keziah (Barber) Cobb.[238] His exact birthdate is not of record, but it is interesting he was born the same year as Ephraim Fox.

When my YDNA was tested by FamilytreeDNA it was a close match to the descendants of John R. Cobb. As it was already established that John's father Samuel was the son of Ambrose Samuel Cobb Jr, researchers believed the historical documents that claimed John was Samuel's son. With more people being tested, results have been refined that now indicate John R. Cobb was not the biological son of Samuel Cobb, but the biological son of either Benjamin Fox or his son Nicholas.

Though unknown if Keziah (Barber) was John's biological mother, it appears she was judging from the spacing between births of her biological children and John; which do not indicate anything unusual. If John was the product of an illicit affair between Kizzie and Benjamin or Nicholas, it was a secret only Kizzie might have known for about two centuries.

When John was born, Benjamin was 50 years old and he and his wife Elizabeth had a son named Henry that was three years old; the couple would have no more children. Benjamin's eldest son Nicholas, on the other hand, would have been only 28 years old and had only begun having children. It seems the odds are that Nicholas was the father but that cannot be said with surety, yet. In any event, John R. Cobb was raised as a son of Samuel and Kizzie Cobb, and there are no documents that indicate he maintained any relationship with the Fox family.

By the time John R. Cobb and Ephraim, or "Eph" as he was known by those familiar with him, were born, Ephraim's cousin Arthur Fox Jr. had lived for many years in the log cabin his father had left him in Mason County, Kentucky. In the year Ephraim and John Cobb were born, in 1822, Arthur Jr. completed a new brick home on the family plantation that he called 'Webster'. In addition, Arthur Jr. had built a race track on his property and was becoming quite well known for racing horses that won awards in places like Memphis and New Orleans. Each year annual races came to be held at Arthur Fox's, Webster plantation, courtesy of the Webster Jockey Club.[181]

When Indian reservations had been established in what had not yet become Missouri, for the Delaware Indians in 1818[282] and the Kickapoos in 1819,[47] they did not occupy the area. The area was mostly unoccupied hunting ground for a number of Indian tribes, who did not live there, but traveled in its wilderness. As White settlements became populated, the Indians moved further into the Missouri wilderness they had been promised.

Even so, in 1818 the first petition to Congress requesting statehood was presented by the Speaker of the House of Representatives. Hostilities followed and by the year Ephraim was born in 1822, conflicts were increasing between Missouri pioneer settlers and the displaced Indians. After an appeal was made to the government on their behalf, the Indians were declared to be within their rights. The White settlers abandoned their claims, for a while.[282]

In 1823 explorer William Henry Ashley brought in Tom (Broken Hand) Fitzpatrick, Jed Smith, Bill Sublette and Jim Clyman for an expedition he was planning. It was an all-star group of mountain men. All of them would be instrumental to mapping 'The West' and leading people through it.

Later in the winter of 1823, Jim Clyman made his way over South Pass, the low and extremely wide sweeping meadow over a low mountain range in the Rockies, which would figure prominently in the expansion of the West. Though Robert Stuart had stumbled through it previously without realizing what it was, Jim Clyman knew what it meant. When he emerged from the mountains, word got back to the

United States pretty quickly about what he had found. This single discovery changed the entire picture for those dreaming of going west.[23]

The discovery came as Ephraim Fox turned a year old. As Eph grew, so did Oregon fever.

It must have been in about 1823, when Mary Sara's brother, Daniel Hammack Jr, a single man of 23 years, left Kentucky, for Indiana. The move created an exodus of the Hammack family. In the coming few years, most of his siblings would follow him there as well, leaving their sister Mary Sara little family left in Knox County but for her own with husband Nicholas Fox.[7]

CHAPTER THIRTY-ONE

MACON COUNTY, MISSOURI

Until 1824 the Fox, Sac and Iowa Indians laid claim to the area that would many years later become Macon County, Missouri in 1836. The earliest settlers were mainly from Kentucky, Tennessee and North Carolina and pushed into the area in the early 1820's. These earliest of settlers came from Howard, Randolph and Chariton Counties in Missouri, continuing their push westward searching to better the lives of their families.[62] Among them were brothers William and James Bunch, as well as Henry and John Bunch, who were likely cousins.

Ephraim was two years old in 1824, when explorer and entrepreneur William Henry Ashley initiated the rendezvous. It was a first of its kind gathering of Red and White trappers who brought their peltry to be traded for money, whiskey, food, supplies, beads and generally anything that you might want. The rendezvous tradition went on for a dozen years, throughout Ephraim's boyhood. The event was reported on in eastern newspapers and romanticized in the hearts of young adventurers, including perhaps Ephraim's 28 year old father, Nicholas Fox.

Nearby, Barton Warren Stone and Alexander Campbell met for the first time and recognized the principles of the "Christians" and "Disciples" were strikingly similar. Once informed about Campbell's great success gaining much support for the movement, publishing the *Christian Baptist*, Stone began publishing *The Christian Messenger*, in 1826.[70]

During the 1820's, opponents of the movement began using the derisive term "Campbellite", which members of the church found slanderous. As the movement grew in numbers and influence the term was used more often and Campbell did his best to end the practice, but wrote, "*Men fond of nicknaming, are generally weak in reason, argument and proof.*"[70[p.8]]

In 1830, Campbell changed the name of his paper to the *Millennial Harbinger*. The movement got positive response from Ohio to Alabama, but its proponents were overly optimistic and it soon became clear there were a great number of Methodists, Baptists, Catholics and Presbyterians that preferred their denomination. These were dismissed as sectarian and in this way the battle lines were drawn between the "Christians" and the "sects". Using the name "Campbellites" on these God-fearing people who despised the use of party names and wanted nothing more than to just be Christians, was a terrible insult.[70]

When Andrew Jackson ran for President of the United States in 1824, he won a plurality of the popular and electoral vote, over John Quincy Adams, but no candidate won an electoral majority. To end the tie, the House of Representatives; following the law; elected Adams. Jackson and his supporters cried corruption between Adams and Henry Clay and in response to the president-elect's ambitious agenda, Jackson's supporters founded the Democratic Party.[150]

The fact Jackson supported slavery is the primary reason Democrats purport today to not like the man. This despite the fact the party was the sole proponent of slavery, Jim Crow laws, the Klu Klux Klan, and opposed equal treatment of Blacks and women throughout the civil rights movement of the 1960's. Leopard's might change their meow, but they don't change their spots.

Six years after the Treaty of Cherokee Agency was signed, President James Monroe expressed his strong belief that all Native Americans should be relocated west of the Mississippi, so to free up the entire east coast to White settlement. For land speculators the statement portended great profit, while for the Indians it spelled the end.[254]

In 1825 Nicholas and Sarah had a second son, that unfortunately died at birth or soon after and remained unnamed.[5] Nicholas dug another grave at the edge of the wood near their cabin. The deaths of now three children, no doubt took a toll on them individually and as a couple. Despite the commonality of it, their babies deaths left scars on their hearts and tested their Christian faith. Though Ephraim was too young to remember his father digging the grave of his infant brother, it was a memory his elder sister Susan must have carried.

That same summer, those members of the Bunch family that had remained in Kentucky, picked up and moved to Tennessee, following their kin, looking for a better future for them all. As friends and neighbors scattered toward frontiers in every direction, the Fox families of Benjamin and Nicholas remained in Knox County, Kentucky.

By 1826 Allen Powell and his wife Mary Polly had brought seven children into the world, five of them boys. These boys grew into some hearty men, indicating the kind of parents that had raised them. As Allen's boys grew, William, David, Jackson, James and John (similarly aged to Ephraim Fox) were reared on stories about mapping and discovering what lied west. Among those whose anxiousness couldn't be contained, these brothers would collectively make great contributions not just along the Oregon trail, but in the territory itself. The brothers were married to Pugh girls, of whom the Fox family were well acquainted and this might be where the Powell's met the Fox's.

Still residing in Knox County, Kentucky, about a year after Nicholas and Sara had lost a son, the couple had a healthy, dark haired daughter they named Phoebe, on January 16, 1826.[118] Her elder sister Susan was eleven and brother Ephraim four years old when Phoebe was born.

Map of Knox County, Kentucky upper right and Jackson County, Tennessee, lower left, 1827. Most of the children of Nicholas Fox and Mary Sara (Hammack) were born in Barboursville, Knox County, KY. Benjamin Fox owned property and lived in Jackson County, TN, but curiously appeared as a neighbor to his son Nicholas in Knox County, KY during the same years. The current day drive from Barboursville, Knox Co. KY to Flynn's Lick, TN is 163.5 miles; quite a distance in 1827. (19)

CHAPTER THIRTY-TWO

FIRST CONTACT WITH THE ROGUE INDIANS

Fort Vancouver, built by the Hudson's Bay Company in the northwest would become pivotal in the coming years to the formation of civilization and settlement of the Willamette Valley in the Oregon country.

The first known contact with the Indians of the Rogue came in 1826, when George Vancouver anchored off of Cape Blanco about 30 miles north of the mouth of the Rogue River and the Indians visited the ship in their canoes. That same year the Hudson's Bay Company led an overland expedition from their new fort in Vancouver to as far south as the Rogue River, encountering Indians.

Their name is believed to be from French trappers who had discovered the river and the Indians that lived along it, considering them to be rogue, perhaps for their willingness to trade with White men, or their mischievousness. At any rate, the first contacts were mutually entertaining and profitable.[71]

In 1827 the Old National Road opened across Ohio to Richmond, Indiana. By the early 1830's, the important trail reached St. Louis and from there, the Mississippi. Suddenly emigration began from points east like Pennsylvania and Maryland, reportedly bringing 100 families a day through Zanesville, Ohio to long established Baptist Brethren communities.

In the years these people from the east had been separated from their people in the west, they had come to worship and behave differently. Ideology clashed among those Baptist Brethren and given the nature of the Second Great Awakening, many churches were drawn toward Church of Christ denominations, or simply went Baptist.[297]

While records indicate George Bunch, the elder, and his second wife, Nancy (Maupin), had been married for 10 years when they had their first child in 1828, it's almost certain there were others. They named the little boy, James Washington Bunch, perhaps after his Revolutionary War veteran grandfather.[96] He was born in the Tennessee county of Washington, also named after America's first president. Step-brother George (known as John) was twelve years old when young James W. Bunch was born.

By the time James was born in 1828 the George Bunch family had left Kentucky and gone to Tennessee. George's youngest brother Nathaniel, called Nat, was born in 1805 and left Kentucky to Missouri with his wife's family who were long time neighbors; the McCollum's.

Also leaving the Bluegrass State, was Mary Sara's widowed mother Agnes (Pruitt) Hammack and Mary Sara's 30 year old brother Ephraim Hammack, who migrated north into Indiana. Though the exact year is unknown, by 1828 the Hammack family had mostly, if not completely relocated to Indiana. Perhaps Sara's younger brother had done well after moving north and that is why more of his siblings had followed. The author has not found documents that would explain the family relocating to Indiana. Most of them spent the rest of their lives there. Perhaps religion was a factor. In any event, Mary Sara had only her immediate family left in Knox County, Kentucky.

In August of 1828, Cader Powell passed away in Pike County, Kentucky so his sons Jacob and George traveled from Georgia, where they lived, to court in Pike County finalizing provisions of his Will. Along with the brothers, were two character witnesses, one of whom was James M Rice, a curious name given the coming events, but perhaps only coincidence.[31]

In his lifetime, Cader Powell was married just once, to Frances Foote, who bore him nine sons and two daughters. As their children grew, most settled bounty claims in Georgia, but not their eldest, Allen, and their seventh, Theophilus, who remained in Pike County, Kentucky, where they had been born. Allen was nine years older than his little brother, Theophilus, who became a circuit preacher early in his life. A very short time after the death of their father, Allen and Theophilus moved from Kentucky to Missouri.[209]

In order to provide incentive to the Cherokee Nation to move west across the Mississippi, the Treaty of Washington was signed in May of 1828.[240] The treaty promised to compensate the Indians for their land and pay their moving expenses for the next year. Few Indian families chose to leave. In response, in December the state of Georgia stripped the Cherokee of legal rights, attempting their forceful relocation. Still, they resisted, going on with their lives, peacefully. Many Indians who owned farms or plantations believed their adaptation to the White men's ways would insulate them from eviction.

That year, along the unexplored west coast of the continent, Jedediah Smith, clerk, frontiersman, hunter, trapper, author, cartographer and explorer came north from California to Oregon on what would become the Applegate Trail, but not for another generation. Fifteen trappers in his party were killed on the Umpqua and Smith was lucky to escape with his life. Jedediah later petitioned the federal government for a grant to help him map the West but was denied, so formed his own expedition just a few years later. He was unfortunately killed by Comanches two months into what became his last expedition.[24]

In the Presidential election of 1828, Andrew Jackson beat John Quincy Adams in a landslide. He ran as the first populist president and was deemed by his supporters as a champion of the common man.[313] For what he would do to the American Indian in the following years, he earned an abiding historical hatred, especially by the Cherokee people.

The following year, in Knox County, Kentucky, 1829, Nicholas and Mary Sara Fox had a healthy baby girl, they named Ann.[92] This little girl, like her elder sisters Susan and Phoebe, and older brother Ephraim, somehow beat the odds and survived birth. The following year, the 1830 census shows that in Knox County, Kentucky, Benjamin and Nicholas Fox remained neighbors. It is also important evidence that Ambrose Cobb (brother of Samuel Cobb), had passed away but his sons, Ambrose and Samuel Cobb remained neighbors. The mysterious James Fox still lived nearby.[90]

In 1830, men who had become larger than life; Bill Sublette, Jed Smith and Dave Jackson, took a caravan of 81 men from St. Louis to the rendezvous in the Wind River Mountains in current day Wyoming. The difference with this caravan is that this one traveled on wheels; 10 wagons drawn by four mules each and 2 one-mule dearborns. The men rode mules and they took a milk cow and a dozen beef cattle.[23]

Among the group was an inexperienced and unknown young nineteen year old, named Jonathon Keeney; a raw but entrepreneurial farm boy from Missouri, drawn to roaming with a penchant for adventure. Jonathon Keeney, like the other men of this caravan if they had not already, soon became living legends. Keeney had procured ponies for the trip and intended to begin on his own hook.[249]

All of these men would play vital roles in opening and leading the way west. In the era they lived, they were looked upon like modern-day rock stars. The truth was there were literally thousands of places to get lost or turned around in the wilderness that stretched from the Missouri River to the Willamette Valley. In order to make a trip of this type, it was necessary to follow someone that had been there before and this was what made these trail blazers famous.

Upon reaching Ft. Laramie the train of wagons met and traded with Jim Bridger who had a party of about 35 men and about as many

Indians. Here young Keeney jumped at what he recognized was a great opportunity and joined Bridger, proceeding forward with him.[249]

Many years later when Keeney was an old man, he related that soon after he joined Bridger they were camped on the Sweetwater River when the emigrant party of Dr. Whitman visited their camp on one of his first trips through the trail. At this time, Jim Bridger had the points of two arrows in his back that had been put there by Indians two years previous. This was his first chance to see a real doctor and Jim took advantage by having the kindly but large and stout Dr. Whitman remove them.

Keeney later related that Bridger laid on his belly as Whitman went to work with a good knife. The first point came out easy but the second one was embedded in bone and the country doctor had to apply quite some force to remove it. While Bridger had to be held down to facilitate the procedure he was said to give but few groans. He quickly healed and went on to the Yellowstone, with thanks to the benevolent Dr. Whitman.[249]

William Henry Ashley's group didn't roll OVER the mountains, but they got up ON them. People noticed and newspapers reflected with great fanfare;[23] it was a matter of time before someone got all the way to the Willamette Valley in a wagon.

This was essential to taking a family across the continent, for personal possessions and tools for the trip, as well as for setting up in Oregon. They had to be able to carry enough supplies to sustain a family not just across the country, but also through the first winter until a crop could be planted. In order to move 2000 miles across little known terrain, wagons most certainly had to come along.

To move into the frontier was seen as patriotic by the nation's first sons. Every generation had pushed westward and they were good at it. There was safety in numbers, so naturally common to move in family groups, subsequently resulting in marriages, babies and more relationships. These groups grew close often, as they closed ranks to survive in the savage land.

When wagons reached the Stony Mountains in 1830, discussions relating to possibilities that lied in the west began to be held in many pioneer cabins.

CHAPTER THIRTY-THREE

MORMONS

The Mormon organization, the Church of Christ, was organized by Joseph Smith in 1830. This action would alter and shape the content of the United States and vastly test the idea of religious freedom. It was the first time of many that Missouri would bleed in the following years for the subject. Claiming divine communication with God, Joseph Smith drew much criticism from fellow religious leaders and skepticism from non-Mormons.[16] One year later as leader of the Mormon Church of Latter Day Saints, Smith laid the foundation in which discourse would be given, when he announced to his followers,

"If ye are faithful, ye shall assemble yourselves together to rejoice upon the land of Missouri, which is the land of your inheritance, which is now the land of your enemies."[175[section 52, verse 9e]]

No matter what state a person called home, those were fightin' words, but especially in Missouri. With that began an exodus of Mormons to Jackson County, Missouri locating centrally in Independence. The differences of the Mormon religion from others isolated them, so when a concentration of them moved the complete town of Massenet to the small county, it riled the locals that felt the Mormons were an invading cult.

Some religious leaders called Joseph Smith's claim of divine communication with God a claim that was of the devil and politicians called the Mormon use of polygamy one of the two relics of barbarism.[317] Despite the criticism, in just a couple years the numbers of Mormons were able to dominate the local economy and it became feared by those already living in Jackson County, that the Mormons would vote in blocs that would re-shape their county, not to mention that Jackson County residents took Joseph Smith's promise of coming to town as their enemy plenty seriously.

Adding another element to their differences, most Mormons were abolitionists and most of the locals, though not necessarily slave owners, defended the practice.[272] There's little doubt that Nicholas and Mary Sara, considering their Christian faith, were among those that found it hard to get past the Mormon's highly publicized belief in Polygamy.

CHAPTER THIRTY-FOUR

INDIAN REMOVAL ACT & WHITE MAN'S MAGIC

As White settlement continued, efforts to dislodge Native Indian tribes had been mostly ignored, so congress passed The Indian Removal Act. Signed by President Andrew Jackson on May 28, 1830. It authorized the president to 'negotiate' with southern American Indian tribes to be relocated west across the Mississippi.[229]

The act did not provide reluctant Indians any choice this time and it was quickly and strongly enforced by President Jackson. The following spring in March of 1831, the decision by Chief Justice John Marshall in Cherokee Nation vs State of Georgia, identified Native American tribes as independent nations within the United States, therefore not afforded the protections of the Constitution.[260] The Trail of Tears had begun.

An incredible, strange but true event occurred in 1831, far to the west, where White men were few and not yet seen as a threat.

The Nez Perce were of considerable intelligence; at least semi civilized and did not see the White man as an adversary. This was decades before the White man had broken treaties and been at war with these Indians, and their dealings til now were usually of mutual benefit. The Nez Perce occupied what is now Oregon and Washington and the Flathead Indians, just as advanced, occupied western Montana.

As with White men, they too had religion. It was obvious to them that the religion of the White men was different than theirs. Their religion was the power of their people much like the White man's religion is their power. They noted the declining business in furs done with the British and that the business was being replaced by Americans. Through some of their business dealings, the Nez Perce and Flatheads noted that the British enjoyed many creature comforts but that the Americans had more of them. They could see the "Bostons" had great power; 'medicine', as they called it, and they believed this resulted in the White man having possessions that Indians coveted.

How could the Indian get the same big medicine so that they could have these things? The Nez Perce got credit for the idea. They would travel all the way to St. Louis to talk to General William Clark who had come to their land in 1805-06, the man who could help them appropriate this religion. The Nez Perce talked with the Flatheads and they liked the idea too, so four Nez Perce and three Flatheads left for St. Louis probably with the great fur trader Lucien Fontenelle, in the summer of 1831.[179]

Three turned back in the August heat of the lower Platte Valley, while four made it all the way to St. Louis; probably around the first of October. One named Man of the Morning was a Flathead and the other three were Nez Perce named Black Eagle, No Horns on His Head and Rabbit Skin Leggings.[223]

While these Native American's who had little experience with White men made a perilous journey across the Great American Desert, seeking White men's knowledge that summer, another subjugated group, generations into slavery, decided they had seen enough of the White men's knowledge.

On August 21, 1831, Nat Turner led a slave uprising in Southampton County, Virginia, from the plantation where he had been owned and served his owner. Nat's own owners died first, then from plantation to plantation, Turner freed slaves and killed the Whites they found, adding to his ranks. Axes, knives and clubs were used initially, so as to not alert response. By the following morning, before a militia could be raised, 60 or 70 White men, women and children were killed.

Turner had been a slave all of his life and looked to God for answers. He was described later as being often at prayer, singing hymns or reading the Bible in an attempt to find justice in this world in the holy book. Nat's story was related by his lawyer and people still argue how accurate the lawyer was, to Nat's answers and claims.[15]

Turner claimed that for some time before the attack he became convinced that the Lord had called upon him to kill the slavers. If that is true, he was suffering an understandable mental psychosis, if it is simply an excuse he gave to a lawyer, to elicit some level of compassion or understanding, we will never know.

In his life, Nat never left Southampton County, Virginia, where he was born a slave and grew up a slave. His entire world of experience was inside the boundaries of a farm that he worked for all of his life with no benefit but scant food and shelter.

He was in fact, later caught hiding nearby. Enslaved as he was, without benefit of money or travel, Nat had gained a brutal education that his slavers died teaching him.

The whole thing only truly lasted a couple days, but over 3000 troops were gathered from a terrified population, shocked at the thought the slaves could revolt. In fact, in answer to the violence, the state of Virginia cracked down on free Blacks, and their right to bear arms was removed there and in many states.

Blacks, chained like animals and treated the same; used for sex or whatever else entertainment a White man wanted, not to mention working for nothing and watching your wife, daughter, son, father, sister, brother, beaten, whipped and sold down the road, never to be seen again, saw this rebellion as a good thing. White Christian society, who knew what they were doing was ultimately a sin in the eyes of God, were in a full blown panic.

It is no doubt or wonder every rotten thing a White slaver ever did to a Black man, woman or child, flashed through their mind as those they had abused had their revenge. While it can be said that this rebellion was a turning point, focusing national attention on slavery, the subject had been argued strongly for decades.[15]

The truth was that there was a day, when all people could and often did indenture themselves or their children to pay a debt, but the idea of lifelong servitude and loss of all human rights, was not always the case.[75] In a time before physical coin, when all a person had to offer was their labor, it is easy to see how labor would become a commodity.

Racism occurred when White men of that era looked upon Black men as not subject to the same laws the Whites were because they were Christians and the Blacks were not.[345]

Seen through the eyes of his victims and their kin, Nat was a murderer, but to his people he was an example of fighting back and had the roles been reversed, White's would have too. But in 1830 Whites knew his example was dangerous and set about to squelch any idea of freedom.

Had White children and women not been killed, it's possible that history might have forgiven him. But the truth is that Nat watched White people treat Black children with absolutely no regard for their humanity, so why would they expect to see him show mercy?

One immediate effect of the uprising was that the subject became widely debated and with that, consciousness began, but still decades before the practice ended in a bloody war. Absolutely terrified of Blacks uniting in their defense, the response was to give Black people less freedom.

In the hysteria and anger that followed the initial night of killings, an estimated 120 Blacks were killed by mobs and militia, many of whom were completely innocent of anything to do with the rebellion. The state tried and executed 55 more and sentenced the rest to be removed from the state, sold far and wide apart (down the road, was the term).[15]

To this day history ignores Nat Turner and few White people have even heard of him, but had he been a White American, fighting for the freedom of White Americans, he would be a household name. Life is most ironic when death and suffering become involved.

In the ensuing days after the arrival of the three Nez Perce and one Flathead Indians in St. Louis, communication was the biggest obstacle. Unfortunately, there were no trappers in town who had learned their language. In the next few weeks however, they got to the point where they could communicate using sign language.

The Whites interpreted that the Indians wanted principally amulets, incantations and instructions in magic, is what it seemed. Which Gen. William Clark, the Red Headed Chief, interpreted as religious instruction, and perhaps it was.

However the Indians having come down from the clear thin air of the Platte were not prepared for the stagnant muggy heat of Missouri. Though they met with Bishop Joseph Rosati and Rev. Edmund Saulnier who agreed with Clark that they needed a missionary, the religious leaders were under-funded.

As all this was figured out, the Indians lingered in St. Louis. They were filled with wonderment at the White men's accomplishments, but soon some low-land disease killed Chief Black Eagle, and he died October 31, 1831. Saulnier baptized him in last rites. Soon after Man of the Morning died with his last rites being administered by Friar Joseph A. Lutz.[223]

By 1831, when Ephraim Fox was nine years old, there was considerable interest in the opportunities that the Oregon country offered. Of those interested, was Hall Jackson Kelley, who began to promote movement west and probably became the earliest propagandist for Oregon. In his widely circulated view, it was patriotic to settle Oregon and the Hudson's Bay Company had no right to it. A talented writer, Hall could write about things he'd never seen and it dripped with authenticity.

Though his interest started 15 years before, in 1831 he circulated a pamphlet that gave directions and advice on a trip he had never taken or seen.[334] The eastern press grabbed it up and ran with it, as nothing like it had ever been claimed before. This 'news' changed the equation. There was a growing obsession focusing on The West, and some of the dreamers couldn't help but put in their two cents, even if it held no water.

In Illinois on April 30, 1831 the Coldbrook Christian congregation that included Thomas Pugh established a Church of Christ on Cedar Fork on the Henderson River in Warren County. Of the seventeen charter members were Elijah Davidson and John Ecles Murphy.

In twenty years Thomas's brothers who were yet neighbors of Ephraim Fox and George Bunch, would join John Ecles Murphy wagon train.[70]

In Oregon, along the Columbia, with the decline in fur trade French-Canadian trappers began moving south with their families and settling in the lush and moderate Willamette Valley. Dr. John McLoughlin of the Hudson Bay Company encouraged the settlement, hoping to discourage American interest in the lush distant valley. The area has been known since then as French Prairie, where the first White settlements were begun in Oregon.[302]

By late 1831 or early 1832, there were at least three farms on the upper Willamette as well as another French-Canadian farmer. These four were reported by British Army officers as being the first to settle *"above the falls"*. Nathaniel Wyeth, an independent trapper and tradesman from New England had a farm southwest of present day Butteville. These were the first farmers in Oregon.[22]

After Elizabeth Ann (Asher), the wife of deceased Revolutionary War veteran James Bunch, passed away in Tennessee, sometime in about 1831, most of she and George's grown children moved away from the state, perhaps feeling unencumbered.

In 1832, two of these sons; George Bunch, born 1794, and his brother Nathaniel, or Nat, born 1805, moved from Tennessee; initially to the frontier of Boone County, Missouri. George was 38 years old and his eldest son by his first wife, George William (John) Bunch, was 16. His second wife Nancy (Maupin) was 33, the mother to 12 year old daughter, Malany and a 4 year old son, James.

George's in-laws, the Maupin family, were some of the earliest pioneers to Boone County and having lived there for at least the last ten years, were well established.[4] This relationship surely had a great deal to do with why and where the elder George Bunch moved his family to in Missouri. Nat was eleven years younger than his brother George and still single.

CHAPTER THIRTY-FIVE

BAD MEDICINE & THE RESTORATION

By spring of 1832 Rabbit Skin Leggings and No Horns on His Head, the two remaining Nez Perce in St. Louis, were on the steamer '*Yellowstone*', headed for the upper Missouri country, on their way home. There they met George Catlin, the early western artist. At the mouth of the Yellowstone River, No Horns on His Head died.

Rabbit Skin Leggings was the only survivor of the Indian trip to the White man's cities to find his medicine. It was fortunate that he was able to tell his story to some Nez Perce he met on a hunt east of the divide, for they would be the only Nez Perce to hear the story. Continuing on his way home, he lost his scalp to Black Foot Indians, who killed him. Such was the end of the Nez Perce and Flathead Indian search for the Holy Grail.[223]

Unconnected to these events, there had been a number of meetings between the "Christians" and the "Reformers", in and around Kentucky, held by Alexander Campbell and Barton Stone. By January of 1832, a large meeting was held in Lexington, Kentucky where both groups decided to unite. Since neither group recognized any higher ecclesiastical authority above the local church, actual union could only be accomplished by going to the congregation and urging them to unite. This was accomplished on a broad scale and soon it was estimated that between the unified Stone-Mulkey and the Campbell's groups, there were 25,000 members of the movement in 1832.

True to their beliefs, there was no particular name designated for local churches. Alexander Campbell preferred "Disciples of Christ", though his father and Walter Scott both liked the name "Christian". Stone and Mulkey both insisted on the name "Christian" and their churches were usually designated "Church of Christ" or "Christian

Church". Throughout most of the nineteenth century both names were used and accepted interchangeably.[70]

Capt. Benjamin E. Bonneville, on leave from the U.S. Army, assembled a train at Fort Osage on the eastern edge of Jackson County, Missouri, in 1832 and moved west by land, past the landings on the Missouri River at Independence and down across its banks. They crossed rock ledges in what became Westport; now downtown Kansas City; and onto the old Chouteau fur trail to the mountains.

His wagons were the first to cross the divide at South Pass and head northwest. He built Fort Bonneville in western Wyoming, on the Green River. In doing so, Bonneville blazed a trail about halfway to Oregon's Willamette Valley.[331]

The milestone hit the newspapers about the same time that in the east, the Erie Canal was completed, connecting New York with the Great Lakes, providing much improved access to points in the northwest Oregon territory.

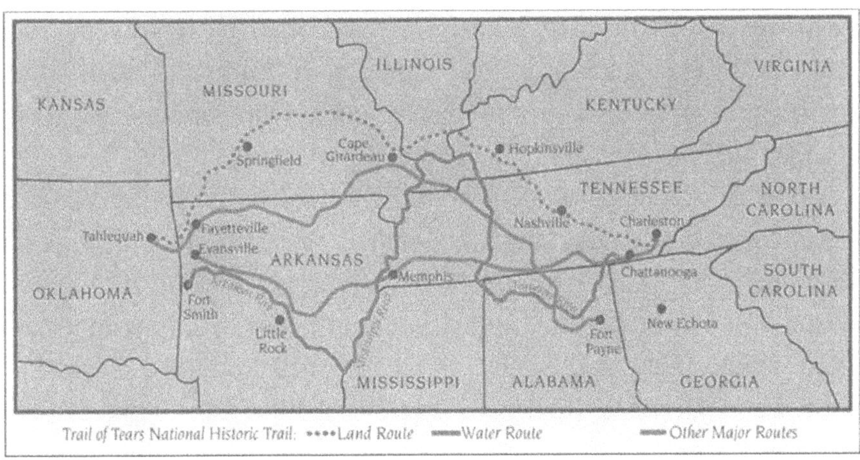

Trail of Tears. (20)

CHAPTER THIRTY-SIX

HENRY FRANKLIN MARTIN

In March 1832, the same month Ephraim and his half-brother John R. Cobb turned ten years old, Henry Franklin Martin was born in Knox County, Kentucky. His mother Martha was the half-Black daughter of David Martin and an unknown Black slave woman.

YDNA indicates Henry Franklin Martin, John R. Cobb and the author share a common father; that being Benjamin or Nicholas Fox. Just like the conception of John R. Cobb, the details that led to these unions will never truly be known. However in the case of the birth of Henry Franklin Martin, there might be clues to where Benjamin Kendrick Fox originally came from and who his biological parents were.

David Martin was a cotton plantation owner that lived in Edgefield, South Carolina, but before that he was an overseer for many years on the Beech Island cotton plantation of Edmund Bacon. There are familial ties between the Martin and Bacon families for many decades leading up to and throughout David Martin's life.[171]

Martin was married to Mary Polly Erfurd in the spring of 1807. Court documents would later relate that he started beating his wife the following fall. Shortly after David Martin began working for Edmund Bacon, in 1810 he began a sexually intimate relationship with a slave there named Lucy. A daughter was born to them named Eliza. At a point when Martin acquired a plantation of his own, Lucy and Eliza went with him.[59]

It might be easy to guess David Martin was not a nice guy, but it took his wife a few months of marriage before she realized just how utterly ruthless he could be. Having beaten Black slaves for a living, it was no great leap for David Martin to take to treating his wife as his own property to do with as he pleased.

His wife Mary took the beatings and might have lived her entire life that way but one day she asked her husband to come with her to her father's and David took serious offense. He tied her to a tree and left her there for about an hour as punishment. He bound her wrists so tightly that her fingers turned black by the time he returned to free her. Even then he continued to berate her for her indiscretion.

David Martin beat his wife with a bridle; he horse whipped her with a tree bough that was being used as a broom. When she was pregnant with his child, he drew up her clothes and beat her on the hip to the point she bled so severely he thought he had mortally wounded her, so he tended the wounds he had made and cuddled her by the fire for the evening.

Mary left David a month after he tied her to the tree, the morning after he beat her with a plow line for telling her mother about the way he was treating her. The day after Mary left him, she was returning to David's plantation with her mother and a man named George Sawyers when they were met by David on the road. Mary told her husband that she would return to him if he would but promise not to beat her like he had. His response was, "that if she would not take such usage as she had received and worst, she might go to the devil." Mary returned to David a number of times to ask him to take her back and treat her right, but he never allowed her entry into the house again.

She divorced him shortly after and because divorce laws were so stringent in that era, requiring very specific reasons, the treatment Mary had received was entered into the court record.[59]

In 1817 David Martin fathered Martha, with an unknown female slave and gave her the Martin surname.[133] Slavery laws in South Carolina required that slave owners not simply release a slave. Instead they had to appear before the court to file a 'manumission' wherein slave and owner agreed that the slave would leave South Carolina when they were freed and never return, or else they could become a slave again.

This law was enacted as a response to what became known as Cato's Rebellion or Cato's Conspiracy; the largest slave rebellion in South Carolina history.[164] This revolt pre-dated the Nat Turner rebellion by many decades and seems to be mostly forgotten, though 25 colonists and 35-50 Black slaves were killed. Manumission was a paranoid response made by a White hierarchy that treated Black people like cattle or inanimate objects, but well understood the truth was Black people were human beings, with the capacity to reason, remember and respond.[48]

As David Martin's health began to fail, in 1827 he began petitioning the court to manumit Lucy, Eliza and Martha. The process took longer than a year and when it was over, the request was denied.

Desperate to see the women freed before he died, the record states that in 1832 David sent Lucy, her daughter Eliza and Eliza's husband, described as an ignorant White man who could neither read nor write, and his daughter Martha, to Knox County, Kentucky.

When the group left Edgefield, South Carolina, Martha was five months pregnant; the father is not mentioned.[184.5] What the record did not state; what was not public knowledge; what was not discovered for almost two hundred years; was that the baby boy Martha carried was the son of Benjamin Fox or his son Nicholas.

Henry Franklin Martin was born in March, 1832, in Knox County, Kentucky.[105] Martha gave the boy her maiden name. As with John J. Cobb, YDNA currently only proves that Henry Franklin, John J. Cobb and the author share a common father, that is ultimately, Benjamin Fox.

This obviously means Benjamin or Nicholas Fox was in Edgefield, South Carolina in about June, 1831. Were it not for DNA proof, this would make no sense, because up until this shocking news, no documents ever placed Benjamin or Nicholas Fox in South Carolina. Which leads one to wonder, what were they doing in the Palmetto State? The answer likely has something to do with Martha's father David Martin's old friend and employee, Edmund Bacon.

Edmund Burke Bacon, 1776-1826 (21)

Edmund Bacon's was known as a Virginia family, though his father moved to Georgia prior to the onset of the Revolution. Edmund was born April 17, 1776. Orphaned young, he was raised by his older sister Mary and brother-in-law, General Thomas Glascock.

At an early age Edmund was provided schooling at one of the best institutions of its type in Georgia. He later attended the first academy in Augusta, GA. His command of dead languages was extraordinary and as a young man he would rather study the topic than pursue a career.

While Edmund was attending the academy in 1791 it was announced that General George Washington would be visiting the city in a tour of the south and as the whole population made ready, Edmund was chosen by his peers to give the address of welcome to the President. His oratory so impressed President Washington that he presented the youth with several law books. This was the impetus for young Edmund to begin studying law.

With the support of his guardian Gen. Glascock, Edmund began study at the celebrated law school at Litchfield. After graduating with honors he returned to Augusta where he became a member of the Georgia bar and began his practice. When his health began to fail, Edmund was told to move to a higher climate and moved to Edgefield, South Carolina, but not before he was married on January 29, 1799 in Augusta.

His wife's name, was Eliza Fox.[195; 84]

Betsy Eliza Fox-Bacon, 1780-1871 (22)

There are few historical documents relating to the wife of Edmund's wife who carried the maiden name of Fox. It is believed that her father's name was James Fox. An important clue can be found in the last will and testament of her husband's father. When Edmund Bacon's father died in 1785 his will and testament was proved February 1, 1786. It names Joseph Pannill of Wilkes County and James Fox as co-administrators.[103] Unfortunately, no one knows who this James Fox is, or anything about him. Edmund and Eliza had five children, one was named James, though he died as an infant.

Circumstantial evidence is that James Fox, who was a friend of John Bacon, was also the father of Eliza Fox who married John Bacon's son, Edmund. Since we can place Benjamin or Nicholas in South Carolina, at the plantation of David Martin in the summer of 1831, we might assume they were there to visit Edmund Bacon's wife Eliza Fox or her father James, who lived nearby and of whom they were related.

This is all conjecture that wouldn't even be possible were it not for YDNA proving Benjamin was not the son of William Fox of Virginia and was the father or grandfather of Henry Franklin Martin. This turn of events seems to indicate Benjamin was born to this South Carolina/Georgia Fox family and then raised by northern cousins, William and Mary Fox in Virginia.

Augustus Baldwin Longstreet began writing "Georgia Scene's" in about 1830. These were short sketches portraying life in the south. The book was a smashing success. The title character was based on two of Longstreet's friends; Dred Pace and Edmund Bacon.

There is no doubt as to the wealth and attendant power that Edmund Bacon controlled in his life. It is a shame that his wife's genealogy is not as detailed as his. At this point, the only way we will know who fathered Benjamin Fox is when or if the correct male descendant is YDNA tested.

When Edmund Bacon died his grave was given a grandiose marker. His wife Eliza lived decades longer and likely lies under a much smaller, but similarly designed marker three feet away.[195]

The grave and marker of Edmund Burke Bacon. His wife, Betsy Eliza (Fox) lies a few feet to the right. (23)

CHAPTER THIRTY-SEVEN

WAY BACK OUT WEST

By 1833 Hall Jackson Kelley had dreamed long enough and assembled a group to head to Oregon. He had a hard time convincing people and perhaps that affected his decision for a route, but inexplicably he went there via Mexico and where he picked up nine converts; eight wanted for horse stealing.

When he finally made it to Oregon, he contracted malaria and nearly died, but was saved, ironically, by Michel la Framboise, brigadier leader of the very organization that Kelley used in his circulars as a focus of his hatred, the Hudson's Bay Fur Company. Though he could have been arrested by Dr John McLoughlin for at the least running with criminals, he was not. He recuperated and disappeared into history, his work promoting Oregon complete. McLoughlin gave him passage to Hawaii and from there he sailed home to Boston with his health and finances in ruins. Kelley never returned west and died decades later in Massachusetts in 1874. Maybe the experience was a disaster for Kelley, but he had added greatly to Oregon settlement excitement.[334]

Back in Missouri the well intentions of the Methodists were printed in the commonly read Methodist journal, the *Christian Advocate*. A letter March 1, 1833 from William Walker, a Wyandot half breed who had learned to read and write, claimed to have met three Flathead Indians at General Clark's house, and they had come to St. Louis in search of the White Mans Book of Heaven. Never mind that he never met them and he couldn't speak a lick of their language, this is the letter he "translated",

"You took me where you allow your women to dance as we would not allow ours, and the book was not there. You took me where they

worship the Great Spirit with candles, but the book was not there. You showed me images of the good spirits and pictures of the good land beyond, but the book was not among them to tell us the way. I am going back the long, sad trail to my people of the dark land. You make my feet heavy with gifts, and my moccasins will grow old and my arms tire in carrying them, yet the book is not among them".[257]

His narrative obviously meant to stir good will in the congregational readership was followed up with fire and brimstone by the businessman named Disoway that sent the letter in. The wealthy New York Methodist businessman who had actually sent the letter in (a letter in a letter), G.P. Disoway added to this letter by declaring in his letter,

"Let the Church awake from her slumber and go forth in her strength to the salvation of those wandering sons of our native forests!"[77p.268]

All of this obviously meant to rouse the religious to act; the result was that financing was finally established for a willing missionary, in a big awkward schoolteacher from Quebec named Jason Lee.

He and mountain man notable Nat Wyeth, headed for Flathead country. Inexplicably, Lee never said why, but after meeting with the Flatheads he continued on to Oregon and the Willamette valley and established the first Methodist mission. It was only the beginning of Jason Lee's work.[55]

CHAPTER THIRTY-EIGHT

FAMILY OF EPHRAIM MOORE

Susan Fox, eldest daughter of Nicholas and Mary Sara, now 18 years old, married Martin Moore on August 6, 1833.[8] Martin's father Ephraim Moore, moved from South Carolina between the years of 1806 and 1809, settling in Knox County, Kentucky on March 15, 1810; not many years behind his contemporary, Benjamin Fox.

When he was 46 years old with a wife and seven children, Ephraim Moore purchased 500 acres on Old Lynn Creek, near the Old Lynn Camp Baptist Church House, about three miles east of Corbin, Kentucky.[50] The couple would have one more child. On August 20, 1819 Ephraim Moore purchased another adjoining 100 acres,[51] thus becoming a neighbor of longstanding with Benjamin and Nicholas Fox, in Knox County.

Nine years earlier in 1824, one Ephraim Moore's four daughters, Keziah, nicknamed Kizzie, had married Spencer Norvell, born 1750,[108] whose brother Thomas Norvell, born 1749, was father of Martha Norvell, who had married Benjamin Fox. Additionally, another daughter of Ephraim Moore, Elizabeth, known as "Lizzie", married James Hammack,[141] the brother of Mary Sara (Hammack) Fox. These marriages and scant few random notes are all that's left to show for decades of close relationships, whose participants died about two centuries ago. Even so, it is evident relationships made decades earlier in Virginia, continued in Knox County, Kentucky.

Considering Ephraim Moore hailed from South Carolina, it might be suspected he was familiar with Benjamin Fox before he came to Knox County, KY. With these relationships in context it's easy to envision Nicholas and his wife Mary Sara welcoming Martin Moore into their family and looking forward to grandchildren.

Two months after the wedding of Martin Moore and Susan Fox in Kentucky, a brilliant young doctor from Ste Genevieve, Lewis F. Linn stepped into service as Missouri's Senator, October 25, 1833.[275] Fellow Missouri Senator Thomas Hart Benton and Linn collaborated constantly on the Oregon question and could easily be considered the best friends of Oregon's settlement.

Meanwhile in Jackson County, Missouri in October 1833, tensions caused by locals harassing and threatening the Mormons resulted in mob violence against them and the Mormons were forced to abandon their homes in Jackson County, with many settling north in nearby Clay County, Missouri.[281]

When the Mormons were refused to return to their property and retrieve their belongings, early in 1834, they organized an informal military expedition they called Zion's Camp. Their purpose was to retrieve their belongings in Jackson County but the Governor refused them support and the attempt failed. Unable to reclaim their properties they had been forced to abandon, they made homes mainly in and around Clay County the adjacent northern county.

While this was the first violent confrontation since the Bunch family had relocated to nearby Boone County, Missouri, there were ongoing smaller hostilities all over the state and they were no doubt drawn into the conflict, in some regard. As hostile confrontations heated up, the subject of the Church of Latter Day Saints became more commonly brought up in daily discourse. But not everyone was compelled to violence. Some were vocal in their support. Others treated their involvement with the vigilance committee's as a secret society and did not speak of it.[281]

By 1834 the decline in the fur market became a contributing factor in a growing financial depression that grew throughout the decade, during Ephraim Fox's teenage years.[267] In Missouri that year, Eph's contemporary, eighteen year old George William (John) Bunch got a little brother named Stokely Dalleson Bunch; son of the elder George Bunch and Nancy (Maupin).[208]

Meanwhile in Kentucky by the end of the year, Mary Sara and Nicholas got their first grand-baby when their eldest; newlywed Susan and husband Martin Moore; had their first child October 6, 1834. They named the healthy baby boy, Jesse.[198]

Nicholas's biological only biological sister Nancy, married to Joseph Chaffin gave birth to the couples eleventh and final child in 1834.[122] Joseph and Nancy were adjoining neighbors to Benjamin's property in Flynn's Lick, Tennessee.

In Knox County, Kentucky, Mary Sara Fox must have known that she herself was pregnant by this time, for just a five months later in the spring, she bore little blonde, green-eyed Nancy Jane Fox; born March 21, 1835.[204]

Despite the fact Mary Sara was still bearing children herself, after Susan had given her mother a grandson she began to be known as Grandma Sara. Perhaps at least in part as a result of her reputation as a pioneer doctor, using techniques and knowledge that even at that time, was being forgotten.[44]

There were few if any families that went unaffected by the rise of the Mormon's Church of Christ, and the Fox family was no exception. Benjamin and Elizabeth's youngest daughter Marinda was married when she was 17 years old, in 1832 (the same year Henry Franklin Martin was born) to Thomas Maxey Ewell, a well-to-do ship's captain.[329]

Marinda if you recall, was the only one of Benjamin's children that was born in Kentucky. The Ewell family had been established in Virginia for generations, in fact letters still exist between Thomas's grandfather Maxcey Ewell and Thomas Jefferson. In addition, one of Thomas's uncle's, Dr. Thomas Ewell, owned an inn that was recommended by Jefferson. [280] On January 26, 1833, the couple had a son they named Richard Leighton Ewell.[207]

Marinda Fox-Ewell-Watkins with son Richard Leighton Ewell. The original daguerreotype including Thomas Maxey Ewell is not available to the public. (24)

A curious portrait of the family survives, painted by an artist in 1905, seventeen years after Marinda had died. The artist worked from a daguerreotype; a type of photography that was not yet available in America when the photo was taken, but was practiced in Paris, France. It is assumed that at some point Richard Ewell took his family to Europe and had one of these earliest types of photographs taken.

In it, Thomas stands by Marinda who is seated with toddler Richard Leighton in her lap. Marinda has brown hair pulled back into a bun and appears somber, yet graceful. She wears a dark dress with small white flowers and collar and a garnet necklace.

The blue-eyed baby in her lap could be no older than 18 months and wore a dress because it was the custom of the time, he would grow up to be a Colonel in the Civil War and lead a highly successful life.

Thomas himself stands rigid; older, with piercing blue eyes, mustached and a little debonair. He wears a long dark blue coat with two rows of large buttons over a white shirt with high stiff collar and a tie. The full portrait is not available to the public.[329]

Within a year of the photograph being taken Thomas Ewell was suddenly gone, having abandoned the young family. To save face, the Fox family claimed he had died, but he had not. To be fair, it's possible that initially Marinda and the Fox family didn't know what had become of him, for he might have just left, but it seems likely they eventually must have learned at least some of his fate.[329]

Evidence suggests that while the young family had been in Europe, Thomas's father, Pleasant Ewell, who had moved from Virginia to the Missouri country, was approached by Mormons, who soon converted the middle aged man. By the time Thomas and Marinda returned from Europe the elder Ewell had relocated to the Mormon capital of Nauvoo, Illinois.

When Thomas left his family, he moved in with his brother John Martin Ewell and remained in Iowa, near Nauvoo, for the rest of his life. He never remarried but remained a faithful Mormon, living with his brother and family to the day he died. Interestingly, if not sad, Thomas's father was the only Ewell to make the trip to Salt Lake City; dying as he reached the touted Promised Land.

Marinda, 'the widow', remained in Kentucky and in 1835 remarried, to Wiley Wellington Watkins.[201] The couple would have six children besides young Richard, all of them born in Laurel County, Kentucky.

In winter of 1834 Jonathon Keeney brought some men from Jim Bridger's party south to look for good pasture for their ponies and the ponies of their Indian guides. Along the Snake River they found good green grass and they found that investor and businessman Nathaniel Jarvis Wyeth had built Ft. Hall.

Having brought supplies all the way up the Columbia intending to trade about $3000 worth of goods Wyeth had gotten as far as the Snake before it was decided he and his men needed to winter up. Fort Hall was unusual because the new 'fort' and its owner were not controlled by the Hudson's Bay Company or the American Fur Company.

When Keeney pulled out of Fort Hall, he could have had little idea it would be twelve years before he would return.[249]

CHAPTER THIRTY-NINE

ENTER, EWING YOUNG

Enter young American trapper Ewing Young, who arrived in Oregon from California in 1834, in the company of Hall Jackson Kelley, with a herd of horses, using the as yet unnamed Applegate Trail.[152] This was the trip that included mostly horse thieves and Kelley nearly died of malaria; barely surviving to make it home to Boston.[334]

Shortly after the group arrived, Young was accused of stealing 200 horses when he left California, but he denied it saying it was some other guys that ended up traveling with him, that stole the additional horses. It enraged Dr. John McLoughlin of the Hudson's Bay Company and he blacklisted Ewing Young from doing business with the HBC.[22]

In addition and perhaps more importantly, along the way from California Young and the other men had camped on an island in a river and for reasons that remain unknown, he and his party killed several Native Americans and buried them on the island, later to be found by their tribe. This was the first recorded hostility of White men and Indians in the Oregon territory, though there were likely confrontations before that were not recorded.[33]

Eventually Young established himself on a claim near the mouth of Chehalem Creek on the Willamette, nearly opposite of present day Champoeg. This house is termed "the first house built on the west side of the Willamette".[39] Dr. John McLaughlin tried to discourage settlement on that side of the river, but Young butted heads and there being no authority to stop him, he did as he chose. Ewing Young was a complicated man, not to forgive or forget and had only begun to have influence in the Oregon country.[271]

Ironically the same year, in 1834, the Methodist missionary Jason Lee arrived to establish Mission Bottom, just north of present day Salem along the Willamette.[305] Coincidentally, the mission was not that far from Ewing Young's property.

East of Oregon, persistent to gain the White man's medicine, historically well-known Flathead Chief named Old Ignace and two of his sons showed up in St. Louis in 1835, looking for a minister for their tribe, as the previous doomed Native expedition had. Gen. Clark was engaged once more on the same question, but again Clark unfortunately couldn't find a missionary to go with them. Turned away, the Indians left again with nothing to show for their effort but worn out moccasins.[274]

By then, in the Oregon country, the Indian tribe had found their murdered family members, left buried by Ewing Young on the island in southern Oregon the year before. Obviously grieving and angry, they happened upon a group of eight fur trappers and retaliated for the grisly discovery by attacking White men who had done it. They killed four of eight trappers and disappeared into the rugged landscape. Ironically, William J. Bailey and George Gay who were friends of Ewing Young, were two of the survivors.[271]

In 1836 when Ephraim Fox was 14, the Mexican army slaughtered the defenders of the Alamo, and as national pride swelled, so did a thirst for revenge. Many young, patriotic men with a hot head wanted to drop everything and go join a mounted volunteer group to kill Mexicans. If young Eph was among them, we will never know. If he was he missed his chance for within a month the Texians chased down Santa Anna, soundly whipping him, sending his troops that yet remained alive, south to Mexico and out of Texas to broad patriotic cheers across the 25 states.[80]

During the summer as Santa Anna was driven back to Mexico by defenders of the Lonestar State, violent tensions were rising in Clay

County, Missouri where Mormons were again settling in large numbers, attracting the ire of locals.

To stave off violence the Missouri legislature formed Caldwell County, carving it out specifically for Mormon settlement and for a time there was relative peace. Though violence was averted, the topic still elicited red-hot emotional opinion and judgment throughout the state of Missouri and its northern neighbor states where the Mormon's made their homes.[57]

Quietly and unobtrusively, though the world around them was violent, isolated by their beliefs and use of the German language, the Brethren in Pennsylvania continued to peacefully prosper. They adopted the name, Fraternity of German Baptists in 1836.[297]

CHAPTER FORTY

DR. MARCUS WHITMAN

In the fall of 1836, well-known missionary Dr. Marcus Whitman and his wife Narcissa were able to pull two wheel carts almost to the Columbia River in a well-publicized trip to his mission at Walla Walla. Dr. Whitman and Samuel Parker, a 56 year old minister from an Ithaca school took two-wheeled carts drawn by men or beast almost to the Columbia. Heading out in a fur caravan led by Lucien Fontenelle there were sixty men, 200 animals and six wagons. They weren't conventional wagons, but he got that far!

With him were two things that were pivotal to showing that The West was open; he brought a wagon and his bride; the articulate Narcissa Prentiss Whitman. The last wagon gave out when they got to the Snake River, but if it had been built sturdier it would have made it. All along the way, Narcissa Whitman wrote letters which somehow got delivered to her parents in the east, and somehow they ended up in print. In her letters she rejoiced when the wagon was finally too far gone to keep going, as it slowed the whole party. But what she proved in those letters was that a wagon made correctly with enough strength would make the trip.

Picking a spot 25 miles up from the mouth of the Walla Walla, Whitman set up his mission in a place called Waiilatpu "Place of the Rye Grass".[312] In negotiations for the mission Parker told the Cayuse Indians,

"I don't intend to take your lands for nothing. After the Doctor is come, there will come every year a big ship, loaded with goods to be divided among the Indians. Those goods will not be sold, but will be given to you. The missionaries will bring you plows and hoes, to teach

you how to cultivate the land, and the will not sell, but give them to you."41[pp.23-24]

There they would Christianize the Cayuse. Then when Whitman met the Flatheads and Nez Perce, he realized that these people wanted the White man's religion, so he skedaddled back to civilization determined to get an outfit together to establish a mission the following year.

Parker stayed and moved into Fort Walla Walla where the river empties into the Columbia, but soon moved on down the Columbia to Lee's outpost of Methodism on the Willamette. Eventually, at the invitation of early Northwest powerhouse, John McLoughlin of the Hudson Bay Company, Parker sailed home to Connecticut to rest his weary bones.

A genuinely good and honest man, Parker did not hold much hope for missionaries in Indian country. He respected Indians and detested Whites that took advantage, stole or killed them with no acknowledgment of their humanity. When he returned home from Oregon, Parker wrote one of the best Oregon guidebooks of the era, and the farmers were reading.[22]

It was clear to men like Nicholas Fox and his son Ephraim, who read about the story of Whitman struggling along a crooked and rugged trail with a handcart, that The West was accessible for the committed. The subject was a common source of conversation throughout the border states; society's would soon be established to discuss the subject.

Meanwhile, intrepid mountain man, businessman, murderer and general schemer, Ewing Young had set up a saw mill on his claim on the Willamette. Then he secured a vat from Nat Wyeth's failed post and began to distill booze. He was not discriminating in who he sold it to, including settlers and Indians alike. His neighbor Jason Lee, just up the river at the Methodist mission plead with him to stop, but he would not. When Dr. John McLoughlin asked him to stop, he laughed. So Jason Lee set up a Temperance Society and working with McLoughlin, who prohibited liquor sales to the indigenous people, they pressured Young to stop his sinful ways. Still he ignored them.[269]

Young didn't stop distilling liquor and selling it until the end of the year when U.S. Navy Lt. William A. Slacum visited him from his ship *Loriot*, and dissuaded him from continuing distilling booze for the Indians. Lt. Slacum was actually a spy for President Andrew Jackson who was interested in the northwest territory. After talking with Methodist missionary Lee, Slacum devised a better idea on how to put the screws to McLoughlin.

Currently McLoughlin rented stock to the emigrants, so Slacum talked Ewing Young into jumping aboard his ship the *Loriot* and as an agent of the President of the United States they sailed to California; bought 630 head of cattle and formed the Willamette Cattle Company in order to sell stock to the emigrants and put a stick in the eye of John McLoughlin.[312]

To the east, which until recently was the west, Macon County was formed in northern Missouri, in 1836. In typical fashion, settlement began on waterways and Indian trails, such was the case of Macon County, where the first county seat of Bloomington, lied along the Great Indian Trail, near another well-known and used Indian pathway, called the Bee Trace, which ran north to south. There was substantial oak, hickory, walnut, cottonwood, linn, hackberry and sugartree that grew in abundance. Initially it seemed like a promised land to White settlers.[62]

The bloody battles between Mormon and anti-Mormon's weren't the only example of the deeply religious nature of society in the nineteenth century. In January 1837, a debate about Roman Catholicism was held in Cincinnati, Ohio between Alexander

Campbell and Bishop John B. Purcell, which drew the focus of the entire country.

Campbell was seen as a worthy spokesperson for American Protestants and Purcell was second only to Bishop John Hughes, the most influential figure in American Catholicism. The battle of religious titans debated five hours a day for nine days to packed crowds with more than five hundred standing in aisles and at the back; hundreds more were turned away each day.[70]

Later in the spring in Oregon country, on Narcissa Whitman's 29th birthday on March 14, 1837, Alice Clarissa Whitman was born. The little girl was a blessing to her mother, who in the isolation of the frontier, doted on the girl. There was little chance to foretell what impact the child would soon have on the survival of the mission; threatening the entire White population.

Back in Kentucky, Eph shared the birthdate and turned 15 that year.[312]

CHAPTER FORTY-ONE

MORMON'S DECLARE WAR OF EXTERMINATION

The little known and strange historic search by Indians for the White man's powerful medicine continued. Flathead Chief Old Ignace and two of his sons had showed up in St. Louis in 1835 and did not find the medicine, but at least they made it home alive. Intent to find the medicine, in 1837, Old Ignace returned with three more Flatheads and a Nez Perce Chief, to St. Louis.

By now the religious hierarchy understood right away that the Indians wanted a missionary to go back with them, but they still had nothing to offer. On the way home from his second trip to the White man's land to ask for spiritual help the chief stopped through Ash Hollow and a group of Sioux Indians scalped and killed Old Ignace.[274]

Mormon conflict had little documented direct effect on the Fox family, living in Kentucky, but was having a direct effect on the Bunch clan, who had moved to Missouri.

In 1837, the Mormon Church moved their headquarters from Kirtland, Ohio to the county seat of Far West in Caldwell County, Missouri. The result caused an exodus from Kirtland, Ohio to Caldwell County, and as the land was taken, they began to settle outside the county.

This was considered by Missourians as a violation of the compromise that had been made, but it was not considered so by the Mormons. The population explosion was again feared politically as Whigs and Democrats remained divided fairly equally in those areas and worried about the Mormons voting in blocs.

Meanwhile the Mormon Church itself fractured and many who left the church owned much land in Caldwell County that had been purchased by them as agents of the Church and yet claimed it as their own. Now the Church wanted it back. The land dispute threatened to become a legal battle.

The church turned on the "dissenters" as they were labeled, and the president of the Church delivered The Salt Speech, wherein he commanded the dissenters to leave and if they refused he demanded they be driven away. In two days eighty Mormons signed the Danite Manifesto that directed the dissenters to leave *"or a more fatal calamity shall befall you"*.[281]

On June 19, the dissenters fled as the church wanted, but wherever they went they complained about the Mormon Church, flaming the hatred that already existed in the state. On July 4, Sydney Rigdon, the president of the Church again delivered an oration with the blessings of Joseph Smith who attended the event. A Liberation Pole was erected as Rigdon delivered what was seen as a threat, when he vowed to not be driven out of anywhere again, from with or without,

"And that mob that comes on us to disturb us, it shall be between us and them a war of extermination; for we will follow them until the last drop of their blood is spilled; or else they will have to exterminate us, for we will carry the seat of war to their own houses and their own families, and one party or the other shall be utterly destroyed..."[281]

Soon after this speech in Gallatin County, a confrontation between 200 Missourians and 30 Mormons coming to vote in a statewide election developed into a brawl. Agitated by a candidate that called the Mormons horse thieves and robbers, the Missourians faced off with the outnumbered Mormons that had come to vote. Refusing to allow them to vote, the confrontation became a violent brawl that resulted in the Missourians been repulsed, vowing to return with guns. When the Missourians returned the crowd had dissolved but the confrontation fed the animosity in the state.

In the next few months rumors circulated that cited certain officials including judges and sheriffs were involved in vigilance committee's to drive out the Mormons. In response, Joseph Smith accompanied by as many as 100 armed men, made visits to these leading citizens and forced them to sign papers disavowing the vigilance committees. Few needed the benefit of being threatened to understand the implication of having a hundred angry armed men surrounding their homes. With their job done Joseph Smith rode home to Caldwell County.[281; *156*]

During the spring and summer of 1837, both Sara Fox and her daughter Susan Moore were again pregnant at the same time. While no doubt exciting for the families to share the experience, there was anxiety as well. Susan gave birth first, on August 1, to she and Martin's second child, they named Elizabeth, perhaps after her grandmother.[*256*] Of course, her grandmother Elizabeth, was her grandfather Benjamin's 2nd wife, not her biological grandmother.

The baby Elizabeth was born healthy and Susan bore the birth in like manner. Children or mothers dying in birth is rare now, so it is hard to imagine the terror that accompanied a woman giving birth. Any complications were life-threatening. Nor do we understand the joy and relief when both mother and child survived.

So we must use our best imagination to understand how a month later on September 9, 1837 when Grandma Sara, now 41 years old, completed a successful birth to she and Nicholas's 2nd surviving son,[10] months of anxiousness fell away. They named the lad John Madison Fox.

There was quite a separation of years in Nicholas and Sara's children and as Sara continued to bear them, nephews and nieces were sometimes older than aunts and uncles. Ephraim Fox, 15 when his brother John was born, was likely working in much the same capacity as a man. The separation of years did not always promote a close sibling relationship between the two brothers.

William J. Bailey and George Gay, having survived the retaliatory Indian attack from two years prior were working for their old boss Ewing Young. The salty pair were working for the Willamette Cattle Company, specifically, herding cattle with other cowboys when the party passed by some Indians. Gay randomly shot a young Indian boy.

With a predisposition to violence and harboring what had become a lifelong grudge against the whole of the Indian race, Gay had been waiting for two long years to make a target of an Indian. He got his wish and following up his revenge for revenge was the dead Indian boys tribe and now they wanted revenge.

Attacking the cattle drive they killed some of the stock and drove a number off, killing Young's horse, leaving the White men rattled but alive.[153] Though the Rogue River Indian War is commonly cited as confined to 1855-56, these initial confrontations were the beginnings of skirmishes between Whites and natives for close to the next 20 years; many of them horrible examples of human violence in an age less civilized and emotionally and ancestrally heated by culture and revenge.

And in Oregon, it all can be tracked back to Ewing Young and friends. While it might seem like Young, Bailey, Gay and friends were not likable guys, they must have been, because other than authorities they were generally well respected and liked by their peers.

On February 7, 1838 Senator Linn introduced the Oregon territorial bill in congress[255] and though he would work the rest of his life to get it passed, his life was short. He passed of an aneurysm in 1843. He had returned to his home in Ste Genevieve to assist in a cholera outbreak that had killed almost half his constituents when he passed himself.[275]

In the spring of 1838, an anti-Mormon that was a major land owner sold much of his land in the nearly vacant town of De Witt in Carroll County, Missouri, to the Mormon Church, prompting it to be quickly populated. That summer concerned citizens in De Witt called a meeting on July 30, in Carroll County discussing what to do with the influx of the Mormons. To keep up appearances, an election followed, just one week later.

When the vote chose overwhelmingly to evict the Mormons who refused, feelings hardened in Carroll County. Vigilance committee's began to form in adjacent counties and isolated Mormon farms were harassed until finally the father of a family was driven from his home and his wife and three children were taken hostage. A week later a company of armed Mormons rescued the family but one of the children was already dead and the remaining children and mother died shortly after being rescued.

On September 20, one hundred-fifty armed men rode into De Witt and told the Mormons to leave, but they refused and informed the Missourians they were prepared to fight. When October 1 the home and stable of a Mormon was burned, the Mormons sent a non-Mormon to plead for assistance from a judge and a general, of a state militia. Meanwhile the anti-Mormons sealed off the town of De Witt, whose residents then trapped, were forced to kill any loose cattle for food, as they waited for assistance.[42]

When General Parks finally showed up, his orders to dismiss were ignored by the vigilance committee's blocking the roads. When his own troops threatened to join the anti-Mormons, he was forced to retreat. On October 9 word came the governor felt the "quarrel was between the Mormons and the mob"[22] and they should fight it out.

Facing certain death, two days later the Mormons agreed to leave and were forced to walk many miles to adjacent counties. It was winter, and so the first night of the march two women died; one of childbirth and another of exposure. Many children got sick that died afterword.

Within a week the adjacent counties that had taken in the refugees were being harassed with homes and barns being burned and pillaged. Anarchy well-ruled the countryside, but Missouri Gov. Lilburn Boggs refused to interdict when he was requested to by General David R. Atchison, and the situation completely unraveled. Meanwhile in northwest Missouri, Daviess County, the same harassment of Mormons continued as homes were burnt and property taken.

By October 14, Colonel William A. Dunn, sympathetic to the Mormon's plight warned the Mormons about Daviess County violence and advised them not to go there or not to go unarmed in small groups, so to not affect more violence. The advice was ignored and Joseph Smith with Mormon militia's and assisted by members of the Danite organization set about for payback. The towns of Gallatin, Millport and Grindstone Fork were attacked and anti-Mormon Missourians were now forced to flee for their lives for neighboring counties. [42]

Though the Fox family remained in Kentucky, a few hundred miles away, such was the social and political discourse Ephraim grew up in and the acceptable response to Mormons. For some in the Bunch family who had moved into the state, the situation had taken on daily implications.

Records are contradictory, claiming that on October 15, 1838, the day after the 'involuntary' evacuation of many counties of Missourians, 22 year old George William Bunch, born in 1816 and Narcissa Moxleyin Chariton County, Missouri had David Bunch,[194] while other records indicate the couple wasn't married until that day two years later in 1840.[85] Considering census records are personal recollections, it's possible the events were transposed. And too, it was not uncommon in the remote wilderness for couples to hold frontier weddings, followed by a formal ceremony when a preacher became available.

Narcissa was the daughter of Henry Moxley who had initially come to Warren County, Kentucky from Virginia just before 1820. It is very possible given the proximity and how few settlers were in the area that while residing in Warren County Henry Moxley was familiar with the grown children of Arthur and Richard Fox, or were at the least acquaintances. That said, considering when the Moxley family came to Kentucky, they may have already known the Fox family before either family came west to Kentucky.

It appears both George Bunch and Henry Moxley moved to Missouri about the same time; perhaps together given the marriage that took place soon after. In any event, the physical proximity of the Moxley's and the Bunch family could be how George Bunch, born 1816, met Ephraim Fox. But as with the Moxley's, George's father, George the elder, born in 1794, might have known the Fox's back when both families lived in Virginia.

There is unfortunately no document to reveal how or exactly when or how George (John) Bunch and Ephraim Fox met. When they did, they would join to complete what might possibly be their ancestral family's greatest adventure.

Benjamin Fox would have been 66 in 1838; his son Nicholas, 42 and his grandson Ephraim, 16, as an exodus of their neighbors began moving northwest into the Missouri country, pushing at the edge of civilization.

CHAPTER FORTY-TWO

HAUN'S MILL MASSACRE

As hostilities worsened between combatants and non-combatants in Missouri, the worst was yet to come. Later in the month of October 1838 even Missourians sympathetic to the Mormons were not spared from the Saint's fury as homes were set to the torch in Daviess County every night for two weeks, laying a smoky haze overhead drifting slowly across the state. Armed Mormons were the terror of the countryside.

Millport, the largest town in the county and a center for commerce, was completely burnt to the ground. It was a full-on war. Atrocities were committed against women and children that with their cabins set on fire were forced outside, chased across icy creeks to hide in the snow for rescue. The violence committed by their own people was so frightening and without restraint, that it rattled some in the Mormon hierarchy. To clear their conscious, two members of the Apostles of Twelve in the Church became concerned enough that on October 19, the day after the town of Gallatin burned, signed affidavits, confirming rumors that two additional towns were planned to be attacked. This set off a panic, that the violence was sure to spread.

Across the state many Missourians held up in neighbors houses and collected for their own protection. Armed militias of both sides patrolled the county lines, each looking for trouble. Eventually, when finally a Mormon group was forcibly disarmed by a Missouri militia that had (arguably) inadvertently crossed onto Mormon ground, the cry went out that the Mormons were under attack.

The following day the groups clashed, resulting in the Mormons winning the ground but sustaining more death and injury. Called the Battle of Crooked River; the reports were exaggerated, thus Governor

Boggs issued *Executive Order 44*, also known as the extermination order.[285] It stated in part, "*the Mormons must be treated as enemies, and must be exterminated or driven from the State if necessary for the public peace...*"[224]

Despite the fact participants had not yet received the order, 250 vigilance committee members slipped into Caldwell County and surrounded 40 Mormons, who trapped in a barn, attempted to parley. Young Mormon Thomas McBride led a handful of others, as he walked out of the barn and approached the Missourians, where he surrendered his rifle to Jacob Rogers. Rogers took the weapon and turned it on McBride, shooting him with his own gun. Falling to the ground, McBride held out a hand pleading for mercy. Rogers pulled out a corn knife and sawed the offered hand off, then plunged the blade into the corpse, further mangling young McBride's body while he was still alive, screaming horribly and flailing.[218]

The Mormons who had accompanied McBride watched in horror as the vigilance committee opened fire sending the horrified Mormons scrambled for cover. Eventually with the Mormons holding up in a blacksmith's shop the vigilance group set it afire, killing nearly everyone inside.

One ten year old boy remained alive the following morning in the wreckage and was summarily shot and killed.[316] While the boy laid bleeding out in the blackened timbers of the fortification that became an oven, his killer stood over him and said,

"*Nits will make lice, and if he had lived he would have become a Mormon.*"[43[pp.671, 673]] It became known as the Haun's Mill Massacre where seventeen men, women and children were killed. Fourteen of the bodies were slipped off a plank the next day into an empty well and covered with a shallow layer of straw and dirt.

Afterward when the Mormon's were collected in the city of Far West inside their headquarters, they were surrounded by the Missouri state militia and Joseph Smith and other church leaders were detained while negotiating for peace, and held overnight without benefit of a roof.

The following morning Smith sent word to Far West that they must surrender. Thus, the Mormon militia marched out of the city and was disarmed while state militia troops under General Lucas, were let loose upon the city. Looting and destroying homes, they shot oxen and let their horses out on the fields of corn to destroy the crops. Taking everything they wanted and leaving the rest in the streets, the militia drew back and left.[174]

Immediately following, Joseph Smith and 60 other Mormon leaders went on trial the evening of the surrender, November 1. In a court martial held by Gen. Lucas they were found guilty, with Lucas giving the order for them to be taken at sunrise and shot. Appointed to the task, General Alexander William Doniphan replied,

"*It is cold-blooded murder. I will not obey your order. My brigade shall march for Liberty to-morrow morning, at 8 o'clock, and if you execute those men, I will hold you responsible before an earthly tribunal, so help me God*!"[174[Siege of Far West]]

After an inquiry, a few days later, all but a few of the Mormon leaders were released except for Smith and five others who were held in the Clay County, Missouri jail on charges of treason against the state, murder, arson, burglary, robbery and larceny.[174]

A few months later, the following spring of 1839 Joseph Smith escaped while being transferred to another prison.[21] Citizens of Daviess County were sent into a mob rage and one of the guards that was responsible was drug by his hair across the town square. When county Sheriff Morgan responded, he was ridden out of town; hoisted upon an iron bar used for a rail. The treatment he received and the injuries he sustained from the bar, killed him after a few days, suffering internal injuries. The Mormon's fled to Illinois and regrouped in a small town called Commerce.[57]

Despite widespread violence, in 1838, David Anderson Bunch and his brothers John and William Maloy Bunch bought property in St. Clair County, Missouri.[137] Few White men had pushed that far north and while most that followed the brothers wouldn't remain there but kept pushing northwest taking advantage of land prices as people followed behind, these Bunch brothers, sons of Jesse Bunch, stayed on their original claims for the rest of their lives.

Incidentally, David Anderson Bunch married Delilah Cobb, whose relatives had come to America through New England colonies, not Virginia and were not at all related to Ambrose Cobb, previously mentioned, however there may be ancestral connections in England.[65]

In Knox County, Kentucky in the spring of 1839, Susan (Fox) and Martin Moore had their third child, a second daughter they named Mary Jane Moore.[101] Perhaps fortunately for Susan, there are no records to indicate she lost children in birth and the spacing between them indicates normal regularity.

Despite these good fortunes, the growing financial depression that gripped the states might have begun to have a real impact on her father, Nicholas Fox, by the end of the 1830's.

CHAPTER FORTY-THREE

YOUNG IGNACE FINDS MAGIC

In the spring of 1839, another delegation of Flathead Indians including Young Ignace; son of Old Ignace; and another Flathead returned to St. Louis, still seeking the White man's great medicine.[336] This time they got a promise of a man who was nearly ready for ordination.

A stocky little Jesuit Pierre-Jean DeSmet left in the spring of 1840 for Flathead country. Intensely sympathetic and affable, DeSmet would do more for all Indians than any other missionary, including Dr. Whitman.[336] The Protestant press did not report on him initially and perhaps that is why history forgets him. Establishing one mission after another along the trail west, DeSmet got them manned, with the concentration on teaching. He crossed the Atlantic time and again raising vast sums to support his Jesuit missions. When he could no longer travel he used his arthritic hands to write letters in support of his efforts.[183] His soothing of Indian tempers in the face of the federal government breaking treaties probably saved more lives than any other man in the west. The by-product of his efforts were missions along the trail that would come in handy to later emigrants and decades later, to the Pony Express.

Leaving Virginia on an exploring mission for the United States was a six-vessel squadron under the flagship, *Vincennes*. In May, 1839, the ship anchored in Discovery Bay and visited missions along the Columbia and Willamette. The captain of the *Vincennes* wrote his impression of the White inhabitants of the Willamette Valley,

"They generally consist of those who have been hunters in the mountains, and were still full of the recklessness of that breed. Many of them, although they have taken farms and built log houses, cannot

be classed among the permanent settlers."[252] Such were the condition of White settlements in Oregon territory in the summer of 1839.

At this point, the Mormons were in a great deal of disarray. Brigham Young grew to prominence when he organized the move of about 14,000 Mormons to Illinois and Iowa from Missouri. As the population of Mormon's grew in Commerce, Illinois, they changed the name to Nauvoo.[163]

Joseph Smith come out of hiding after his escape, was back at the helm of the church, safe from the state of Missouri. Promoting the view of having been persecuted, Smith went to Washington DC and met President Martin Van Buren and asked for reparations, but was refused. He returned to Commerce, Illinois seething for retribution.[163]

Joseph Smith (left), founder of Mormonism (25) & a young Brigham Young (26)

About this time, it's likely that David Bunch was born to George and Narcissa Moxley in Chariton County, Missouri, despite aforementioned contradictory records.[194] Though documents don't directly indicate David Bunch was born in Chariton County, Missouri, only the state itself, documents relating to his parents residency indicate this was the case.

CHAPTER FORTY-FOUR

SAMUEL COBB, GUIDE TO MISSOURI

By the end of the 1830's, as the national economy flagged due in part to the collapse of the fur industry, settlers began emigrating to the border states of Missouri and Iowa. In fact, Samuel Cobb, now nearing 50 years old, moved his family to Macon County, Missouri in about 1840 and found enough demand for a guide that he then began working in that capacity, leading others moving from Kentucky to Missouri.[298]

At a point in the mid-1840's Nicholas Fox and his immediate family, except for his two eldest married daughters, moved from Knox Co. KY first to Linn County, then Macon County, MO. Considering this information, it is possible if not likely that it was Samuel that led Nicholas Fox and his family from Knox County. KY to the Show Me state.

Did Samuel Cobb realize Nicholas or Benjamin Fox had fathered his son John? It certainly seems possible. Nicholas Fox appears in the 1840 federal census, still living in Knox County, Kentucky, where his father Benjamin had brought the family just after 1800.[91].

His father Benjamin, however, is not listed in this census. Nor is Benjamin listed in Jackson County, Tennessee, as one might suspect. Further, the 68 year old does not appear to be living with one of his children. Oddly enough however court records created many years later in an ugly divorce proceedings reveal that Benjamin, on Dec 5, 1839, claimed a tract of 150 acres on the north side of Flynn's Creek, in Jackson County, Tennessee, alongside a 100 acre tract of land to the east, owned by Abner Chaffin, being part of a grant of that date.

In between, was property Benjamin had given as an early inheritance to daughter Sarah Ann Fox, who married Miles Alfred Dennis, a decidedly mean and cruel man. Fifteen years later, after

Benjamin had passed away, Sarah Ann accused her husband of pulling a knife on her, whipping her and further - had intentions to sell the property her father Benjamin had left her.[246] While this salacious information is interesting, it provides an important glimpse into how close the Fox and Chaffin families lived. These documents claim Benjamin lived on this property.

Benjamin may have purchased this property and was engaged in moving there from Kentucky when the census was taken. In any case, he was not counted in Knox County, near Nicholas, who for his part is shown in the 1840 census as a neighbor of many whose names would someday all be connected to each other in one historic effort pushing west.

Later that year after the census was taken, Sara bore Nicholas a third son, they named William J. Fox.[121] The newborn might have been named after his 'grandfather', William Fox. Even if this were the case, it would neither prove nor disprove that Nicholas knew that his father was adopted by William Fox. It's likely the middle initial of Nicholas's third son stood for James, however there is no evidence he ever recorded his full name to prove this theory. If William J. Fox had a nickname, it also is unknown. It must have seemed as if the worst were behind Nicholas and Sara, as her births were more successful than they had been earlier in their marriage.

CHAPTER FORTY-FIVE

HISTORIC YEAR OF 1841

Its estimated that there were no more than 40 Americans living between Alaska and San Francisco, then called Yerba Buena, in 1840. That year, the families of frontier doctor Robert Newell, mountain man Joseph L. Meek and trapper Caleb Wilkins left for Oregon. They like their contemporaries, had seen the fur trade waning and were looking to settle down in a place of promise. Upon reaching Fort Hall, they met another small group, going the same way. Meek, knowing the way, offered to lead the group. When they reached Fort Walla Walla with their families and three wagons, they held the distinction of being the first wagons to complete the last leg of the trip, from Fort Hall, up and over the Blue Mountains.[258; 277]

The following spring, the WOLF organization was formed in 1841 in the communities that had formed along the Willamette and Columbia Rivers in Oregon. It had been common practice for generations to offer bounties for predators. Accordingly, Oregon settlers loosely formed a WOLF organization for the control of predators.

Discussions abounded about many topics, one of which was the death of Ewing Young and the settling of his estate. In a strange example of historical irony, prominent Oregon settler (also bootlegger, Indian murderer, profiteer and agitator of Dr. John McLaughlin), Ewing Young, died suddenly in the Willamette Valley without a will or an heir. Even in his death, old Ewing Young was a thorn. In all his dealings along the Pacific coastline he had made some serious money and was well known and liked in the settlements along the Willamette despite how we might view him historically or through the eyes of Dr,

McLaughlin. His death created a need for a probate court because he had plenty of debtors and creditors among the settlers.

The legal and political activities that took place to settle his estate led to the creation of a provisional government in Oregon.[22] A historical marker marks the spot where his farm was and he is buried, under a round topped oak tree that was planted from an acorn planted on his grave. Ironically after all the chaos the man caused he was responsible for both the formation of a provisional government in the territory of Oregon while simultaneously for the initial hostility with Indians of the area.

Ewing Young in life and death shaped the world around him, for better and worse, by hook or by crook. General internet searches do not tell the full story of Ewing Young; the totality of his involvement in so many events contributing to the formation of Oregon is typically revealed piecemeal according to the narrative of the writer. He is a sinner or a saint, depending on perspective.

In response to his death, the first meeting of the Oregon Territorial provisional government was February 17, 1841 in Champoeg, along the banks of the Willamette River. The meeting, organized by the earliest settlers and Methodist missionaries as well as Catholic priests, accomplished little, but laid a foundation for later meetings. The meeting was attended by 150 people; the vast majority of the settlers in the Willamette valley. The initial meeting had little impact on anything; separating into opposite minded groups that decided nothing.[22]

Easterners looking west saw it as mostly un-mapped, untamed and wild, but still full of prospect. Though the fur trade had collapsed by 1841, there was still unlimited promise in the vast frontier. Of course those to be affected by this first were the trappers. Some of the hardened breed saw advantages in the creeping changes on the frontier.

During the year, James Douglas, working for the HBC established a post at the bay in Yerba Buena. Also, experienced mountain man Jim Bridger and fellow trapper Louis Vasquez built a trading fort on the Black Fork of the Green River. They had been in this wilderness long enough to see the writing on the wall and while they saw the fur trade was waning, they knew that the trails heading west would soon bring throngs of settlers needing supplies.[267]

A month later in Kentucky, on March 10, 1841 Susan (Fox) Moore gave birth to she and husband Martin's fourth healthy child; this time a son.[196] They named him Ephraim; probably after Martin's father, though would also be the same as Susan's little brother, Ephraim Fox.

As the birth occurred that spring, hundreds of Kentuckians, Tennesseans, and Missourians, full of anxious excitement and promise, amassed on the shore of Sapling Grove, for the Bartleson-Bidwell wagon train.[156]

Expansion of American families into the Oregon country was to become a reality. Near Westport, the beefy farm wagons prepared to test the trails with a planned five month journey, the first of its kind. Tom 'Broken Hand' Fitzpatrick, leading a contingent of Jesuit missionaries including Father DeSmet, had joined the group for safety sake.

Being a collection of some different parties they first had to agree on their destination. After some discussion, it was decided that their goal was California. However by the time they got to Soda Springs, near Fort Hall, the treacherous path over the Cascades and up the Snake intimidated many of them so about half the party of between 60 and 100 men split off continuing to California while the other half moved toward the easier route, to Oregon.

Those that decided for California headed west along the north shore of the Great Salt Lake. Crossing the desert west of the lake, they were forced to abandon their wagons as the stock was failing. They walked or rode their stock until they made it to Mary's River and followed it into Nevada. Crossing the desert to the south they reached the Walker River and followed it up and over the Sierra Nevada's where Jedediah Smith had mapped a trail in 1827.[156]

Narcissa (27) and Dr Marcus Whitman (28)

About the time these first pioneers reached Oregon, in October 1841, a Payuse Chief near the Walla Walla mission of Marcus Whitman died. Upon his death his brothers, perhaps in a competition for leadership of their people, demanded payment from Whitman for use of the fort on their land. Harsh words were spoken and the hot-headed Indians left. Some days later one of the brothers entered the mission and was told to leave, by W.H. Gray, Whitman's assistant. This offended the Indians so one turned and threw his rope around a mission horse to lead it away. Gray responded by cutting the rope.

Later in the afternoon the Cayuse Indian brothers appeared with some additional braves and the one who had attempted before to take the horse, did so again brazenly in front of Whitman, who asked him if he wanted to become a horse thief. The second brother threatened Whitman that he would kill all the cattle and Whitman too. Whitman responded that he had shown his true heart.[156; 359]

In a few days, a relative of the brothers arrived at the mission with a handful of young men and told W.H. Gray that he must leave the mission and then further berated Whitman for taking Gray's side and bemoaning that they had labored to build Gray's house.

The argument got heated and the Indian pulled Whitman's ear and thumped him on the chest a number of times, getting no reaction from the missionary. Finally the Indian jerked Whitman's hat from his head and threw it to the mud at his feet. Whitman would only pick it up. The Indian ripped the hat off again and threw it down. And again. And again. The Indian left in disgust when Whitman asked him, “perhaps you are playing?” An Indian among the group named McKay hollered to the other Indians at the mission to quit working there and return to their tribes. With that the irate Indians spun about and rode away. Meant to defuse the situation, the lack of aggression on Whitman’s part actually fed the coup mentality of the Indians.[252]

An interpreter was sent to relay a message of warning to the commander of the Hudson's Bay Company fort in Walla Walla, that Whitman thought these Indians were acting like dogs. The interpreter, perhaps caught up in the moment, added a threat that Governor Simpson and a party in Cowlitz had removed their cattle to safety in readiness for the retaliation that was sure to come.

That evening the Cayuse Indian brother that began the original argument, returned to the mission house brandishing a hammer first at the door and then at the window, while his brother forced the door. When they came in a struggle ensued and Whitman was able to disarm the Indians of their hammer and an axe. The Indians beat him with their fists instead. Narcissa, his wife and W.H. Gray removed the weapons upstairs as the fight went on.

The next day one of the Indian brothers returned with a club and hollered insults and threats at Whitman, who ignored them, further enraging the Indian who retrieved a rifle and continued his threats. Finally, in disgust, the Indian told Whitman that he could not be shamed into fighting and they argued more until the Indian told Whitman that a part-Iroquois at Grande Ronde had told him how the Iroquois had killed White men until they were paid for their land.

Though the angry Cayuse did not identify the Iroquois as Enos Thomas,[214] this would not be the last time that the Indian from the east would agitate and initiate the murder of Whites. The foul contributions and true end of Enos "Acnes" Thomas, is mostly left incomplete, but his story was only beginning in 1841.

When the Indians left this time, Whitman sent word to the HBC that the Indians were going to the fort. The next day not many of the friendly Indians came to worship and someone broke valuable glass windows out of the house that had been carefully carried all the way from the United States.

The Indians set out armed for Fort Walla Walla but the commander met them peacefully. He explained to the Cayuse that while the fort did not need any help, he had sent for reinforcements from Fort Vancouver anyway, and they were coming to aid Whitman. The meeting ended well and the Cayuse vowed peace.

This news slowly unraveled in news articles and rumor many months later as it was related in letters carried on horseback, taking nearly a year to reach the United States. It was reported with great petulance and fear that the Cayuse and Snake (Shoshone) Indians were so infamous for their savagery that they were feared by Blackfoot and Sioux. As winter settled in, Indian provocations slowed, but hostilities were far from over.[214]

CHAPTER FORTY-SIX

WAGON TRAINS OF 1842

While Barton Stone contributed greatly to the origin of the Church of Christ, Alexander Campbell became the face of the movement. His Bethany College chartered in 1840, opened in 1841 and became the principal training school for a new generation of Christian teachers. The strength of the church came from seven contiguous states comprising Tennessee, Kentucky, Ohio, Indiana, Illinois, Missouri and Iowa. By 1842 the movement was in the process of becoming a religious body of significant size.[70]

The following spring in 1842 there weren't a great number of wagons moving west, though there was one group of note, of 112 people (60 women and children) accompanied by 18 wagons plus horses, mules and cattle that headed out of Missouri along the southern Sante Fe Trail.

This particular train was led by Dr. Elijah White and ambitious self-promoter Lansford Hastings who put out a guide book to California for a route that he had yet to see.[212] Lansford's book was later picked up and followed by the Donner Party. Despite breaking up after reaching Fort Hall and the single men running ahead, the families slowly followed and arrived later.

These initial trips west were creating an important framework of organization that those following would also practice, or not. All their arguing, racing ahead and splitting up was read about and served also, as early warnings, to a public hungry to learn through the eyes of letters and reports sent home.

From gathering outside Westport in Sapling Grove or Indian Creek campground, to convenient campsites along the way, their organizational skills and experiences were recorded in journals and letters, which found their way back to the public who were watching their every move.

When these emigrants reached Oregon there were only about 700 to 800 White men there, and most of those were French-Canadian fur trappers and traders. There were only 150 Americans in the entire territory. By then Dr. John McLoughlin had moved from Fort Vancouver to a small village at the Willamette Falls, near present-day Oregon City. Most of these emigrants settled nearby. Some of these emigrants found work at the already established Lee mission with the remainder scattered about the Willamette Valley.[211]

That spring Nicholas and Ephraim might have found particular interest in the construction of the simple heavily built, high sided farm wagons with arched canvas covers that were used to cross the plains.

While there were likely others, the only member of the Restoration Movement that is documented coming west that year is Reuben Lewis.[70] He traveled with likely member, Gabriel Brown, whose daughter was later a member of the Aumsville Church, as well as Allan Davie. One letter that survives claims Lewis was so successful at hunting that "*he just about supplied the whole train of sixteen wagons, killing as many as eleven buffalo in a day*".[70[p.19]]

Sometime in April or March of 1842, 46 year old Sara must have realized she was pregnant with yet another child. Considering the deaths of children she and Nicholas had endured, news of the pregnancy of a woman of her advanced age might likely have filled them with special concern. It turned out by the fall that those fears were misplaced; instead, they faced perhaps an even greater, crushing loss.

During the summer of 1842 on a steamboat heading up the Missouri River, Lt. John Fremont, preparing for his first expedition into The West met Kit Carson. Fremont intended to travel to South Pass, which was the most popular if not the most reasonable way, over the mountains. Kit Carson offered his services as scout as he had spent much time in the area.

Kit Carson standing, Lt. John Fremont seated (29)

The expedition was an unqualified success and both men became national heroes. The story of the five month journey, taken with 25 men was printed in newspapers offering a vision of the west; not dangerous but wide open and inviting. Fremont superimposed his maps over those of Jedediah Smith, in order to verify his accuracy, but that part was little known at the time.[69] The report so impressed Henry Wadsworth Longfellow that he remarked, *"Fremont has touched my imagination. What a wild life, and what a fresh kind of existence! But ah, the discomforts!"* [303]

Among those thousands who followed these adventurers in news accounts was Nicholas Fox and his son Ephraim. Along with the other dreamers, they seem to have begun to see the goal as achievable. At least Ephraim must have. The discomforts were of little importance to toil-toughened farmers.

As Fremont's report captivated the nation, Senator Thomas Hart Benton, "Old Bullion", a popular Senator in Missouri emerged a champion of westward expansion. He reasoned in congress and in newspapers that if Oregon was easily reached by wagon and Americans might indeed find a better life there, Oregon should be given territorial status and protection by the government of the United States.

Those kinds of statements helped to give legitimacy to serious notions men like young Ephraim must have had. Surrounding the Fox's were families like theirs, born and raised in Kentucky, now leaving for Missouri, led by guides like Samuel Cobb.[298]

Fox Cemetery in Flynn's Lick, Jackson County, TN (30)

Diary's don't reveal, nor any other hints indicate if Benjamin Fox was sick for long, before he died on the 3rd of August, 1841. No Will has been located to indicate he knew his time was close.

It is a real mystery why Benjamin kept residences in Knox Co, KY and Jackson Co, TN; and most of his children were birthed in Jackson County, except Marinda, born in Knox County, KY. When Benjamin passed, he was buried honorably in Jackson County, on property he owned.[193] In the following years as Elizabeth followed Benjamin in death, then their children followed; all were buried there.

At some later point, probably within just a few years as more graves were dug, the resting place was formally given the name, The Fox Cemetery.[253]

Benjamin's gravestone in the Fox Cemetery (31)

Indications certainly are Benjamin and Nicholas were close, by evidence that the father kept his residence in Knox County, KY, near his eldest son, even though he owned vast amounts of land in Tennessee and the balance of his adult children lived there. If a rift in relationships existed it seems to have been between Nicholas and his step-siblings; even his own sister Nancy, who remained in Jackson County as well.

Though it seems like a response, it might not have been; but after the death of Benjamin Fox, his son Nicholas left Knox County. The 48 year old had lived in Kentucky since he was six or seven years old, leaving him scant few if any, faded memories of Virginia. The Bluegrass State was his home. Sara too, had grown up in Knox County, but with most of her family moved to Indiana long ago, there was little holding her there.

Questions abound almost 200 years later to why Nicholas chose to leave Kentucky at this point. Was he already planning the relocation, before his father died or was his father's death the impetus? Was there an ugly probate ahead, so he walked away? Perhaps he simply left Kentucky for the prospect of profiting in Missouri, with no ill-will between him and his family.

Perhaps the best indication of a lack of family warmth between Nicholas, his sister Nancy and step-siblings was that none joined him, as historically happens when families migrated. It's worth noting Nicholas left Knox County within six months of his father dying, despite his wife giving birth just three months after his father passed.

When Nicholas Fox left Kentucky with his family, it severed any connection with his siblings; to such a degree, that the relationship between Nicholas and his step-siblings was only discovered because of DNA almost 200 years later.

Question remain; in the course of their lives what did Benjamin, his son Nicholas and grandson Ephraim know about the adoption of Benjamin? Was that knowledge a factor in the decision Nicholas and Ephraim made to move away from everyone in their family and everything they had ever known? Did moving away from Knox

County, KY have something to do with the illegitimate births of John J. Cobb and Henry Franklin Martin?

It is a stark fact indeed that none of their family ever joined them. Why the dual residency of Benjamin? Did Nicholas leave Kentucky because the only family he felt he really had there was his father, Benjamin? It might be Nicholas and Ephraim were simply following the common migratory pattern of many thousands who left Virginia to Kentucky, then to Missouri and finally across the continent. But there were so many personal issues going on with the Fox family that it's impossible to say.

Whether Nicholas or his son Ephraim knew details about the adoption of Benjamin, or what they knew about John Cobb and Henry Franklin Martin will probably never be known. Regardless the fact is, that by virtue of the decision, Nicholas and his son Ephraim certainly set out determined for a separate, different and better future. Whatever the past was for Benjamin, his son Nicholas and grandson Ephraim would make a new start in Missouri.

Mary Sara had another son, named Nicholas, just three months before Benjamin passed, in November of 1842.[120] Some records later in his life indicate his initials were C.N.; likely for Charles Nicholas, but predominantly most records identify him as Nicholas Fox.[102] He would be the last of the couples 11 children; the 8th to survive birth.

Throughout the winter, the Fox family prepared to leave Knox County. The news must have struck Susan hard; married with children and building her life as a 2nd generation Knox County pioneer, she might have thought her family would, like her, remain there. Though the neighbors that accompanied them have not yet been identified, there surely were those that did.

A month before young Nicholas Fox was born, far to the west, Narcissa Whitman, wife of Marcus, in their mission at Walla Walla recorded by October 6, 1842 that 24 settlers had passed through the humble mission. Among them, Jim Bridger sent his six year old daughter to live with the Whitman's for a while, arriving with a group of overland travelers.[362] Narcissa wrote her thoughts in her diary that fall,

"Doubtless every year will bring more & more into this country.... These emigrants are nearly destitute of every kind of food when they arrive here & we were under the necessity of giving them provisions to help them on. Our little place is a resting spot for many a weary, way-worn traveler and will be as long as we live here. If we can do good that way, perhaps it is as important as some other things we are doing."[252]

Waiilatpu Mission Established by Marcus Whitman and wife, Narcissa, near current day Walla Walla, WA. (32)

CHAPTER FORTY-SEVEN

LEAVING KENTUCKY, 1843

At some point early in 1843, Nicholas and Sara said goodbye to their eldest daughter, Susan, her husband Martin Moore and the couples four children.[11] Rolling out of Kentucky with the balance of their family, Nicholas, Sara would never see their eldest child again. Susan was 28 years old and likely pregnant because she gave birth sometime that year.

Nicholas and Sara were both 47 years old. Because Susan remained with her family in Knox County, Ephraim, at 21 years old, became the eldest of the siblings; then 17 year old Phoebe, 14 year old Ann, 8 year old Nancy Jane, 6 year old John Madison, 3 year old William J. and newborn C. Nicholas. Of these siblings, William nor Nicholas would have recollection of their eldest sibling, nor of Kentucky and memories of Ann would be vague for Nancy Jane.

Susan's children were also very young and of the four, perhaps only the eldest, 9 year old Jesse would have clear memories of his mother's family. While it would be comforting to know there was correspondence between Susan and her family, if there was, it's not been found.

On their farm in Knox County, Nicholas and Sara left behind three little graves, they would never forget. Whatever the impetus for leaving Kentucky, Nicholas was surely pursuing a better life for his family, satisfied they had left Susan in good hands. It was over 150 miles from Knox County, KY to Flynn's Lick, TN where Nicholas's father Benjamin was buried and his siblings lived. Due to the physical and possible emotional distance, Nicholas may never have seen his father's grave, nor his siblings to say goodbye. He would never have known that the original marker on his father's resting place was replaced many years later by some of his step-brothers, who remained in Flynn's Lick, in Jackson County. Today in the Fox Cemetery, in Flynn's Lick, the patriarch remains buried, undisturbed; the progenitor of a unique family line. He carried a lot of secrets to his grave that 240 plus years later only YDNA could uncover. Yet we still don't know who his father was.

Early in 1843, the same year the Nicholas Fox brought his family to Missouri, William Gray, an early settler in Oregon living on the Willamette River, organized another "wolf meeting" to discuss predators and setting up a bounty on the animals. Convened, on February 2, 1843 for the purpose of discussing protecting cattle and horses from predators. It was decided to pay a bounty on killing predators and decided on how to go about it fairly.[64]

To pay the bounty, a herd tax was voted on and approved. A vigorous discussion was held about the organization of a government as well and in late March the committee sent a strongly worded petition against the HBC and the British, signed by 65 settlers at Oregon City. Another meeting was set for May 2, 1843, again referred to as a 'wolf meeting', most of the settlers in Oregon attended the meeting; many of them French Canadians who remained loyal to the Hudson Bay Company.

The Organic Laws of Oregon, providing a framework of laws to govern the sparsely populated pioneer settlements, was voted on and rejected, primarily by the French Canadians who opposed naming an office of Governor. Another meeting was set for July 5.[252]

There is no single document that in itself proves Nicholas Fox left Knox County, KY in the spring of 1843, after living there for 32 years. However his youngest son Nicholas was born November of 1842 in Knox County, KY and six months later Nicholas's daughter Phoebe, 17, married George William Bunch, 27, in Macon County, MO, May 13, 1843.[148]

The task of moving 500 miles through what was still considered dangerous Indian country, was not to be taken lightly. They, like their peers, used the wagons they had on their farms, upgrading pieces and parts, as necessary. Considering Samuel Cobb lived in Knox County, Kentucky and was employed in the practice of leading people from Knox County, Kentucky to the Show Me state at that time, it seems very likely that it was he who led the Fox's out of the Bluegrass State, to Missouri.

There is an indication that they initially settled in Chariton County, for within a year a U.S, General Land Office Record indicates Nicholas bought 80 acres in Linn County, Missouri, referring to him as 'Nicholas Fox of Chariton County'.[138] Linn County lies just west of Macon County and north of both Chariton and Randolph counties where many of the Bunch family had settled.

Did Nicholas know his father's questionable heritage? If he did, did he harbor a grudge against his uncles and aunts for never accepting his father? Was there animosity between him and his sibling Nancy and half-siblings? And just as importantly, did he move to Missouri with a longer range goal to reach Oregon? These are the questions I would ask my Grandpa Nicholas if I could.

Likely barely settled, Phoebe married George William (John) Bunch in Macon County, Missouri on May 13, 1843. There is no document that cites the date of death of George's first wife Narcissa, but she must have passed away the previous fall, in 1842 or early in 1843 at 29 years old. George remarried in May of that year.

In any event, George and Phoebe had a short courtship, making it very likely the families were acquainted before the Fox family relocated to Missouri. George had been born in Clay County, Kentucky, about 25 miles from Knox County, but left for Tennessee 11 years before when Phoebe was only six.

In any case, one thing seems evident; of all the marriages investigated in this work, Phoebe Fox and George (John) Bunch's commitment to each other and their children stands out. Phoebe Fox might have been young when she married, but she married well and the couple obviously complimented each other.

No documents exist to prove Phoebe was a loving step-mother to David, who was about six years old when his mama died and Phoebe married his father, but documents do exist that show the step-son remained living reasonably near Phoebe for the rest of their lives; many years after George had passed away.

Pictures of Phoebe that exist were taken later in her life, but in them a person might be able to imagine what she looked like when she married George at 17 years old. She had dark hair, was short and stout of build. Phoebe surely had a sense of humor, but she appears to be of serious temperament. She wasn't beautiful but she was not unattractive. Of Sara's daughters, it was Phoebe who may have become the family physician when her mother was gone.[44]

The year the Fox family moved to Missouri, was called "The Great Migration of 1843", as emigration to Oregon was up to nearly 1000 in that spring, due primarily to the famed Applegate party.[213] Consisting of 120 wagons and several thousand loose cattle and horses the group was promoted by Dr. Whitman, who was returning home from a trip back east, pleading for more funding to continue his work.

Horace Greeley espoused Whitman's cause and Whitman was able to return with a little more funding.[25] One train was led by Peter Burnett in a true-life rags to riches story. Burnett was a frontier lawyer with debts totaling $15,000 and a wife seriously ill with consumption. He was trying to make a living running a store in Weston, Missouri, between Independence and St. Joseph; right in the heart of Oregon emigration fever. Hopelessly in debt, Burnett saw the prospect of free land as a dream come true. Since he had a wife and six children, he could lay claim to 1600 acres. After receiving permission from his creditors Burnett set out, in his words, "*to work most vigorously to organize a wagon company. I visited the surrounding counties, making speeches wherever I could find a sufficient audience and succeeded even beyond my expectations.*"[70[pp20-21]]

Burnett was himself a member of the Restoration movement and member of the Church of Christ. During the winter before he led a wagon train west, many other members agreed to follow him. These included the Newby's, Gray's, Gilmore's, Wilson, Holman, Howell, Hembree and in particular, Catherine Blevins Baker, the 20 year old wife of John Gordon Baker who was not a member of the church. It is believed the Baker family shared familial relations with the Bunch family, through the McCullough family. The Bakers traveled in a single wagon, with two small sons under the age of four. They had five children more in Oregon.[70]

Behind them came the hunting party of Sir William Drummond Stewart traveling under an alias with Bill Sublette as guide. One of the drivers was Baptiste Charbonneau, now almost 40; he was the son of Sacagawea, only an infant while she was in the service of Lewis and Clark. This group settled Oregon City and within a few months it went from a village of three or four structures to a respectable town containing more than thirty buildings. Some found work at the already established Lee mission with the remainder scattered about the Willamette Valley.

These earliest pioneers were made up of close knit families and friends that often shared the same religious beliefs and traveled together for support, as was a generational custom since Daniel Boone cleared a path through the Cumberland Mountains. These earliest settlers like their colonial ancestors, would logically set the corner posts of their claimed land where ever the land was optimal to be divided into 640 acre segments as opposed to the Rectangular Land

Survey System that was adopted by Congress in 1785 and still used today. Oregon was surveyed using this method in 1850.[323] Maps before that date show an eccentric patchwork of polygonal and other irregularly-shaped plats of land; boldly pointing out those earliest of pioneers.

The historically benevolent Dr. John McLoughlin, though operating Fort Vancouver for the British Hudson's Bay Company, would barter to the early settlers for seed and other items. This was frowned on by his superiors. When many of the settlers arrived they were destitute and were desperately in need of supplies. McLoughlin's aid helped those settlers get a foothold in the Willamette Valley.[310]

In a journal, he wrote that in 1843, 800 settlers came to Oregon. As the first stragglers were coming in on canoes that first year of so much migration, he overheard some Indians on the riverbank talking, when one of them tested his veracity by purposely stating loudly, *"It is good for us to kill these Bostons!"*[268] at which he charged them with his cane and chastised them, calling them dogs. The Indian who had made the statement said a Snake Indian told him that was how they felt and McLoughlin said if that was how they felt they were dogs.[268]

The Snake Indian who made the remark is believed to have been instructed in this belief by Enos Thomas, who gave the same advice to the Cayuse who had threatened Dr. Whitman in the same manner, two years before in 1841.[214] The Iroquois who harbored a deep hatred for White men was nicknamed, Acnes, for his complexion, Enos, as he is more known by history, would be the instigator of much violence in the next 20 years. He was traveling west spreading hate and discontentment wherever he had stayed and he spent some time with Snake Indians.

McLoughlin never spoke of this exchange, knowing the trepidation the settlers already had for the Natives and that if tensions were raised to conflict, the settlers would be wiped out. Understanding

Indian psychology, he knew that his stepping up to the insolent threat gave the intended effect.[268] Surely as history will show, Dr. Whitman could have learned much from this lesson on Indian psychology from Dr. McLoughlin.

In congress, Senator Benson had a plan to keep Oregon in the national eye. He saw to it that the Congress appointed Lt. John Charles Fremont to head a federal exploring expedition to the Columbia. Admirably suited to the task the young ambitious surveyor, geographer and celebrity of last year's exploration also just happened to be the husband of Jesse Benton Fremont, the Senators daughter.[68]

Attributed to the success of Fremont's first expedition, he was named to lead another in the summer of 1843. And this one was far more ambitious. Proven guide, Kit Carson joined him again as they took a route just north of the Great Salt Lake and up the Snake River to the Columbia. Much the same route as today's interstate highway.

Stopping east of the Cascade Mountains, they generally mapped Mt. Hood and Mt. St. Helens. They turned south and traveled the eastern side of the Cascades until they were on the east side of the Sierra Nevada. Kit Carson led them through a new pass in the Sierra's being some of the first Americans to see Lake Tahoe. From there they crossed and followed Jedediah Smith's trail north, back to South Pass and in the process, they mapped much of the Great Basin.[332]

A group of settlers in Oregon met again on July 5, 1843, at Champoeg on someone's farm. Here they presented a model of government based on the Iowa Organic Law and the Ordinance of 1787 and agreed on a slate of candidates. This time it passed as a general outline of a government, utilizing an Executive Committee of three, rather than a governor, satisfying the French Canadians.

The Organic Laws of Oregon were created to organize land claims within the Oregon country. The Willamette Valley was divided into four districts, each with a justice of the peace and constables and elected a triple executive (three presidents), a supreme judge, a secretary, a treasurer and four magistrates with their force of constables under captains and a major. All told, the police force in Oregon numbered about twelve guys. The provisions were adopted and all positions filled on the spot. They would last as the territory's basic government until 1849.[22]

The preamble states that the settlers only agree to the laws only "until such time as the United States of America extend their jurisdiction over us".[14p.131] Married couples were granted at no cost (except for the requirement to work and improve the land) up to 640 acres (a section or square mile), and unmarried settlers could claim 320 acres. As the group was a provisional government with no authority, these claims were not valid under United States or British law.[14p.131] This one fact held back many who understandably still felt trepidatious about selling everything but what would fit in a wagon or two and walking across 2000 miles of strange and unfamiliar wilderness, only to find their land claims invalidated.

Near the end of the year, Senator Lewis F. Linn died unexpectedly on October of 1843, passing of an aneurysm. He had returned to his home in Ste Genevieve, Missouri to assist in a cholera outbreak that had killed almost half his constituents when he passed himself.[58] Linn was one of two of the greatest political champions of the settlement of Oregon, Thomas Benton being the other, and sadly he died before he saw it made into a territory of the United States. Benton would pick up the torch.

After the Nicholas Fox family had relocated to the wilderness of Linn County, Missouri, only established a half dozen years before, Samuel Cobb continued to act as a guide. He traveled back and forth through the inhospitable wilderness, leading his neighbors in Kentucky to Missouri, until he simply disappeared. After a period of waiting with no word from what had happened to him, his widow

Kizzie, moved to Monroe County, Iowa, nearer her children. Samuel was neither seen, nor heard from again.[298]

The suspicious disappearance was the end of any connection between the Fox and Cobb families. It is a mysterious end for Samuel Cobb, who like Benjamin Fox, took many secrets with him to the hereafter.

CHAPTER FORTY-EIGHT

ANDREW JACKSON FOX

Ephraim became a father on February 4, 1844, when Andrew Jackson Fox was born in Missouri.[127] Documents however claim Ephraim was not married until two years later, to Louisa Frances Wells, called Lucy. In his lifetime Andrew filled out a number of documents claiming his mother's maiden name was Turner, however this woman has not been identified.

DNA confirms Lucy's father was John William Wells but not the biological daughter of his wife, Eliza Payne-West-Wells; this fact lends credence to Andy Fox's claim his mother was a Turner.

Eliza Payne married young to James Craik West, but six years later he died of unknown causes, leaving Eliza a widow with three small children. Eliza remarried to John William Wells in 1821 and Lucy would later claim to have been their first born child, claiming she was born both in 1827[93] and 1834.[129]. The former date seems the most logical.

When Lucy was about 10 years old Eliza Payne-West-Wells passed away in 1837. Lucy's father, John William Wells, was born in Bracken, Kentucky in 1795; about the same age as Nicholas Fox.[126] The family was some of the earliest to move to Missouri, in about 1837 and that's when Lucy's mother passed away, though her death date is undocumented. Lucy's father remarried and had many more children in Dallas County, Missouri, some distance south of Macon or Linn counties.

It is unknown when Ephraim met Lucy but the original marriage certificate claims the couple was wed two years after Andy was born, September 17, 1846.[119] Sometimes people were joined in frontier marriages, then later had the union made legal by a justice of the peace, but this seems unusual in this case, given they did not live far from civilization and Andy's lifelong claims to be the son of a woman named Turner.

Andrew's birth is recorded on his death certificate and in various Oregon pioneer files, but this was an era without much documentation when many went from memory, without proof. It's interesting that in the 1860 census Andrew was 15 years old and rather than be listed among his siblings, he was listed at the bottom of them, as if he were not of the same couple, however he appears correctly in the 1850 census. Sometimes elder children were set apart from their siblings in this way to show that they were independently living and working and maybe this was the case.

No record can be found of Ephraim marrying before Andrew was born. It is wholly possible that Ephraim had been married to a woman named Turner that died before documents could be created. At any rate whatever his mother's name was, Turner or what, 22 years old native Kentuckian Ephraim Fox was in Missouri in the winter of 1843-44 and became a father.

That spring in the Oregon country, Molalla Indians led by a Wascopam, or Dalles Indian by the name of Cockstock was causing a fair amount of mayhem in the settlement of Oregon City. His antics had been related in newspapers and they embellished his stature so he was believed by some to be a chief, but was only a leader of a group of disgruntled young braves. The Indian Agent Elijah White offered a $100 reward for the errant Indian.

On March 4, 1844, his antics boiled over when he and seven or eight of his braves rode wildly into Oregon City with war paint on, brandishing bows and firearms. Their intimidation of settlers was only temporary. Two Christian friends, Reuben Lewis and William H. Wilson working in a nearby sawmill were among the pioneers to respond to the threat. Everything turned to chaos as settlers rushed the braves in an attempt to apprehend the desperado.

Before he was pulled from his horse the warrior fired his pistol into the crowd, setting off a flurry of gunfire and filling the air with arrows. William Wilson, standing on a bridge at the time, fired at Cockstock just as Col. James Nesmith followed suit as the brave spun about. The ball creased across the back of the Indian's head as he fell from his horse. Just as Wilson fired he was hit with a poisoned arrow, deeply penetrating his hip. Two settlers died in the exchange and the Indians scattered.

Before he thought about it, in an instant, Wilson jerked the arrow out of his wound, inadvertently breaking off the broad head, deep inside. His friends urged Wilson to be seen by doctors at McLoughlin's fort but he said he was more afraid of the doctors there, than the wound itself. He carried the Native arrow head in his hip until the day he died, well over 50 years later, but said it was only tender for the first 20.

The Indians poisoned their arrow heads by catching a rattlesnake and presenting it with the liver of a deer, inducing it to strike until its venom was exhausted into the organ. Arrows were gouged into venom-soaked organ and then removed and allowed to dry.[46; 70]

Nesmith forever claimed that it was his ball that brought Cockstock down and Wilson never made a point to publicly argue about it, but later said this, "*I believe that was my bullet for I was a good shot in those days,*" and in addition, "*Col. Nesmith thought that shot was his and I never disputed the honor, if it is honor it was, with him. However, ours were the only shots fired at that time. It was one of us and it was a good job, whichever did it.*"[70[p.43]]

Andrew Jackson, 'Tennessee Gentleman', by Ralph E.W. Earl c1831.(33)

CHAPTER FORTY-NINE

THE RETRIBUTION OF JOSEPH SMITH

As the spring of 1844 approached along the Missouri, there was little rain and by April it was already unnaturally dry. However rains began in May and continued for six straight weeks.[155]

That same spring Joseph Smith wrote to the candidates for President in the election of that year seeking their support for reparations and when he got no response he became a candidate himself from his Mormon headquarters in Nauvoo, Illinois.[16]

Meanwhile Smith had confrontations with a half dozen close associates over how best to run the Nauvoo economy and two of them accused him of proposing to their wives. Smith excommunicated them and again labeled them as "dissenters", as he had labeled those before that had crossed him. These dissenters published a one-time issue of a paper called, the "*Nauvoo Expositer*", that communicated the concerns they had about Smith as a moral and wise leader.

Outside the incessant rain had swollen the Missouri and nearby Mississippi Rivers to raging, cascading torrents. When Smith moved to seize the *Nauvoo Expositer* press on orders that he deemed the paper a "public nuisance", he faced backlash and was brought up on charges filed by the dissidents of perjury and polygamy. Response to his seizing a newspaper press got quickly heated and fearing a mob attack, amid the raging rainstorm outside, Smith called for martial law in Nauvoo.

The reaction from Illinois Governor Thomas Ford was a threat to raise a larger state militia unless Smith and the city council surrendered. Smith initially fled to Missouri but returned to turn himself in at the Carthage, Illinois jail along with his brother Hyrum on June 23.[16]

The rain outside beat down at a steady rate and filled streams then streets, turning most of the established United States to mud. Carthage was just 10 miles from the Mississippi River, which jumped its banks, flooding the lowlands. The raging water of the Missouri did the same.[155]

For Joseph Smith in Carthage, once locked up, the charges stiffened to treason. On June 27, 1844, an elder of the church visited Smith and his brother and two others in the makeshift jail and upon removing himself from the crowd, produced a small pepperbox pistol, offering it to Smith who readily took it in hand. With the pistol secretly tucked into his pants pocket the group took their dinner and wine, sharing it with the guards.

When they had finished the wine, one of the prisoners saw a group of nearly 100 men with faces painted black coming toward the two story stone jail. The men stormed the front door and quickly climbed the stairs, firing at the locked door to the two rooms that served as jail cells. Inside the prisoners jumped away from the solid plank door as the second shot that tore through it struck Hyrum Smith in the face, to the left of his nose, dropping him to the floor. He cried out,

"I'm a dead man".[311[section 135]] As Joseph knelt over him he replied,

"Oh, my poor dear brother, Hyrum."[311[section 135]]

Meanwhile a lethal battle went on at the door where the other two prisoners worked to block it from opening while using a stick to strike hands or barrels that exposed themselves through the door. Joseph stood up from the body of his brother and went to the door, firing all six shots from the revolver through the open crack, though three of the shots misfired. In answer, bullets came in a hail through the door and one of the other prisoners was shot four times as Smith stepped desperately toward the second story window.

As Smith reached the window the door blew open and two pistol shots blew through his back and another from a muzzle-loading rifle below shot him through the window in the head as he leaped. Smith hollered, *"Oh Lord, my God!"*, as he fell to the earth.[311[section 135]]

Some said he was dead when he hit the mud, others maintained he survived long enough to be drug to a sitting position and killed by an informal firing squad. In any event, as his corpse was about to be mutilated a deep rolling thunder began to boil and bark to such a point it caused panic in the crowd, and the mob, believing the Mormons were coming, dispersed.[73]

Joseph Smith lied against a wooden wall, smeared with mud and blood, his eyes closed to the world forever, while the rain just kept coming down.

The assassination of Joseph Smith, as depicted in newspapers of the day (34)

CHAPTER FIFTY

EXCLUSIONARY LAWS OF OREGON

In the Oregon Territory, gatherings still being referred to as 'wolf meetings' continued, and at one such meeting in June of 1844 the provisional government enacted laws governing the issue of slavery. While the earliest pioneers were willing to fist fight over a political argument, most who came to Oregon simply wanted to avoid the subject of slavery.[14]

The result were exclusionary laws meant to keep the issue from becoming contentious as it was in the established United States they had fled. Thus, owning slaves was outlawed and citizens owning slaves were required to set them free within three years. Male Blacks over 18 years of age were required to leave Oregon within two years and Black women within three years. Black children were allowed to stay in Oregon until they were 18, when they were require to leave. A lash law was enacted that required Blacks who violated these laws be whipped no less than twenty and no more than thirty-nine times. This punishment was initially deemed proper to be administered every six months, "until he or she quit the territory".[14]

The verbiage was seen as too severe and was never used before it was replaced with a punishment of forced labor. The next law required that Black people tried and convicted of being in Oregon illegally would be hired out publicly by whomever employed them the shortest time. This law was never used before it too was rewritten.[14] The exclusionary laws were proof the issue was as contentious in Oregon as it was in the United States, east of the Missouri River.

The rainstorms that summer along the border states finally crested July 16. The result was known as The Great Flood of 1844.[155] It was the largest flood of the Mississippi and Missouri Rivers ever on record.

The disease that the receding waters created killed 100 Wyandot Indians and forever altered the course of every stream from its discharge.[63] A sandbar was created in front of Wayne's Landing at Independence. Missouri, blocking all access for use. The result was that commerce and emigrants began to use the solid rock port at Westport, coincidentally much closer to Macon County than had been Wayne's Landing.

The flood was certainly the worst natural disaster that Nicholas and Sara or their family had ever seen or survived. Along every stream fences were replaced by fields of silt and debris. Vast fields of crops were underneath feet of mud. Receding waters along rivers left stinking buffalo carcasses in tree tops.[155]

By end of the year the clean-up continued while anti-Mormon sentiment grew. In Illinois, by December 1844, the state government removed the city charter of Nauvoo further removing Mormon protections.[16] The stage was set for something big.

Emigration in 1844 was down from what it might have been,[238] partly due to how wet the spring was. Official reports claim that about 1500 people walked to Oregon and another 53 to California and of these, four were murdered by Indians.[76]

Worthy of note is one particular pioneer that year, named William Henry Hawk, born in Indiana.[131] Besides being one of the earliest pioneers to Oregon, his descendants would someday marry into the Fox family. Those earliest of pioneers were the toughest of the lot and William Hawk was no exception.

Among those in the emigration of 1844 were two talented Christian Church leaders, named Amos Harvey and John Foster. Both would be responsible the following year for establishing churches.[70] In Oregon, a message from the provisional government in 1844 claimed the rising settler population was beginning to flourish among the savages, who were *"the chief obstruction to the entrance of civilization"* in a land of *"ignorance and idolatry"*.[14p131.]

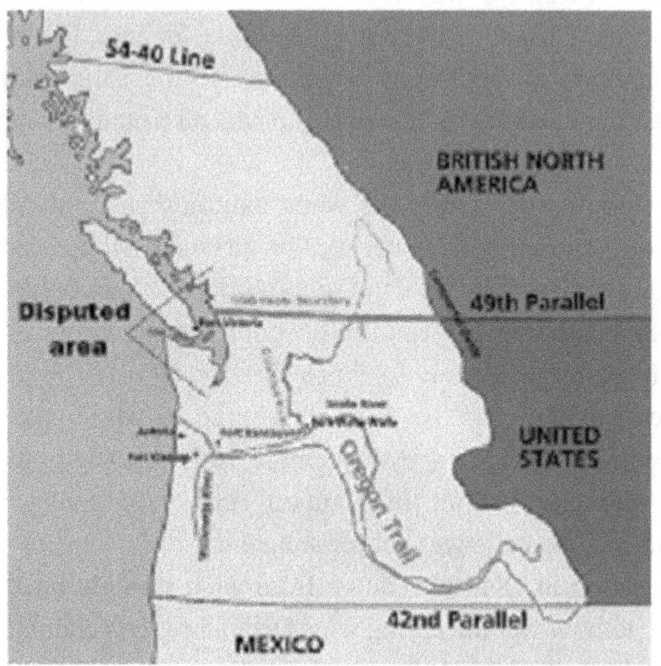

The slogan 54, 40, or fight referred to where the US/ Canadian border would be located (35)

The presidential election of 1844 between James Polk and Henry Clay was decided primarily over expansionism in the United States. The slogan "54 (degree), 40 (degree) or fight" referred to the U.S./Canadian border and where it would divide the countries.[38]

Those supporting James Polk wanted 54 degree, 40 degree and they wanted it NOW! Polk claimed he did too, but as is common in American politics since George Washington left office, once James Polk won election he didn't want it that bad. Negotiations settled at the 49 degree parallel.[38]

CHAPTER FIFTY-ONE

1845

In the spring of 1845 Col. Stephen Kearney, a veteran of the War of 1812, rode west with several companies of dragoons (later called cavalry), led by accomplished guide Tom "Broken Hand" Fitzpatrick, who had led the ground breaking Bartleson-Bidwell train of 1841. It was the first time that such a military force had done so.

Part of their mission was to respond to a number of Indian atrocities. Upon reaching Ft. Laramie, Kearney sent part of his command further west while dispatching messages to the local Indians, many of them Arapaho, to meet him at the fort. It was here that the Indians first saw the White warriors and as ruminants of the natural world, they were predictably impressed. The uniformity of movement, the arms they carried, the horses and equipment they possessed, were all impressive to the simple Natives.

In no uncertain terms he warned them that he was aware of the recent violence against White people and if it happened again, he would return with all the force and might of his dragoons and kill every one of them. That evening he accentuated his remarks by firing both a howitzer and a rocket into the air above the gathering. Many of the Arapaho fell prostrate to the ground, shaking in fear from the fiery messenger sent to the Gods. Throughout the night and the next day the Indians stole away, back to their villages and camps, sufficiently frightened of angering the powerful, colorful, well-armed White warriors. With their job well done, the troops marched home.[66]

To this point, Indians from Missouri to Oregon had been reasonably friendly to travelers and typically when the Indians approached the emigrants it was for mutually beneficial trades or to help the emigrants in some fashion many times at water crossings. The show of force had the intended effect on the Native tribes who saw or heard about it. Though this event is not found in most historical accounts, it was more important to relative peace than is given credit and is in fact a first-hand account.[66]

Characteristically Indians lived in small band, with no central leader. They were bonded by their superstitions and language but held no allegiance to any other band. Their leaders were only given respect and obeyed as far as his personal qualities could be feared.

In this form of hierarchy some chiefs were more powerful by their magnetism, much like King Philip and Tecumseh. Nothing bound these independent tribes to each other, but instead committed raids on fellow bands. They fought with other tribes as well, but would not unite to help each other in this regard; historically, this is why they could never repel the White European advance across the continent.[66]

Hollywood would have us believe that chiefs of tribes were rich and lived opulently, but this is absolutely false. In fact, chiefs made great efforts to appear as if they did not have any appearance of outward wealth; he knows how tenuous his position is so gives most of what he has to other men in the village, many of which live much better than he does.

Chief's were related to many different families in the band; this ensured he had many people who cared about him. The chief's power relied upon keeping good will among these many relatives who also assumed varying positions of power in this loose framework of government.

Many times a year the bands gathered as such they could manage and held great celebrations of war that they then committed upon their hated enemies of neighboring tribes. These encounters gave the young men chance to gain glory. The caricature of the stoic Indian is stolen from reality, for this emotionless, uncaring distant stare was a cultivated look for the simple Natives, who felt showing no reaction was a sign of strength.[66]

White men had much to fear from Indians as Indians had good reason to fear White men. In Oregon that year a band of Indians killed on old ox on the Tualatin Plains and White settlers quickly organized to gain recompense. For their transgression, the Indians were compelled to give up eight horses and a rifle. In another instance, when peaceful Indians from near Whitman's Mission organized a cattle drive from California, they were stopped enroute by California highwaymen. In the ensuing fight the Indians took 22 horses. When the Indians reached the settlements to purchase cattle, they were accused of stealing the horses and argued their innocence under the circumstances. In the fight that followed a young chief was killed.[46]

At the beginning of the year 1845, there were approximately 2100 White settlers in the Oregon country and nearly half of them were less than 18 years of age. Only seven percent were older than 45. Among the settlers were about 100 members of the Christian Church.

Emigration that year across the Oregon Trail topped 2500, doubling the population of White men. Over 1000 wagons surrounded by families that had sold everything and turned their back on everything and everyone they'd ever known, walked out of the United States, across the Missouri River out of sight into the prairie knowing their survival lied completely in their ability to overcome any and all perils. For those that dared begin, the consideration to stop along the way or turn back, was unimaginable, for it would likely mean death. The heartiest of men didn't want to risk their parents, wives or children's lives in that position.[70]

Of those who were stout enough of heart, body and mind to risk these things that year, were Church of Christ followers Theophilus (son of Cader and brother of Allen) and Rachael Powell, as well as his nephews David and Jackson. Theophilus and Allen had a brother named Nelson who had passed away twenty years before. His widow, married Jones Kendrick, making Theophilus a brother-in-law of wife of first cousin 7x removed, of mine, though these relationships occurred prior to Benjamin being adopted, so there is no biological relationship.

Theophilus and his brothers were later joined by their married sister Jane, wed to Wilson Pugh.[74; 247] Included among these Christian family members were distant relatives William David Pugh, born 1790 in Indiana[130] and John Pugh, born 1779 in North Carolina.[200] These men were related so many generations before that it is unknown if they even realized it. The Pugh family emigrated to the New World in the mid-1600's from Wales.[190]

It's possible that when some of these families vacated Macon County, Missouri, their farms were then inhabited by Sara Fox and her son Ephraim, as the next records available list Ephraim and his mother living as neighbors to the balance of the Powell brothers, James and John as well as their sister Jane Powell and her husband, Wilson Pugh.[93]

The Pugh's were among many other Christian Church members that went west in 1845 whose remaining family in the United States would be in the company of the Murphy Wagon train of 1852. Amos Harvey, Isaac Butler and Thomas C. Davis were just a few that shared some relationship with Ephraim Fox through the Powell and Pugh families.

The number of Church of Christ members living along the Willamette soon led to a new derisive observation that began making the rounds in the Oregon country, "*The Campbellites and the fern are taking over the Willamette Valley*"[182]; one Baptist Missionary posted on the Clatsop plains near Astoria observed, "*the Campbellites are industriously engaged in making proselytes*".[182] There were many families of other religious beliefs who would become related to the family of Fox, who made the journey to Oregon in 1845.

John Lewis was a member of the Church of Christ and his eldest son served that year as captain of the Lewis train traveling, among others. Two events occurred during their trip that are worth repeating. First, along the Platte the wagons encountered many Indians who were making pests of themselves, following and milling about their wagons when they camped. They could not be persuaded to move along, before one of the Christians came upon a brilliant idea. The following day a young child's face was painted with red spots and placed prominently in the back of a wagon as the procession began. When the Indians saw the spots they suspected measles and disappeared from the trail.

The second event took place toward the end of the journey when a number of young men, bored with the monotony of travel wanted to leave the trail to hunt buffalo. Capt. Lewis admonished them with the warning the hills were dangerous with Indian's but they were persistent. Relenting, Lewis told them they might go but he would not provide any support to defend them or find them if they did not return in a timely manner. The young men rode away, never to be heard from again; along the trail or after their families reached Oregon. Despite their family pleading through sobs, Lewis would not relent and the balance of the wagon train reached its destination.[70]

Groups named for the families that had organized them, gathered together, such as the Griffith-Findley train that came to Oregon in spring of 1845. Partly organized by Elisha Griffith, a shoemaker and brick maker, it included his wife Betsey, as well as her father and mother David and Janett Findley and many more of the Findley relation.[124; 52] The great great grandson of Elisha and Janett Findley would someday wed Ephraim Fox's daughter. Just as the trip began, a daughter was born to Elisha and Betsey Griffith along in Nebraska, in May of 1845.[203]

It was a fateful year for these families and would surely serve as a lesson well learned by their kin back in Missouri who read about their relatives not just in letters, but also in newspapers. The trail was new and it was rough. Few had built a bridge or a ferry across any creek or river; indeed few at all had crossed. Among this group were men who became famous like Joel Palmer and Sam Barlow. Others like Stephen Meek would earn a reputation of another sort and be lucky to survive himself.

The Powell family gathered with family, friends and neighbors with the great train of 1845 in Independence, Missouri, on May 11, as part of a smaller train under the command of Capt. Solomon Tetherow (his brother's son John M. Tetherow, seven years old in 1845, would someday wed Martha (Mary) Jane Pugh, born in Oregon to Jesse Washington Pugh four years later in 1849.[202]

After a few days of travel complicated by bickering and fighting Tetherow resigned and a Capt. English took over.[30] It took these emigrants six months to reach 'the settlement', as Oregon City was then called. This would have been a month longer than would generally be expected. But these families fate was bound for a special route. Though it was rare to do so, circumstances required that Theophilus's elderly mother in law and his wife's crippled sister, rode in a wagon as much as was possible. Finally on April 8, the members of this train left St. Joseph for Oregon.[247]

Along the way this train joined with others and perhaps more than any other, would have the greatest impact on those who would follow. These emigrants improved the trail by necessity and by sheer force of their numbers, however those numbers had a starkly adverse effect on the trail as well.

Trees that had been landmarks since the first White man had inadvertently found the trail, were stripped first of the limbs easy to reach, then the trees themselves were dumped to the ground so the rest of the limbs could be used. Most of these landmark trees were too large to cut into firewood, so they were left a limbless corpse on the ground. The impact of hunting along the trail to Oregon was devastating to wildlife.[52]

Weeks after the last wagons had left for Oregon, Nicholas Fox purchased property in Linn County, Missouri, on June 1, 1845. This might have been property sold by an emigrant now on their way to Oregon. This is the final document that cites Nicholas Fox's name. In fact it is the last document to record any of the family until they appear five years later in the federal census for Macon County, Missouri and Nicholas is not among them.

There is no hint to the date, circumstances, or location of the death or burial of Nicholas Fox, he simply disappears. Eerily, suspiciously, just like Kentucky to Missouri guide Samuel Cobb. Is there a connection?

If Nicholas relocated the Fox family in Missouri in preparation to jump off to Oregon, it was a goal he never saw realized. The fate and future of the Fox family was now in the hands of he and Mary Sara's son, Ephraim.

Even more than his grandfather Benjamin that brought the family through the Cumberland Gap, into Kentucky and Tennessee, Ephraim Fox would lead the family in a direction that would forever alter their future.

Benjamin had been among the last of his brothers to leave Virginia and may have learned that he wished he had made the move earlier. Ephraim's grandfather, Benjamin, might have felt that those who were the most intrepid and first to settle, were the most likely to prosper. Certainly, his eldest brothers Arthur and Richard had proven that. The example set by these relatives might have provided Ephraim and his father Nicholas with powerful examples.

Benjamin transplanted his family to Kentucky and Tennessee, surrounded by his siblings (which now we know were his step-siblings) and their children. His son and grandson left this cradle of family and struck out on their own.

A half century after Benjamin Fox brought his family from Virginia to Kentucky, his grandson Ephraim moved the family west across the Oregon Trail.

Ephraim Fox was the product of the experiences of his father Nicholas and his grandfather Benjamin; of the relationships they nurtured and those that failed. The drama of their lives were directly responsible for bringing Ephraim to the edge of civilization; ready to gamble everything in order to get to Oregon; in order to leave the secrets of Benjamin Fox behind completely.

My third grandfather Ephraim led his family across the continent, as far from the Virginia Fox's as was physically possible. It would be a fresh start where he would stand alone to define his family.

It was a bold move, but it didn't come without a cost.

But that is another story.

EPILOGUE

Benjamin Fox probably spent his life trying to move on from the events that led to his birth and adoption by William and Mary Fox. And the jury is still out on if it was he or his son Nicholas who fathered John J. Cobb and Henry Franklin Martin; a subject both men kept quiet about.

A decade ago Benjamin was a complete mystery and though DNA discoveries have identified who his children are, his paternal heritage remains unknown, with but few hints pointing to his biological father. One can be sure in the coming years more will be unearthed and when they are, if I am yet alive, this book about the secrets of my fifth great grandfather Benjamin Kendrick Fox will be updated.

At least we, the grandsons of Benjamin and Nicholas have discovered their progenitor. For the descendants of John R. Cobb the news is probably shocking because there was no indication in historical documentation that John wasn't Samuel and Kizzie's biological son. But for the descendants of Henry Franklin Martin and Nicholas Fox (my family), who already knew something was amiss, the DNA discoveries have provided answers, but raised others.

My suspicion is Benjamin was the biological son of a family of South Carolina Fox's who were also related to David Martin's wife, Eliza (Fox). Why he was raised by Virginia cousin, William Fox is anyone's guess. Time will tell if my suspicions are correct.

As to how fathers affect sons, it seems obvious the relationships or lack of them that Benjamin shared with his adopted Virginia Fox family and/or his son Nicholas had with his stepsiblings was the catalyst for Nicholas abandoning Kentucky when Benjamin died. Surely there were personality traits passed forward, but there is no record of them, particularly.

My take is Benjamin was not filled with rancor for his adopted Fox family as his son Nicholas was for his stepsiblings. Even so, Benjamin held a strange dual citizenship, almost as if he promoted the distance between his eldest son Nicholas in Knox County, KY and the rest of his many other children in Flynn's Lick, Tennessee.

When Benjamin died, Nicholas took his family immediately and left Kentucky, none of his relatives would ever follow. These facts point to a rift between Nicholas and his family.

If Nicholas Fox was a brooding man, his father Benjamin may have provided the blueprint. The complicated relationship the men shared with their family was uncomfortable at best. The effect he saw it had on them may have been part of the reason Ephraim Fox wanted so badly to go to Oregon.

It seems like Nicholas Fox left Kentucky because he planned to organize a trip across the Oregon Trail, but we will never know because he died before it could be accomplished. Whether Nicholas had Oregon Fever or not is unknown, but his son Ephraim sure did, as is chronicled in book two of this series, *Ephraim Fox on the Oregon Trail, 1852.*

ACKNOWLEDGMENTS

While conducting genealogical investigation it has been my pleasure to interact with a number of individuals who are experts in their fields. This book would not be possible were it not for being able to exchange emails with DNA expert and author Joseph Fox. It is an honor to be able to ask questions of someone as knowledgeable and well respected in his field.

It has also been an honor to exchange emails with Oregon historical writer and investigator Stephanie Flora and 19th century writer Kathy Weiser of Legends of America, whom I admire greatly.

Fellow genealogists Nora Brashear and Lynn Ware Sprattling were gracious enough to offer the use of the photographs of Edmund Bacon and wife Eliza Fox and their graves, respectively.

This book is really a compilation of the works of genealogical friends and distant cousins I have met. I am the author, but this is OUR book. Relationships I have made in the research of this book are very special to me.

I cannot thank Bev Moltzau and Brenda Martin enough for all they have done. Bev has been a cousin-friend for years and we have shared many discoveries.

I have been privileged to have spent a number of fine hours on the phone being schooled by Brenda in everything from the lay of the land in Kentucky, South Carolina and Georgia, but in deciphering DNA and using it to expand my research.

Research has revealed that I am the last living male of the Ephraim Fox family that came to Oregon. I feel it is my responsibility to leave an accurate record of my family before I am gone.

This fact is why it is a matter of personal importance that American Fox Tales books be as accurate as possible. To that end, I invite anyone who has information about this Fox family to use the contact information at the beginning of this book.

There are more shadowy secrets out there; all but forgotten in attics, basements, storage boxes; even in blood that may only be illuminated by DNA. The research never ends, and I am committed to updating each book in the series until the day I join the family I chronicle.

I would like to dedicate *The Secrets of Benjamin Fox* to my father James Royal Fox, Sr., who was my hero as a little boy, my guide as a teenager, my business partner as an adult and my friend all my life. He is my best angel now. It is my honor to be his son and bear his name.

Thank you for the opportunity to tell you my family's story.

BIBLIOGRAPHY

AUTHOR'S NOTES

[1] Birth nor death date, or place of burial is known for Martha Norvell-Fox. Her death is estimated from the date of remarriage of her widow, Benjamin Kendrick Fox.

[2] No documents cite the 1800 birth of Henry Fox's son Benjamin other than Ancestry.com family trees. The source of this information is unknown. There are no other documents relating to this Benjamin Fox including his date of death.

[3] No documents citing the parents of Mary Sara Hammack were Daniel Sr. and wife Agnes Pruitt were found other than Ancestry.com member trees. The couple's birth and death dates are of similar nature. Ancestry.com Thrulines has established 28 DNA matches between each one of the couple and me, establishing the relationship to be legitimate. Accessed Thrulines matches 21 Oct. 2020.

[4] Migration patterns of parents can be tracked by birth records of their children. p.161, 182

[5] Ancestry.com member trees are the only source for the birth and subsequent death of the unnamed children of Nicholas Fox and his wife, Mary Sara Hammack.

[6] The death date of Martha Elizabeth Morris-Bunch is assumed as her widow remarried in March, 1818.

[7] Hammack family trees on Ancestry.com indicate Mary Sara Hammack's father died in Knox County, Kentucky in 1818. Within a few years the balance of the Hammack family, except for Mary Sara, relocated to Indiana.

[8] The marriage date of Susan Fox and Martin Moore is widely circulated on Ancestry.com on member trees, however I can find no document to confirm the date.

[9] An anomaly exists regarding the marriage of Martha Norvell. "*Mecklenberg, Marriage Index, 1765-1810*" cite her marriage to Benjamin K Fox 9 May 1792 while the "*Virginia, Select Marriages, 1785-1940*)" claim she was married to John Bernard 16 Jul 1792. This is likely a different Martha Norvell, but that has not been established.

[10] The birth date for John Madison Fox, 9 Sep 1837, originates from Ancestry.com member trees. U.S. Federal Census only confirms year of birth and no other documentation can be found to substantiate month or day.

[11] The departure date for Nicholas Fox and his family is estimated based on activities the family were involved in, in Missouri and the time it took to travel from southeast Kentucky to north-central Missouri.

PRINT RESOURCES

[12] *Boddie, John Bennett. Historical Southern Families. Vol. 1. Baltimore, MD: Clearfield; 1998*

[13] *Bradley SE. Brunswick County, Virginia Deed Books. Lawrenceville, Va.: S. Bradley; 1997. [p.296]*

[14] *Brown J Henry. Brown's Political History of Oregon : Provisional Government : Treaties, Conventions and Diplomatic Correspondence on the Boundary Question ; Historical Introduction of the Explorations on the Pacific Coast ; History of the Provisional Government from Year to Year, with Election Returns and Official Reports ; History of the Cayuse War, with Original Documents. London, Forgotten Books, 2016 [p.131][p.131][p.131]*

[15] *Burnett, Charles. Nat Turner: A Troublesome Property. Frank Christopher, Docu-drama. 22 Aug. 2003. Accessed 25 Oct. 2020*

[16] *Bushman, Richard Lyman (2005), Joseph Smith: Rough Stone Rolling, New York: Alfred A. Knopf*

[17] *Carl Bert Albert, Olive May (Chaffin) Peterson. Abner Chaffin of Jackson County, Tennessee, and sons, Bailaam, Elias, Joseph, William: an account of their migrations to Missouri, Illinois and Montana. OMC Peterson. The University of Wisconsin – Madison, 1966*

[18] *Charles Russell Logan, Arkansas Historic Preservation Program. "The Promised Land" : The Cherokees, Arkansas and Removal, 1794-1839. Arkansas Historic Preservation Program; 1997*

[19] *Cobb J. Cobb and Cobbs, Early Virginians. Durant Pub. Co; 1977*

[20] *Cocke, Ellen Mookler. Some Fox Trails in Old Virginia; John Fox of King William County, Ancestors, Descendants, Near Kin,. Richmond, VA., Dietz Press; 1939.[p.9]*

[21] *Columbia Patriot. "The Mormon Prisoners Escaped." Columbia Patriot, 27 May 1839. Boone County, Missouri*

[22] *Corning, Howard Mckinley. Dictionary of Oregon History. Portland, Or., Binford & Mort Pub, 1989*

[23] *Dale, Harrison Clifford, The explorations of William H. Ashley and Jedediah Smith, 1822-1829, Lincoln: University of Nebraska Press, 1991*

[24] *Dale Lowell Morgan. Jedediah Smith and the Opening of the West. Univ. Of Nebraska Pr; 1971*

[25] *Drury, Clifford M. Marcus and Narcissa Whitman and the Opening of Old Oregon, in Two Volumes. 1973. Vol. Two, Chapter 18, Glendale, Cal.: Arthur Clark*

[26] *Eaton, Rachel Caroline. John Ross and the Cherokee Indians. Hardpress Publishing; 2012*

[27] *Eiler, Homer C, and Shelcounty Historical And Genealogical Society (Shelbyville, Ill. History of Tower Hill and Vicinity. p.14. Illinois, Shelby County News Gazette, 1973*

[28] *Engelman FL. The Peace of Christmas Eve. Hart-Davis; 1963*

[29] *English, William Hayden. Conquest of the Country Northwest of the River Ohio, 1778-1783 : And Life of Gen. George Rogers Clark. Indianapolis: Bowen-Merrill Co; 1898*

[30] *Field Jr., James Journal. 1845, "Crossing the Plains," Willamette Farmer, Portland, Oregon, beginning with issue dated 18 Apr. 1879, and ending with issue dated 1 Aug. 1879*

[31] *Folmar, Kathlyn J, and Pike County Historical And Genealogical Society. Papers of the Pike County Historical and Genealogical Society : Names from Pike County Court Minutes, 1828-1845. Troy, Ala., Pike County Historical And Genealogical Society, 1997*

[32] *Grassley, Ray Hoard. Indian Wars of the Pacific Northwest. Portland, Or.: Binfords & Mort; 1972*

[33] *Hale NC. Roots in Virginia; an Account of Captain Thomas Hale, Virginia Frontiersman, His Descendants and Related Families.*

With Genealogies and Sketches of Hale, Saunders, Lucke, Claiborne, Lacy, Tobin and Contributing Ancestral Lines. Editorial: [Philadelphia; 1948

[34] *Hamilton EL. Indian Atrocities along the Clinch, Powell and Holston Rivers of Southwest Virginia, 1773-1794. Virginia? E.L. Hamilton; 1965*

[35] *Harman, John Newton. Annals of Tazewell County, Virginia from 1800 to 1922 in Two Volumes. Richmond, Va.: W.C. Hill Printing Co., [p.25]; 1922*

[36] *Hatcher, Patricia Law. Abstract of Graves of Revolutionary Patriots. Vol. 2, E-K. Westminster, Md: Willow Bend Books; 2001*

[37] *Himes, Sharon. Cavalier's Adventures: The Story of Henry Norwood. Bowie, Md.: Heritage Books; 2002*

[38] *Hough, Emerson. 54-40 or Fight. 1909. Grosset and Dunlap or The Bobbs-Merrill Company*

[39] *Hussey, John A. (1967). Champoeg: Place of Transition, A Disputed History. Oregon Historical Society*

[40] *Jackson, Sally. Register of the Kentucky Historical Society, Vol. II, Chapter 3 The Young and Jackson Ancestry of Mrs Virginia Crittenden and Miss Sally Jackson, Sisters. Genealogical Publishing Company. 1981*

[41] *J B A Brouillet. Authentic Account of the Murder of Dr. Whitman and Other Missionaries, by the Cayuse Indians of Oregon in 1847, and the Causes Which Led to That Horrible Catastrophe. [pp.23-24] S.J. McCormick, 1869*

[42] *Jenson, Andrew. Encyclopedic History of The Church of Jesus Christ of Latter-Day Saints. Salt Lake City, Utah, Corp. Of The Pres. Of The Church Of Jesus Christ Of Latter-Day Saints, 1941*

[43] *Jensen, Andrew (December 1888). The Historical Record. [pp. 671, 673] Salt Lake City, Utah: Andrew Jenson*

[44] *Johnson, Hattie. The Other Side of the Mountain. Old West. Spring 1965: [p.16-21, 50, 57-59]*

[45] Johnston W. *The Glengarry Light Infantry, 1812-1816 : Who Were They and What Did They Do in the War?* Winston Johnston; 2011

[46] *Journals of the Continental Congress, Vol. II, May 10-September 20, 1775. [p.31] Washington, DC: Government Printing Office. 1905*

[47] *Kappler CJ. Treaty Of Edwardsville, Illinois with the Kickapoo on July 30, 1819. Government Printing Office; 1904:Indian Affairs. Laws and Treaties. Vol. II. (Treaties.)*

[48] *Kars, Marjoleine (2008).* "1739 – Stono Rebellion". *In* Campbell, Ballard C. *(ed.). Disasters, Accidents, and Crises in American History: A Reference Guide to the Nation's Most Catastrophic Events. New York: Facts on File. [pp.*22–23*].* ISBN *978-0-8160-6603-2*

[49] *Kennon W. Luke Matthews of Brunswick County, Virginia, 1739-1788, and His Descendants,. Editorial: Kobe, Japan, H. Kodama, Printer; 1937*

[50] Knox Co. KY Court Clerk. *Deed Book B*. 1810, [p.89]

[51] Knox Co KY Court Clerk. *Deed Book C*. 1819, [p.209]

[52] *Lang, HO. History of the Willamette Valley. Portland, Or.: George H Himes, Book and Job Printer; 1885*

[53] *Lareine Warden Clayton, and Jane Gray Buchanan. Stories of Early Inns and Taverns of the East Tennessee Country. Nashville, National Society Of The Colonial Dames Of America In The State Of Tennessee, 1995*

[54] *Lawrence F. Struggle for the Gulf Borderlands : The Creek War and the Battle of New Orleans, 1812-1815. University Of Alabama Press; 2000*

[55] Lee, Daniel, and Joseph H Frost. *Ten Years in Oregon*. Salem, Or, Commission On Archives And History, Oregon-Idaho Conference, United Methodist Church, 1994

[56] Lee, Lucy, Morton. *Register of the Kentucky Historical Society*, Vol. I, No. 3. History of the Lee Family of Kentucky. September 1903

[57] *LeSueur, Stephen C. "Missouri's Failed Compromise: The Creation of Caldwell County for the Mormons." Journal of Mormon History; Published By: University of Illinois Press, vol. Vol. 31, no. 2 (Fall 2005), [pp. 113-144]*

[58] *Linn, E A, and Nathan Sargent. The Life and Public Services of Dr. Lewis F. Linn. Charleston, S.C., Bibliobazaar, 1857*

[59] *Mary Martin vs. David Martin for Separate Maintenance. 1823-1857 Mins. Edgefield Court of Equity, Microfilm #'s110 & 112, SC Dept. of History and Archives, Columbia, SC (Docs #29 & 30)*

[60] *The Mason County Genealogical Society. Historical Sketch of Dover, Newsletter. Vol. IX, No. 4.; 1991*

[61] McKenna B, McKenna T. *War of 1812*. Multicom Entertainment Group. Television Broadcast 1999.

[62] *National Historical Company. History of Randolph and Macon Counties, Missouri : Written and Compiled from the Most Authentic Official and Private Sources, Including a History of Their Townships, Towns and Villages. [p.199] Salem, Mass., Higginson Book Co., 1884*

[63] *Ohio Genealogical Society, Jackson County Chapter. Jackson County, Ohio : History Nd Families, 175th Anniversary, 1816-1991. Paducah, Ky. (P.O. Box 3101, Paducah 42002-3101) : Turner Pub. Co., 1991*

[64] *Oregon Native Son and Historical Magazine, Vol I, Oregon Pioneer Association, Indian War Veterans and Historical Society.*

Oregon Native Son. Editorial: Portland, Or.; Native Son Pub. Co., Approximately 1899

[65] *Park, Alice Crandall, Voss, Avis Park. Park/e/s and Bunch on the Trail West: With Allied Families: Benton, Duvall, Foster, Greenwell, Jones, Loveless and Tally. Baltimore: Gateway Press; Washington, D.C.: 1982*

[66] *Parkman, Francis Jr., Rosenthal, B..The Oregon Trail. Oxford England; New York: Oxford University Press; 2008*

[67] *Philip Alexander Bruce, Lyon Gardiner Tyler, Morton RL, American Historical Society. History of Virginia. Chicago, New York, American Historical Society; 1924*

[68] Richards, Leonard L. (2007). *The California Gold Rush and the Coming of the Civil War*. New York: Vintage Books Random House Inc. ISBN 978-0-307-27757-2

[69] *Roberts, David. A Newer World : Kit Carson, John C. Frémont, and the Claiming of the American West. Editorial: New York, Simon & Schuster, 2001*

[70] *Rushford, Jerry. Christians on the Oregon Trail: Churches of Christ and Christian Churches in Early Oregon 1842-1882. Editorial: Eugene, Or.; Wipf &I Stock. 2008. ISBN 1-892435-10-1. [p.8][p.19][pp.20-21]*

[71] *Schwartz EA. "The Rogue River Indian War and Its Aftermath, 1850-1980." Norman, Okla. University Of Oklahoma Press; 2010*

[72] *Solomon K. A History of Knox County, Kentucky. Daniel Boone Festival; 1976 [p.294]*

[73] *Taylor, John, and Mark H Taylor. "Witness to the Martyrdom : John Taylor's Personal Account of the Last Days of the Prophet Joseph Smith." Salt Lake City, Utah, Deseret Book, 2017. p.236*

[74] *Thwaites, R. Gold. (190407). Early western travels, 1748-1846: a series of annotated reprints of some of the best and rarest contemporary volumes of travel, descriptive of the aborigines and*

social and economic conditions in the middle and far West, during the period of early American settlement. Cleveland, O.: The A. H. Clark company

[75] *Tomlins, Christopher L, and American Bar Foundation. Reconsidering Indentured Servitude : European Migration and the Early American Labor Force, 1600-1775. Chicago, Ill., American Bar Foundation, 1999*

[76] *Unruh, John David (1993). The Plains Across: The Overland Emigrants and the Trans-Mississippi West, 1840–60. University of Illinois Press*

[77] *Van Ravenswaay, Charles and O'connor, C. St. Louis : An Informal History of the City and Its People, 1764-1865. St. Louis, Mo., Missouri Historical Society Press, 1991[p.268]*

[78] *William. Genealogies of Virginia Families Vol 1. Baltimore, Md Clearfield, In.; 1982*

[79] *Zebulon Montgomery Pike, Coues E. The Expeditions of Zebulon Montgomery Pike : To Headwaters of the Mississippi River, through Louisiana Territory, and in New Spain, during the Years 1805-6-7. Vol I, II and III. F.P. Harper; 1895*

WEB RESOURCES

[80] *The Alamo. "Battle and Revolution." Www.thealamo.org, Alamo Trust, Inc., 2021,* Battle and Revolution | The Alamo *Accessed 26 Feb. 2021*

[81] *Albert, Carl, et al. "The Children of Joseph and Martha " Nancy" Fox Chaffin: 1. Benjamin Franklin Chaffin (B." Jackson Historical Society, 1812. [pp.94,95]The Story of Joseph Chaffin, PDF. "[PDF* Story€of€Joseph€Chaffin*", Jun. 1966. Accessed 17 Oct. 2020*

[82] *"Ambrose&Rachel(Black)Cobb." Cobbsasser.com, Cobb-Sasser Family Lineage Website" Page,* Ambrose&Rachel(Black)Cobb - Cobb-Sasser. *Accessed 26 Feb. 2021*

[83] *American Genealogical-Biographical Index, Www.ancestry.com, Ancestry.com Operations Inc., Provo, UT, USA, 1999. Henry Fox 1766-1819, American Genealogical-Biographical Index (AGBI) - Ancestry.com Accessed 13 Apr. 2021*

[84] *Ancestry.com. "Biographical Sketches of the Bench and Bar of South Carolina." Www.ancestry.com. Ancestry.com Operations, Provo, UT, 2005.* Biographical sketches of the bench and bar of South Carolina – Ancestry.com. *Accessed 25 May 2021*

[85] *Ancestry.com. "Chariton County, Missouri, Marriage Records, 1821-1852." 2004. Ancestry.Com Operations, Inc. Provo, UT. W*ww.ancestry.com. *Chariton County, Missouri, Marriage Index, 1821-1852 - Ancestry.com George W Bunch & Narcissa Moxley. Accessed 1 Nov. 2020*

[86] *Ancestry.com. "DNA Insights for James R Fox, Jr." Www.ancestry.com. AncestryDNA® Insights Accessed 7 Oct 2020*

Ancestry.com. "1810 United States Federal Census." [Online Database] *Www.ancestry.com*, Ancestry.com Operations Inc., Provo, UT, USA. 2010.

[87] Benjamin K. Fox 1772-1842, *1810 United States Federal Census – Ancestry.com*. Accessed 18 Oct. 2020. pp.127

[88] *Henry Fox 1766-abt.1818. 1810 United States Federal Census – Ancestry.com. Accessed 18 Oct. 2020*

[89] Ancestry.com. "1820 United States Federal Census." [Online Database] Www.ancestry.com, Ancestry.com Operations Inc., Provo, UT, USA.2010. Benjamin K. Fox 1772-1842, 1820 United States Federal Census - Ancestry.com Accessed 10 Apr. 2021

[90] Ancestry.com. "1830 United States Federal Census." [Online Database] *Www.ancestry.com*, Ancestry.com Operations Inc., Provo, UT, USA. 2010. Benjamin K Fox 1872-1842, *1830 United States Federal Census - Ancestry.com* Accessed 4 Mar. 2021

[91] *Ancestry.com. "1840 United States Federal Census." [Online Database] Www.ancestry.com, Ancestry.com Operations Inc., Provo, UT, USA. 2010. Nicholas Fox 1796-Bef.1850, 1840 United States Federal Census - Ancestry.com Accessed 3 Nov. 2020*

Ancestry.com. "1850 United States Federal Census." [Online Database] *Www.ancestry.com*, Ancestry.com Operations Inc., Provo, UT, USA. 2009.

[92] Ann Fox-Mendenhall 1829-Aft.1884, *1850 United States Federal Census - Ancestry.com* Accessed 24 Oct. 2020

[93] Ephraim Fox 1822-1899, *1850 United States Federal Census - Ancestry.com* Accessed 3 Mar. 2021

[94] Henry W Fox 1766-1819, Henry W Fox - Find A Grave Memorial, Accessed 3 Mar. 2021

[95] *Henry Fox 1819-1894,* 1850 United States Federal Census – Ancestry.com. *Accessed 12 Apr. 2021*

[96] James Washington Bunch 1828-Bef.1900, *1850 United States Federal Census - Ancestry.com* Accessed 24 Oct. 2020

[97] Mary Sara Hammack-Fox 1796-1852, *1850 United States Federal Census - Ancestry.com* Accessed 24 Oct. 2020

[98] Richard O Fox 1817-unknown, 1850 United States Federal Census - Ancestry.com Accessed 12 Apr. 2021

[99] Sarah Ann Fox-Dennis 1811-1860, 1850 United States Federal Census - Ancestry.com Accessed 19 Oct. 2020

[100] Stokely Bunch 1797-1868, *1850 United States Federal Census - Ancestry.com* Accessed 15 Oct. 2020

[101] Susan Fox-Moore 1815-1870, 1850 United States Federal Census - Ancestry.com Accessed 2 Nov. 2020

[102] *Ancestry.com. "1870 United States Federal Census." [Online Database] Www.ancestry.com, Ancestry.com Operations Inc., Provo, UT, USA. 2009. Charles Nicholas Fox 1842-1913, 1870 United States Federal Census – Ancestry.com. Accessed 5 Mar. 2021*

[103] *Ancestry.com. "Extract from the Will of John Bacon." Www.ancestry.com. Administrators and Guardians Bonds Division of Estates, Etc., 1777 to 1830.* Richmond County, Georgia. Georgia D. A. R. [p.72]. Posted by Lynn Ware Spratling, 18 Feb. 2013. John Bacon Will Extract (ancestry.com). Accessed 7 May 2021

[104] *Ancestry.com. Forks of Elkhorn Church [database on-line]. Provo, UT, USA: Ancestry.com Operations Inc, 2006. Original data: Darnell, Ermina Jett. Forks of Elkhorn Church. Baltimore, MD, USA: Genealogical Publishing Co., 2002* Forks of Elkhorn Church - Ancestry. *Accessed 8 Feb. 2021*

[105] *Ancestry.com. "Kentucky, Death Records, 1852-1963." [database on-line] Www.ancestry.com. Ancestry.com Operations Inc, Provo, UT, 2007. Henry Franklin Martin. Accessed 15 Oct. 2020*

[106] *Ancestry.com. "Kentucky, County Marriage Records, 1783-1965." [database on-line] Www.ancestry.com. Ancestry.com Operations Inc, 2016. Henry Fox & Sarah Parke, Kentucky, U.S., County Marriage Records, 1783-1965 - Ancestry.com Accessed 17 Oct. 2020*

[107] *Ancestry.com. "Kentucky Soldiers of the War of 1812." [database on-line] Www.ancestry.com, Ancestry.com Operations Inc. Arthur Fox Abt.1793-1855, Ancestry.com - Kentucky Soldiers of the War of 1812 Accessed 20 Oct. 2020*

Ancestry.com. Dodd J. "Kentucky Marriages, 1802-1850". 1997. *[database on-line]. Www.ancestry.com.* Ancestry.com Operations, Inc. 2016.

[108] Kentucky, U.S., Compiled Marriages, 1802-1850 - Ancestry.com – Spencer Norvell & Keziah Moore. *Accessed 28 Feb. 2021*

[109] *Kentucky, U.S., Compiled Marriages, 1802-1850 - Ancestry.com -Arthur Fox & Lucretia Taylor. Accessed 28 Feb. 2021*

[110] *Kentucky, U.S., Compiled Marriages, 1802-1850 – Ancestry.com – George Bunch & Nancy Maupin. Accessed 28 Feb. 2021*

[111] *Kentucky, U.S., Compiled Marriages, 1802-1850 – Ancestry.com – Henry Lee & Mary Young-Fox. Accessed 28 Feb. 2021*

[112] *Ancestry.com. "Kentucky, U.S., Soldiers of the War of 1812" [George Bunch 1794-1849] [database on-line] Www.ancestry.com, Ancestry.com Operations Inc, 2002. Ancestry.com - Kentucky, U.S., Soldiers of the War of 1812 Accessed 19 Oct. 2020*

[113] *Ancestry.com. "Madison County Kentucky, Marriage Index 1786-1844." [Database Online]. Ancestry.com Operations, Inc., Provo, UT. Dentian Bunch & Isham Boling, Madison County, Kentucky, Marriage Index, 1786-1844 - Ancestry.com Accessed 19 Mar. 2021*

[114] *Ancestry.com. "Mecklenburg, Virginia, Marriages Index, 1765-1810" [Sally Fox & Thomas Norvell] [database on-line]. Www.ancestry.com, Ancestry.com Operations, Inc., 1999,*

Mecklenburg, Virginia, Marriages Index, 1765-1810 - Ancestry.com Accessed 28 Feb. 2021

Ancestry.com. Heritage Consulting. *Millennium File* [database on-line]. Ancestry.com Operations Inc, 2003. Accessed Oct. 14, 2020.

[115] Bunch, George 1794-1849, Millennium File – Ancestry.com

[116] Bunch, James 1750-1820, Millennium File – Ancestry.com

[117] Fox, Nicholas 1796-Aft.1845, Millennium File – Ancestry.com

[118] *Fox, Phoebe 1826-1913, Millennium File – Ancestry.com*

[119] Ancestry.com. "Missouri Marriage Records, 1805-2002." [Ephraim Fox & Frances Louisa (Lucy) Wells] [Database Online] *Www.ancestry.com*, Ancestry.com Operations, Inc., 2007, *Ancestry.com - Missouri, U.S., Marriage Records, 1805-2002* Accessed 6 Nov. 2020

Ancestry.com. "1900 United States Federal Census." [Online Database] *Www.ancestry.com*, Ancestry.com Operations Inc., Provo, UT, USA. 2004.

[120] Charles Nicholas Fox 1842-1917, 1900 United States Federal Census - Ancestry.com Accessed 4 Mar. 2021

[121] William J Fox, 1840-1917, 1900 United States Federal Census - Ancestry.com Accessed 3 Nov. 2020

[122] Ancestry.com. "North America, Family Histories, 1500-2000 :Book Title: Peabody Genealogy" [database on-line] [Joseph Chaffin & Nancy Norvell Fox] *Www.ancestry.com*, Ancestry.com Operations, Inc., 2016. North America, Family Histories, 1500-2000 – Ancestry.com. Accessed 12 Feb. 2021

[123] Ancestry.com. "North Carolina, Marriage Records, 1741-2011." [database on-line]. *Www.ancestry.com*, Ancestry.com Operations, 2015. *North Carolina, U.S., Marriage Records, 1741-2011 - Ancestry.com* Cader Powell. Accessed 18 Oct 2020

Ancestry.com. "Oregon, Biographical and Other Index Card File, 1700s-1900s." [database on-line] *Www.ancestry.com*, Ancestry.com Operations, Inc., 2014.

[124] Elizabeth Ann Findley, Oregon, Biographical and Other Index Card File, 1700s-1900s – Ancestry.com. Accessed 23 Oct. 2020

[125] Ephraim Fox, Oregon, Biographical and Other Index Card File, 1700s-1900s - Ancestry.com Accessed 23 Oct. 2020

[126] John William Wells, Oregon, Biographical and Other Index Card File, 1700s-1900s - Ancestry.com Accessed 23 Oct, 2020

Ancestry.com. "*Oregon, U.S., Early Oregonians Index, 1800-1860." [database on-line]. Www.ancestry.com*, Ancestry.com Operations, Inc., 2014.

[127] Andrew Jackson Fox, 1844-1907, Oregon, U.S., Early Oregonians Index, 1800-1860 - Ancestry.com Accessed 13 Oct 2020

[128] Benjamin J Hardman, 1787-1864, Oregon, U.S., Early Oregonians Index, 1800-1860 – Ancestry.com. Accessed 13 Oct 2020

[129] Frances Louisa (Turner) Wells-Fox, 1827-Bef. Sep 1870, Oregon, U.S., Early Oregonians Index, 1800-1860 - Ancestry.com Accessed 13 Oct 2020

[130] William David Pugh 1790-1846, Oregon, U.S., Early Oregonians Index, 1800-1860 - Ancestry.com Accessed 13 Oct 2020

[131] William Henry Hawk, 1824-1901, Oregon, U.S., Early Oregonians Index, 1800-1860 - Ancestry.com Accessed 13 Oct 2020

[132] Ancestry.com and Smith. "The Coneto Creek Taylors." *Www.ancestry.com*, Ancestry.com Operations. 2021. The Coneto Creek Taylors | Ancestry® 2004. Accessed 15 Oct 2020 [p.44]

[133] Ancestry.com. South Carolina Manumission Attempts by David Martin. *Www.ancestry.com*. Attempts to manumit Lucy, Eliza, and Martha from enslavement (ancestry.com). Posted by Nora Brashear, 24 Oct. 2020. Accessed 3 Nov. 2020

[134] Ancestry.com. "Tennessee, Early Land Registers, 1778-1927." *Ancestry.Com*, database on-line]. Lehi, UT, USA: Ancestry.com Operations, Inc., 2016, www.ancestry.com. Accessed 3 Nov. 2020. Tennessee State Library and Archives; Nashville, Tennessee; Series Number: 06; Series Title: Adjudication. [Benjamin K Fox]. Tennessee, U.S., Early Land Registers, 1778-1927 – Ancestry.com

[135] *Ancestry.com. "U.S. Census Reconstructed Records, 1660-1820" Www.ancestry.com, Ancestry.com Operations, Inc. Territorial Papers of the US*; Volume Number: *Vol 4*; Page Number: *459*; Family Number: *9 [John Bunch 1752-1828].* [database on-line] 2011. U.S., Census Reconstructed Records, 1660-1820 - Ancestry.com

[136] Ancestry.com. "U.S., Encyclopedia of American Quaker Genealogy, Vol I–VI, 1607-1943." *Www.ancestry.com*, Ancestry.com Operations, Inc., Provo, UT, USA, 2013, U.S., Encyclopedia of American Quaker Genealogy, Vol I–VI, 1607-1943 - Ancestry.com Accessed 12 Oct. 2020

[137] Ancestry.com. "U.S. General Land Office Records, 1796-1907." Www.ancestry.com. Ancestry.com Operations Inc, [Database on-line]. Provo, UT, USA, 2007, [David Anderson Bunch] U.S., General Land Office Records, 1776-2015 – Ancestry.com. Accessed 8 Mar 2021

[138] Ancestry.com. "U.S. General Land Office Records, 1796-1907." *Www.ancestry.com*, Ancestry.com Operations Inc, Database Online, Provo, UT, USA: 2008, [Nicholas Fox] U.S., General Land Office Records, 1776-2015 – Ancestry.com

Ancestry.com. Yates Publishing. *U.S. and International Marriage Records, 1560-1900.* [database on-line]. Provo, UT, USA: Ancestry.com Operations Inc, 2004.

[139] Richard Fox/Mary Blanton. U.S. and International Marriage Records, 1560-1900 – Ancestry.com. Accessed 9 Mar. 2021

[140] *Mary Fox-Jones & Samuel Jones. U.S. and International Marriage Records, 1560-1900 – Ancestry.com. Accessed 12 Oct. 2020*

[141] *Elizabeth Moore & James Hammack. U.S. and International Marriage Records, 1560-1900 – Ancestry.com. Accessed 27 Oct. 2020*

[142] Ancestry.com. "U.S., Quaker Meeting Records, 1681-1935." *Www.ancestry.com*, Ancestry.com Operations, Inc., Provo, UT, USA, 2014, U.S., Quaker Meeting Records, 1681-1935 – Ancestry.com. Accessed 15 Oct. 2020

[143] Ancestry.com. "U.S., Quaker Meeting Records, 1681-1935." *Www.ancestry.com*. Ancestry.com Operations, Inc., 2014, U.S., Quaker Meeting Records, 1681-1935 – Ancestry.com. Accessed 15 Oct. 2020

[144] *Ancestry.com. "Virginia, Compiled Marriages, 1660-1800." [Charles Bunch & Mary Bellamy] Www.ancestry.com, [Database Online] Ancestry.com Operations Inc., 1997 Virginia, U.S., Compiled Marriages, 1660-1800 - Ancestry.com Accessed 15 Oct. 2020*

[145] *Ancestry.com. "Virginia, Select Marriages, 1785-1940." [Benjamin Fox & Elizabeth Anderson] [Database Online] Www.ancestry.com, Ancestry.com. Operations Inc., Provo, UT, USA, 2014, Virginia, U.S., Select Marriages, 1785-1940 - Ancestry.com Accessed 16 Oct. 2020*

Ancestry.com, West, Edmund, comp. *Family Data Collection – Individual Records*. [database online] Provo, UT, USA: Ancestry.com Operations Inc, 2000.

[146] James Bunch *1750-1820.* Family Data Collection - Individual Records – Ancestry.com

[147] *Mary Kendrick-Fox 1738-1795. Family Data Collection - Individual Records - Ancestry.com*

[148] *Phoebe Fox-Bunch-Anderson.* *Family Data Collection - Individual Records - Ancestry.com* *Accessed 5 Nov. 2020*

[149] *Ancestry.com. "The Wilderness Road to Kentucky: it's location and features." [database online]. Provo, UT, Ancestry.com Operations Inc., 2005. Original by Pusey, William Allen, New York: G.H. Doran, c1921.* *Ancestry.com - The Wilderness Road to Kentucky : its location and features* *Accessed 9 Mar. 2020*

[150] *Andrew Jackson's Hermitage. "Candidacy | Andrew Jackson's Presidential Campaign." The Hermitage, Andrew Jackson Foundation, 2014,* *Candidacy | Andrew Jackson's Presidential Campaign (thehermitage.com)* *Accessed 24 Oct 2020*

[151] *Astoria Oregon.com. "Astoria Oregon." Www.astoriaoregon.com, Astoria Chamber of Commerce,* Astoria Oregon. *Accessed 19 Oct 2020*

[152] Barbour, Barton. "Ewing Young (C. 1796–1841)." *Www.oregonencyclopedia.org*, Portland State University and the Oregon Historical Society, 22 Feb. 2021, "Ewing Young (c. 1796-1841) - The Oregon Encyclopedia Accessed 26 Feb. 2021

[153] Bassett, Karen, et al. "Ewing Young's Cattle Drive Route." *Archive.is*, Oregon Trails Coordinating Council, 1 Sept. 2006, Ewing Young's Cattle Drive Route (archive.is) Accessed 26 Feb. 2021

[154] *"Battle of Tippecanoe, the Forgotten War to Save the Republic. The War of 1812." theuswarof1812.org. US War of 1812.org,* The War of 1812 - (Battle of Tippecanoe) (theuswarof1812.org). *Accessed 20 Oct. 2020*

[155] *Bene, Terry A. Del. "Deadly Flood of 1844." True West Magazine, True West Magazine, 31 Mar. 2016,* Deadly Flood of 1844 - True West Magazine *Accessed 26 Feb. 2021*

[156] *Bigler, David L. "Utah History Encyclopedia." Www.uen.org, Utah Education Network, 1994,* "Utah History Encyclopedia" *Accessed 26 Feb. 2021*

[157] *Blanton-Wilcox, Jenelle. "American Revolution 1775." Blanton Family War Veterans, 2013, American Revolution 1775 - Blanton Family War Veterans (webs.com) Accessed 26 Feb. 2021*

[158] *Blodgett, Ralph. "Adams-Onís Treaty | the Encyclopedia of Oklahoma History and Culture." Www.okhistory.org.* Adams-Onís Treaty | The Encyclopedia of Oklahoma History and Culture (okhistory.org). *Accessed 26 Feb. 2021*

[159] *Bockstruck, Lloyd DeWitt, comp.. "Land Grants."* www.carothers-carruthers.com, *2007,* Land Grants (carothers-carruthers.com). *Accessed 13 Oct 2020*

[160] *Brant I. James. "James Madison – Madison's Presidency" Encyclopædia Britannica. 24 Jun 2020.* James Madison - Madison's presidency | Britannica *Accessed 20 Oct 2020*

[161] Bryant, Ron D. "The History of the Battle of Blue Licks." *Www.battleofbluelicks.org*, battleofbluelicks.org, 2019, History. Accessed 26 Feb. 2021

[162] *Buckley Jay H. "Lewis and Clark Expedition" Encyclopædia Britannica, 22 Oct. 2020,* Lewis and Clark Expedition - Pacific Ocean and return *Accessed 26 Feb 2021*

[163] *Bushman, Richard L.. "Joseph Smith". Encyclopædia Britannica, 19 Dec. 2020, Joseph Smith | Biography & Facts | Britannica Accessed 25 Oct. 2020*

[164] *Butler, Nic. "Private Manumission: An Intimate Path to Freedom." Charleston County Public Library, 21 Feb. 2020, Private Manumission: An Intimate Path to Freedom | Charleston County Public Library (ccpl.org). Accessed 7 June 2021*

[165] Carol. "Early Settlements & Surnames of Tennessee 1756-1780." *piedmonttrails.com,* Piedmont Trails, 30 Jan. 2020, Early Settlements & Surnames of Tennessee 1756-1780 – Piedmont Trails. Accessed 23 Feb. 2021

[166] *Carson, Phil. "Among the Eternal Snows | History Colorado." Www.historycolorado.org, HistoryColorado.org, 3 Sep. 2020,"* Among the Eternal Snows | History Colorado *Accessed 19 Oct. 2020*

[167] Center for the Study of the Pacific Northwest. "Return to Lesson Eight: Settlement of the Oregon Boundary Question, 1818-1846". *Washington.edu*. 2020. "Return to Lesson Eight: Accessed 23 Oct 2020

[168] *Chaffin, William Ladd, "History of Robert Chaffin and his descendants: and of the other Chaffins in America", Appendix D. New York: Frederick H. Hitchcock, 1913. Ancestry.com Operations Inc, Provo, UT. 2005.* History of Robert Chaffin and his descendants ... - Ancestry.com *Accessed 14 Oct. 2020*

[169] Chakra, Hayden. "British Colonization of the United States of America – About History". 7 May 2018. British Colonization Of The United States Of America - About History. Accessed 22 Feb. 2021

[170] Chandler, Linda L. 'The List of Virginia Company of London Members'. *Www.oocities.org*, 1999, The list of "Virginia Company of London" members Accessed 8 Oct. 2020

[171] Chapman, John Abney, and The Library of Congress. *History of Edgefield County from the Earliest Settlement to 1897. Internet Archive*, Newberry, S.C., E. H. Aull, 1897, History of Edgefield County from the earliest settlement to 1897 : Chapman, John Abney, 1821-1906. [from old catalog] : Free Download, Borrow, and Streaming : Internet Archive. archive.org/details/historyofedgefie00chap. Accessed 11 May 2021

[172] "Cherokee Treaty. Manuscript/Mixed Material" July 8, 1817". *Library of Congress, Wash, D.C. 20540 USA*. Library of Congress. Source Collection: Andrew Jackson papers, 1775-1874 Accessed 23 Oct. 2020. Cherokee Treaty , July 8, 1817 | Library of Congress (loc.gov)

[173] ChristianLight.com Editors. "The Germans Come To North America". *www.anabaptists.org*. The Germans Come to North America - Anabaptists. Accessed 9 Oct 2020

[174] The Church of Christ of Latter Day Saints. "Chapter Sixteen: Missouri Persecutions and Expulsion." *Www.churchofjesuschrist.org*, 2018, Chapter Sixteen: Missouri Persecutions and Expulsion. Siege of DeWitt, Siege of Far West". 2018. *Www.Churchofjesuschrist.Org*. Accessed 31 Oct. 2020 [Siege of Far West]

[175] *The Church of Jesus Christ of Latter Day Saints. "Doctrine and Covenants – Church of Jesus Christ".", www.Churchofjesuschrist.Org.* Doctrine and Covenants - Church of Jesus Christ, *Accessed 25 Oct. 2020 [section 52, verse 9e]*

[176] "Cobb Name Meaning, Family History, Family Crest & Coats of Arms." *HouseOfNames*, Cobb Name Meaning, Family History, Family Crest & Coats of. Accessed 26 Feb. 2021

[177] "Cobb Pages Link Table." *Cobbsasser.com*, Cobb-Sasser Family Lineage Website Page, Cobb-Sasser Family Lineage Ambrose b1760, Samuel b1794, John Cobb b1822. Accessed 26 Feb. 2021

[178] "COBB Y-Chromosome DNA Surname Project." *familytreedna.com*. FamilyTreeDNA - COBB Y-Chromosome DNA Surname Project Accessed 7 Oct. 2020

[179] *Collins, Cameron. "The Indian Delegation of 1831." Distilled History, 14 Oct. 2015,* The Indian Delegation of 1831 – Distilled History *Accessed 26 Feb. 2021*

[180] *Combined History of Shelby and Moultrie Counties, Illinois. Edenmartin.com.* The History of Shelby and Moultrie Counties, Illinois. *Accessed 18 Nov. 2020*

[181] Curran, Arthur Fox. "The Story of a Kentucky Town-Dover, Mason County." *The Courier-Journal*, 24 Aug. 1902, p.26, The Story of a Kentucky Town-Dover, Mason County - Newspapers.com Accessed 14 Oct. 2020

[182] Dailey, Charles. "Pioneer History in Oregon: Wild Growth." *Www.ncbible.org*, 4 Feb. 2006, Pioneer History in Oregon: Wild Growth. Accessed 8 Nov 2020

[183] *Davis, Wm L. "Biography – de SMET, PIERRE-JEAN – Volume X (1871-1880) – Dictionary of Canadian Biography." Www.biographi.ca, University of Toronto, 1972, Biography – DE SMET, PIERRE-JEAN – Volume X (1871-1880) – Dictionary of Canadian Biography (biographi.ca) Accessed 27 Feb. 2021*

[184] *Dykeman, Wilma, and Wilford Allen Bladen. "Kentucky | History - Geography." Encyclopædia Britannica, 24 Jan. 2019,* Kentucky | History, Capital, Map, Population, & Facts | Britannica *Accessed 26 Feb. 2021*

[185] *Eddins, Ned. Robert "Stewart Pacific Fur Company and South Pass". © 2021 The Fur Trade, furtrader.com.* Robert Stuart | American Western Expansion. *Accessed 19 Oct. 2020*

[186] Encyclopædia Britannica, Editors, "Louisiana Purchase | Definition, Date, Cost, History, Map." *Encyclopædia Britannica,* 2019. Louisiana Purchase | Definition, Date, Cost, History, Map Accessed 20 Oct. 2020

[187] *Encyclopædia Britannica, Editors, "Winfield Scott | United States General." Encyclopædia Britannica, 9 Jun. 2020.* Winfield Scott | United States general | Britannica. *Accessed 20 Oct. 2020*

[188] *Eschner, Kat. "The True Story of the Short-Lived State of Franklin". 23 Aug. 2017. Smithsonian Magazine. The True Story of the Short-Lived State of Franklin | Smart News | Smithsonian Magazine Accessed 13 Oct. 2020*

[189] FamilyTreeDNA is a division of Gene by Gene, a commercial genetic testing company based in Houston, Texas. FamilyTreeDNA offers analysis of autosomal DNA, Y-DNA, and mitochondrial DNA to individuals for genealogical purpose. DNA Testing for Ancestry & Genealogy | FamilyTreeDNA Accessed 7 Oct. 2020

[190] "FamilyTreeDNA - Genetic Testing for Ancestry, Family History & Genealogy." *Www.familytreedna.com*, Pugh - Background | FamilyTreeDNA Accessed 11 Apr. 2021

[191] Ferguson Joe L. "Kentucky Counties: History and Information". www.ereferencedesk.com. Kentucky Counties: History and Information (ereferencedesk.com) Accessed 16 Oct. 2020

Find A Grave. Findagrave.com, 2021

[192] Bartlett Anderson Fox (1806-1878) - Find A Grave Memorial

[193] Benjamin K Fox (1772-1842) - Find A Grave Memorial

[194] David Bunch (1838-1907) - Find A Grave Memorial

[195] Edmund Bacon (1776-1826) - Find A Grave Memorial

[196] Ephrom M. Moore (1841-1919) - Find A Grave Memorial

[197] George W Bunch (1816-1867) - Find A Grave Memorial

[198] Jesse Moore (1834-1909) - Find A Grave Memorial

[199] John Kendrick Fox (1802-1878) - Find A Grave Memorial

[200] John Pugh Jr. (1779-1822) - Find A Grave Memorial

[201] Marinda Fox Watkins (1816-1888) - Find A Grave Memorial

[202] Martha Jane Pugh Tetherow (1849-1888) - Find A Grave Memorial

[203] Mary Elizabeth Findley Griffith (1805-1874) - Find A Grave Memorial

[204] Mrs Nancy Jane Wilkinson (1835-1917) - Find A Grave Memorial

[205] Nancy Norvell Fox Chaffin (1793-1859) - Find A Grave Memorial

[206] Nathaniel "Nat" Bunch (1805-1885) - Find A Grave Memorial

[207] Richard Leighton Ewell (1833-1917) - Find A Grave Memorial

[208] Stokely Bunch (1835-1910) - Find A Grave Memorial

[209] Theophilus Powell (1792-1861) - Find A Grave Memorial

[210] William Fox (1804-1875) - Find A Grave Memorial

[211] Flora, Stephanie. "Emigrants to Oregon in 1842" www.oregonpioneers.com, 2017. Oregon In 1842 (oregonpioneers.com) Accessed 4 Nov. 2020

[212] Flora, Stephanie. "Emigration to the Oregon Country In 1842." Www.oregonpioneers.com, 2004. 1842trip (oregonpioneers.com) Accessed 23 Nov. 2020

[213] Flora, Stephanie. "Emigrants to Oregon in 1843". www.oregonpioneers.com, 2017. Oregon Pioneers of 1843 Accessed 5 Nov. 2020

[214] Flora, Stephanie. "Whitman Massacre Preliminary Events." www.oregonpioneers.com, 2004, Whitman Massacre Preliminary Events (oregonpioneers.com) Accessed 4 Nov. 2020

[215] Fox, Joseph. "Fox Y-DNA Surname Project." *www.familytreeDNA.com*, 15 Dec. 2019. Fox Y-DNA Surname Project - Goals | FamilyTreeDNA Accessed 28 Sep. 2020

[216] Fox III, Joseph M. "Genetic Testing of a Paper Trail." 13 Aug. 2016. Journal of Genetic Genealogy. Fox: Genetic Testing of a Paper Trail (jogg.info). Accessed 26 Sep. 2020

[217] "Fox Last Name Origin." *www.surnamedb.com*, The Internet Surname Database. 1980, Surname Database: Fox Last Name Origin (surnamedb.com)

[218] From the Most Authentic Official and Private Sources. "History of Caldwell and Livingston Counties, Missouri." *Cdm16795.Contentdm.oclc.org*, Missouri Digital Heritage, Digitally published 2007., originally 1886, Title Page - MISSOURI STATE LIBRARY SPONSORED PROJECT - Missouri County Histories - Missouri Digital Heritage Hosted Collections (oclc.org). Accessed 28 Feb. 2021

[219] "The Frontier General (1812–1814) | The Historic New Orleans Collection". *www.hnoc.org*, The Frontier General (1812–1814) | The Historic New Orleans Collection (hnoc.org). Accessed 19 Oct. 2020

[220] Giesecke, E.W. "Winship Settlement." *Www.oregonencyclopedia.org*, 17 Mar. 2018, Winship Settlement - The Oregon Encyclopedia. Accessed 27 Feb. 2021

[221] Gigantino, Jim. "Land Lottery System." *New Georgia Encyclopedia*. 28 Sep. 2020. Land Lottery System | New Georgia Encyclopedia Accessed 25 Dec. 2020

[222] Graves, Dan. Infamous Indulgence Led to Reformation - 1501-1600 Church. *Christianity.com*. May 2007. Accessed 28 Sep. 2020

[223] Green, Jordan. "*How The Quest for The Book of Heaven Changed the West Forever. Stark & Main*, 16 May 2019, How The Quest for The Book of Heaven Changed the West Forever — Stark & Main (starkandmain.org). Accessed 25 Oct. 2020

[224] Greene, John P (1839). Facts Relative to the Expulsion of the Mormons or Latter Day Saints, from the State of Missouri, under the "Extermination Order". Cincinnati, Ohio: R. P. Brooks. OCLC 4968992. (pp. 8, 26). Accessed 31 Oct. 2020

[225] GSMD Webmaster. "Pilgrim History - The Mayflower Society." *Themayflowersociety.org*. 2012, Pilgrim History - The Mayflower Society. Accessed 8 Oct. 2020

[226] "A Guide to the Mecklenburg County (Va.) Will Books, 1782-1798. Mecklenburg County (Va.)" Reel 23, Local government records collection, Mecklenburg County Court Records. *www.lva.virginia.gov*, Virginia Heritage, The Library of Virginia, Richmond, Va. 23219. A Guide to the Mecklenburg County (Va.) Will Books, 1782-1798 Mecklenburg County (Va.) Will Books, 1782-1798 1146671-1146672 (virginia.edu). Accessed 25 Oct. 2020

[227] Haden K. "Some Descendants of Col Richard Fox." *Rootsweb.com*. 2013, First Generation - Ancestry® | Genealogy, Family Trees. Accessed 11 Oct. 2020

[228] Haining Kirsty M. "Hainings and Related Families". Cader POWELL *hainings.org.net*. 2018. Hainings and Related Families . Accessed 18 Oct. 2020

[229] *Harold Whitman Bradley. "Andrew Jackson | Facts, Biography, & Accomplishments." Encyclopædia Britannica, 12 Oct. 2018,* Andrew Jackson | Facts, Biography, & Accomplishments *Accessed 26 Feb. 2021*

[230] The Hermitage. "Orphan | Childhood & Early Life of Andrew Jackson." *The Hermitage*, 2014, Orphan | Childhood & Early Life of Andrew Jackson (thehermitage.com) Accessed 21 Oct. 2020

[231] Hickman, Kennedy. "A Signal Defeat: Siege of Detroit". *ThoughtCo.com.* 3 Sep. 2019. Accessed 19 Oct. 2020. Siege of Detroit in the War of 1812 - ThoughtCo

[232] *History.com Editors. "Benedict Arnold." HISTORY.com, 21 Aug. 2018, Benedict Arnold – HISTORY Accessed 22 Feb 2021*

[233] History.com Editors. "Continental Congress." *HISTORY.com*, 13 Sept. 2019, Continental Congress – HISTORY Accessed 26 Feb. 2021

[234] History.com Editors. "George Washington" *HISTORY.com*, 29 Aug. 2018, George Washington: Facts, Revolution & Presidency – HISTORY Accessed 23 Feb. 2021

[235] History.com Editors. "King Philip's War". *HISTORY.com,* 7 Jun. 2019, King Philip's War - Definition, Cause & Significance – HISTORY Accessed 9 Oct. 2020

[236] History.com Editors. "Quakers". *HISTORY.com*, 6 Sep. 2019, Quakers - Definition, History & Beliefs – HISTORY. Accessed 8 Oct. 2020

[237] History.com Editors. "Revolutionary War." *HISTORY.com*, 11 Sep. 2018, Revolutionary War - Timeline, Facts & Battles – HISTORY. Accessed 22 Feb. 2021

[238] History.com Editors. "A Thousand Pioneers Head West as Part of the Great Emigration". *HISTORY.com*, 6 Jul. 2020, Great Emigration Heads West – HISTORY. Accessed 8 Nov. 2020

[239] Hokanson D. "Re: BEAN STATION, TN." *www.genealogy.com.* 18 Aug. 2000, Re: BEAN STATION, TN. - Genealogy.com. Accessed 15 Oct. 2020

[240] "Indian Removal Timeline." *Uh.edu*, Digital History, 2019, Digital History (uh.edu) Accessed 24 Oct 2020

[241] Indians in the Colonial Wars and the American Revolution | *Encyclopedia.com*. 24 Oct 2020. Accessed 11 Oct 2020

[242] Jeffers, Joshua J. "Christopher Gist." *George Washington's Mount Vernon*, Mount Vernon Ladies' Association, 2021, Christopher Gist · George Washington's Mount Vernon. Accessed 27 Feb. 2021

[243] Jewett, Thomas. "James Wilkinson: America's Greatest Scoundrel." *www.varsitytutors.com*, 2020. James Wilkinson: America's Greatest Scoundrel". Accessed 21 Oct. 2020

[244] "The John Punch Court Decisions and the Advent of Slavery in Virginia." *www.americanevolution2019.com*, PDF-The-John-

Punch-Court-Decisions-and-the-Advent-of-Slavery-in-Virginia-Full-Lesson.pdf (americanevolution2019.com). Accessed 8 Oct. 2020

[245] "John Smith Quotes." *quotes.yourdictionary.com,* LoveToKnow, Corp., Quotes By John Smith (yourdictionary.com). Accessed 8 Oct. 2020

[246] Johnson, Mary Lu. "Jackson County, TN Court Records." *Tngenweb.Org*, Jackson County TNGen Web, Jackson County, TN Court Records (tngenweb.org). Accessed 3 Nov. 2020

[247] Johnston-Elkins, Vesta May (1892-1984). "History of the Wagon Train of 1845." *Www.ancestry.com*, Bef. 1984, History of the Wagon Train of 1845 (ancestry.com). Accessed 28 Feb. 2021

[248] Karst, *Kentucky Geological Survey*, University of Kentucky. *www.uky.edu*. 12 Mar 2020, Karst, Kentucky Geological Survey, University of Kentucky (uky.edu). Accessed 11 Oct 2020

[249] *Keeney, Ralph Ray. "Section 1 of Wagon Ruts West." Www.k-f-g-Online.info, 1983,* Section 1 of Wagon Ruts West (k-f-g-online.info). *Accessed 22 Feb. 2021*

[250] Kleen M. "Second Battle of Sackets Harbor." *michaelkleen.com*, 18 Nov. 2018, Second Battle of Sackets Harbor – M.A. Kleen (michaelkleen.com). Accessed 21 Oct 2020

[251] Knoll, USN (Ret.) Radm. DW. "Battle of Lake Erie: Building the Fleet in the Wilderness." *public1.nhhcaws.local*. 1979, Battle of Lake Erie: Building the Fleet in the Wilderness (navy.mil). Accessed 21 Oct 2020

[252] Kohnen, Patricia. "Oregon Trail Time Frame." *Oregonpioneers.Com*, OREGON TRAIL TIME FRAME (oregonpioneers.com). Accessed 2 Nov. 2020

[253] Lambert, Audrey J, and Bobby Fox. "Fox Family Cemetery." *http://www.ajlambert.com/*. 15 Feb. 1999, cmty_fox.pdf (ajlambert.com). Accessed 4 Nov. 2020

[254] Landry, Alyssa. "James Monroe: Pushed Tribes Off Land, But Boosted Indian Education." *IndianCountryToday.com*. 13 Sep. 2018, James Monroe: Pushed Tribes Off Land, But Boosted Indian Education - Indian Country Today. Accessed 24 Oct. 2020

[255] Lang, William L. "Petitions to Congress, 1838-1845." *Www.Oregonencyclopedia.Org*, Portland State University and the Oregon Historical Society, Aug. 2020, Petitions to Congress, 1838-1845 (oregonencyclopedia.org). Accessed 31 Oct. 2020

[256] *Legacy Report. "Ancestors of Bobbie Ann Howard." Freepages.rootsweb.com,* Legacy Report - Ancestry *Accessed 26 Feb. 2021*

[257] Light House Trails, author. "Native American Men Who Longed For 'the Book' and Were Denied." *www.lighthousetrailsresearch.com*, Lighthouse Trails Publishing, Inc., 2 Jun. 2019; Original by Egerton Ryerson Young, "Stories From Indian Wigwams and Northern Campfires" Written latter 1800's, Native American Men Who Longed For "the Book" and Were Denied - Lighthouse Trails Research Project. Accessed 26 Oct. 2020

[258] Mapes, Ginny. "Hillsboro Historical Society." *Hillsboro Historical Society*, Hillsboro Historical Society | … protect and preserve our historic properties and to educate and engage the public in appreciating the value of our heritage … (historichillsboro.org). Accessed 4 Nov. 2020

[259] "March 1, 1812 – Andrew Jackson's Call for Militia Volunteers | Tennessee State Militia." *The Tennessee State Militia*, March 1, 1812 – Andrew Jackson's Call for Militia Volunteers | Tennessee State Militia. Accessed 19 Oct. 2020

[260] Marshall, John. "Cherokee Nation v. State of Georgia John Marshall | 1831 | AMDOCS: Documents for the Study of American History." *Vlib.us*, 1995. AMDOCS: Documents for the Study of

American History, 1831, Cherokee Nation v. State of Georgia John Marshall | 1831. Accessed 26 Feb. 2021

[261] McNamara, R. "Surrender of Fort Detroit: Early Disaster for America in the War of 1812." *www.thoughtco.com,* 26 Jan. 2020. The Surrender of Fort Detroit In 1812 (thoughtco.com). Accessed 20 Oct. 2020

[262] "Meaning of Ephraim in the Bible." *Www.biblestudy.org*, Meaning of Ephraim in the Bible. *Accessed 23 Oct 2020. p.166*

[263] "Missouri Became the 24th State." *www.americaslibrary.gov*. Library of Congress. Missouri Became the 24th State (americaslibrary.gov) Accessed 23 Oct 2020

[264] Missouri Gazette and Public Advertiser. "American Enterprise." *www.newspapers.com*, 15 May 1813, p.1, 15 May 1813, 1 - Missouri Gazette and Public Advertiser at Newspapers.com Accessed 19 Oct 2020

[265] Missouri Gazette and Public Advertiser. "To Enterprising Young Men." *www.newspapers.com,* 13 Feb. 1822, p.2, 13 Feb 1822, 13 Feb 1822, 2 - Missouri Gazette and Public Advertiser at Newspapers.com. Accessed 23 Oct 2020

[266] Morris L.. "Astor Expedition (1810-1813)." *www.oregonencyclopedia.org*. Portland State University and the Oregon Historical Society. 17 Feb 2020, Astor Expedition (1810-1813) - The Oregon Encyclopedia. Accessed 19 Oct 2020

[267] "Mountain Men and the Fur Trade." *Www.xroads.virginia.edu*, Mountain Men and the Fur Trade (virginia.edu). Accessed 27 Oct. 2020

[268] Mulhern, David. "Sir John's Handwritten Note." *Medium.com*, 30 Nov. 2018, Sir John's Handwritten Note. This document was found in Sir John… | by David Mulhern | Sir John | Medium. Accessed 5 Nov. 2020

[269] Munford, Kenneth, and Charlotte L Wirfs. "The Ewing Young Trail (1981)." *Bentoncountymuseum.Org*, Benton County Historical Society, 2020, www.bentoncountymuseum.org/index.php/research/sites-of-interest/horner-museum-tour-guide-series/the-ewing-young-trail/. Accessed 30 Oct. 2020

[270] Nameberry.com. "*Ephraim: Name Meaning, Popularity, and Similar Names*." *nameberry.com*, Nameberry, LLC, 2014, Ephraim: Name Meaning, Popularity, and Similar Names | Nameberry. Accessed 23 Oct 2020

Nemec, Bethany. *historicoregoncity.org*, The End of the Oregon Trail Interpretive Center,

[271] "Ewing Young Route." 2 Apr. 2019, Ewing Young Route – End of the Oregon Trail (historicoregoncity.org). Accessed 26 Sep. 2020

[272] Newill, Cody. "The Bloody History Of Mormonism In Jackson County." *www.*kcur.org. Kansas City Public Radio, 2020, The Bloody History Of Mormonism In Jackson County | KCUR 89.3 - NPR in Kansas City. Local news, entertainment and podcasts. Accessed 25 Oct. 2020

[273] *New World Encyclopedia contributors. "Battles of Lexington and Concord - New World Encyclopedia." Www.newworldencyclopedia.org, 29 Dec 2020,* Battles of Lexington and Concord - New World Encyclopedia. *Accessed 22 Feb. 2021*

[274] Nicholson, Nancy. "Old Ignace and Friends Native American Witnesses to Our Holy Catholic Faith." Www.chcweb.com, Catholic Heritage Curricula, 2001, oldignace.pdf (chcweb.com)

[275] *Office of the House Historian, et al. "Biographical Directory of the U.S. Congress - Retro Member Details."* Biographical

Directory of the U.S. Congress - Retro Member *Accessed 26 Feb. 2021*

[276] Ohio History Central. "Ohio Company." *ohiohistorycentral.org*, Ohio Company - Ohio History Central. Accessed 10 Oct 2020

[277] Oldham, Kit. "Robert Newell and Joseph Meek Reach Fort Walla Walla with the First Wagons Driven Overland to the Columbia River in September 1840." *Www.Historylink.Org*, The Free Encyclopedia of Washington State History,18 Feb. 2003, Robert Newell and Joseph Meek reach Fort Walla Walla with the first wagons driven overland to the Columbia River in September 1840. - HistoryLink.org. Accessed 4 Nov. 2020

[278] "Oliver Hazard Perry." *Navy.mil*. Naval History and Heritage Command, 10 Sep. 2019, Oliver Hazard Perry (navy.mil). Accessed 21 Oct. 2020

[279] O'Neill A. "United States: child mortality rate 1800-2020." *www.statista.com*, Statista, 6 Sep. 2019, • United States: child mortality rate 1800-2020 | Statista. Accessed 22 Oct. 2020

[280] Our Family Genealogy Pages. "Maxcey Ewell b. Abt 1743, Virginia, d.Bef 1 Dec 1800, Albemarle, Virginia: Ewell Family Historical & Genealogical Association." *Ewellfamily.Org*, Maxcey Ewell b. Abt 1743 , Virginia, USA d. Bef 1 Dec 1800 , Albemarle, Virginia, USA: Ewell Family Historical & Genealogical Association. Accessed 28 Oct. 2020

[281] Parkin, Max H. "Missouri Conflict - The Encyclopedia of Mormonism." *Eom.Byu.Edu*, The Encyclopedia of Mormonism, 1992, Missouri Conflict - The Encyclopedia of Mormonism. Accessed 27 Oct. 2020

[282] Partridge D. "Lands of the Delaware Indians – Kansas Genealogy." *kansasgenealogy.com*, Missouri Digital Heritage. 2020.

Lands of the Delaware Indians – Kansas Genealogy. Accessed 24 Oct 2020

[283] "Paul Revere - The Midnight Ride." *paulreverehouse.org*, Paul Revere House. 2016. Paul Revere - The Midnight Ride (paulreverehouse.org). Accessed 11 Oct. 2020

[284] "Pennsylvania Mutiny of 1783." *enacademic.com*, Academic Dictionaries and Encyclopedias. 2010. Pennsylvania Mutiny of 1783 (enacademic.com). Accessed 12 Oct 2020

[285] Pettinato, Tony. "Missouri Governor Ordered Mormons Expelled – or Exterminated." *blog.genealogybank.com*, GenealogyBank.com, 27 Oct. 2020, Missouri Governor Ordered Mormons Expelled – or Exterminated (genealogybank.com). Accessed 2 Nov. 2020

[286] Phifer, Dolores. "Ambrose Cobb (Birth: 1729, York County, VA m Sarah Howell (Birth: 1734, Halifax." *www.genealogy.com,* Genealogy.com. Ambrose COBB (BIRTH: 1729, Yo – Genealogy.com. 24 Jan. 2004. Accessed 11 Oct. 2020

[287] Pitch, Anthony S. "The Burning of Washington." *WHHA (en-US)*. 2019. The Burning of Washington - White House Historical Association (whitehousehistory.org). Accessed 21 Oct. 2020

[288] *Public Archives of Canada, et al. "Documents Relating to the Invasion of Canada and the Surrender of Detroit, 1812." Internet Archive, Ottawa, Government Printing Bureau, 1912,* Documents Relating to the Invasion of Canada and the Surrender of Detroit, 1812 *Accessed 26 Feb. 2021*

[289] *"Queen Elizabeth Charter (1584)." explorationofamerica.weebly.com, Exploration and Colonization.* Queen Elizabeth Charter(1584) - Exploration and Colonization. *Accessed 27 Sep. 2020*

[290] *Rafferty JP. "New Madrid earthquakes of 1811–12 | United States | Britannica." Encyclopædia Britannica. Encyclopedia*

Britannica, Inc; 2019. New Madrid earthquakes of 1811–12 | United States | Britannica. *Accessed 19 Oct. 2020*

[291] *Random Acts of Genealogical Kindness. "Historical Facts of the State of Tennessee Counties Guide." raogk.org, 15 Dec 2014. Accessed 16 Oct. 2020.* Historical Facts of the State of Tennessee Counties Guide (raogk.org)

[292] *Reed, Paul C, et al. "Descent of the Bunch Family in Virginia and the Carolinas." www.ancestrycdn.com, Ancestry.com Operations, Inc., 15 Jul. 2012,* [PDF]DESCENT OF THE BUNCH FAMILY IN VIRGINIA AND THE *CAROLINAS. Accessed 15 Oct. 2020*

[293] Rice JD. Anglo-Powhatan War, Second (1622–1632). *Www.encyclopediavirginia.org*. Virginia Humanities, 30 Nov. 2015. Anglo-Powhatan War, Second (1622–1632) – Encyclopedia Virginia Accessed 8 Oct. 2020

[294] *Rohr N. "I'll Drink To That: John Dunn's Tavern Ledger Huntsville, Alabama 1843." huntsvillehistorycollection.org. Huntsville History Collection, 22 Jan. 2014.* I'll Drink to That: John Dunn's Tavern Ledger - HHC (huntsvillehistorycollection.org). *Accessed 16 Oct. 2020*

[295] *"Ruddles Station, VA/KY 1780." frontierfolk.org,* Ruddles Station, VA/KY 1780 (frontierfolk.org). *Accessed 12 Oct. 2020*

[296] Rummel MC. "Brethren Frontier." *www.cob-net.org, Brethren Frontier (cob-net.org)*. Apr. 1998. Accessed 10 Oct. 2020

[297] *Rummel MC. "Brethren Migrations." www.cob-net.org,* Brethren Migrations (cob-net.org). *Apr. 1998. Accessed 13 Oct. 2020*

[298] *"SamuelCobb&KeziahBarberCobb." Cobbsasser.com, Cobb-Sasser Family Lineage Website Page,* SamuelCobb&KeziahBarberCobb - Cobb-Sasser Family Lineage. *Accessed 26 Feb. 2021*

[299] Sawyer W. "The Six Nations Confederacy During the American Revolution - Fort Stanwix National Monument." *Nps.gov,* U.S. National Park Service, 2016, The Six Nations Confederacy During the American Revolution - Fort Stanwix National Monument (U.S. National Park Service) (nps.gov. Accessed 11 Oct. 2020

[300] *Saylor Academy. "The Anglo-Powhatan Wars" resources.saylor.org, Saylor Academy Resources.* HIST321-11.2.2-Anglo-Powhatan-Wars.pdf (saylor.org)*. Accessed 8 Oct. 2020*

[301] *Shine Gregory P. "North West Company." Www.oregonencyclopedia.org, Portland State University and the Oregon Historical Society, 16 Aug. 2018,* North West Company (oregonencyclopedia.org)*. Accessed 18 Oct. 2020*

[302] Shine, Gregory P. "John McLoughlin (1784-1857)." *Www.Oregonencyclopedia.org*, Portland State University and the Oregon Historical Society, 1 May 2019, John McLoughlin (1784-1857) - The Oregon Encyclopedia. Accessed 26 Oct. 2020

[303] *Sides, Hampton. "What a Wild Life! - Blood and Thunder: An Epic of the American West." Erenow.net, Erenow, 2006, What a Wild Life! - Blood and Thunder: An Epic of the American West (erenow.net). Accessed 4 Nov. 2020*

[304] *"Slavery Takes Root in Colonial Virginia." Www.digitalhistory.uh.edu, Digital History, 2019, Digital History (uh.edu) Accessed 26 Feb. 2021*

[305] *Soden, Dale E. "Jason Lee (1803-1845)." Www.Oregonencyclopedia.Org, Portland State University and the Oregon Historical Society. 23 Jan. 2020, Jason Lee (1803-1845) (oregonencyclopedia.org) Accessed 29 Oct. 2020*

[306] "The Starving Time | Historic Jamestowne." *Historicjamestowne.org*, Jamestown Rediscovery Foundation, The Starving Time | Historic Jamestowne. 2012. Accessed 8 Oct. 2020

[307] *Steadman, Joseph E, Sr. "Ancestry of the Fox family of Richland and Lexington counties, South Carolina."* www.familysearch.org, *The Church of Jesus Christ of Latter-day Saints. 1972.* FamilySearch Catalog: Ancestry of the Fox family of Richland and Lexington counties, South Carolina — FamilySearch.org. *Accessed 11 Oct. 2020*

[308] *Swope CL. "Chief Opechancanough (O-pech"un-kä'nO) of the Powhatan Confederacy."* www.cynthiaswope.com, *2003,* Opechancanough (cynthiaswope.com). *Accessed 9 Oct. 2020*

[309] *Tague M, Engel E. "Senator Thomas Hart Benton - Historic Missourians." historicmissourians.shsmo.org. The State Historical Society of Missouri,* Senator Thomas Hart Benton - Historic Missourians - The State Historical Society of Missouri (shsmo.org). *Accessed 23 Oct. 2020*

[310] Tate, Cassandra. "McLoughlin, John (1784-1857)." Www.historylink.org, The Free Encyclopedia of Washington State History, 24 Sep. 2013, McLoughlin, John (1784-1857) – HistoryLink.org. Accessed 5 Nov. 2020

[311] *Taylor, Elder John. "Doctrine and Covenants 135." Www.Churchofjesuschrist.org, The Church of Christ of Latter-day Saints,* Doctrine and Covenants 135 (churchofjesuschrist.org). *Accessed 8 Nov. 2020*

[312] *Thompson, Erwin N. "Whitman Mission National Historic Site." Www.Gutenberg.Org, Project Gutenberg EBook. 22 Nov. 2019,* Whitman Mission National Historic Site, by Erwin N. Thompson—a Project Gutenberg eBook. *Accessed 30 Oct. 2020*

[313] TPK. "U. S. President #7: Andrew Jackson (Part I)." *Tpksstories,blogatwordpress.com,* 9 Jun. 2020, U. S. President #7: Andrew Jackson (Part I) – TPKs Stories (wordpress.com). Accessed 22 Oct. 2020

[314] *Trye, Capt J H.* "Colonel Henry Norwood of Leckhampton" *(PDF). (pp.113–121) Bristol & Gloucester Archaeological Society, Transactions, 1925. Accessed 9 Oct 2020*

[315] *Tucker G. "Tecumseh | Facts, Biography, & Significance." www.britannica.com, Encyclopædia Britannica, 2019. Tecumseh | Facts, Biography, & Significance | Britannica. Accessed 25 Jan. 2021*

[316] *Tullidge, Edward W. & University of California Libraries. "The Women of Mormondom." Internet Archive, New York, 1877 [p.127],* The women of Mormondom. : Tullidge, Edward W. (Edward William), 1829-1894 : Free Download, Borrow, and Streaming : Internet Archive. *Accessed 4 Mar. 2021*

[317] *The Ultimate History Project Staff. "We Were To Be Nothing." ultimatehistoryproject.com. Americanpolygamy - The Ultimate History Project Accessed 25 Oct. 2020*

[318] *U.S. Govt. Compact of 1802 – document." amindians.tripod.com. 24 Apr 1802.* Compact of 1802 - document – amindians.tripod.com. *Accessed October 18, 2020*

[319] *U.S. Natl. Park Service " 1768 Boundary Line Treaty of Fort Stanwix - Fort Stanwix National Monument." www.nps.gov, NPS, May 11, 2020, 1768 Boundary Line Treaty of Fort Stanwix - Fort Stanwix National Monument (U.S. National Park Service) (nps.gov). Accessed 11 Oct. 2020*

[320] *U.S. Natl. Park Service. "Summer 1812: British General Isaac Brock and Shawnee Leader Tecumseh form an alliance." Nps.gov. 2017, Summer 1812: British General Isaac Brock and Shawnee Leader Tecumseh form an alliance (U.S. National Park Service) (nps.gov). Accessed 19 Oct. 2020*

[321] *U.S.OfficialData.org. "1800 dollars in 2019 | Inflation Calculator." Officialdata.org. 13 Oct. 2020, Value of 1800 dollars today | Inflation Calculator (officialdata.org) Accessed 21 Oct. 2020*

[322] *"U.S., Sons of the American Revolution Membership Applications, 1889-1970." [Database Online] Www.ancestry.com, Ancestry.com Operations, Inc., Provo, UT, USA, 2011.* U.S., Sons of the American Revolution Membership Applications, 1889-1970 – Ancestry.com. *Accessed 8 Mar. 2021*

[323] *Vaughan, Champ Clark. "Willamette Stone and Willamette Meridian." Www.oregonencyclopedia.org, Portland State University and the Oregon Historical Society, 13 Apr. 2020,* Willamette Stone and Willamette Meridian. *Accessed 26 Feb. 2021*

[324] *"Walker T. Dr. Thomas Walker's Journal (1749-1750)." 1888,* www.tngenweb.org, *TNGenWeb/TNGenNet. 2001,* Dr. Thomas Walker's Journal (1749-1750), TNGenWeb/TNGenNet, *Accessed 10 Oct. 2020*

[325] *"The War of 1812 - Siege of Fort Meigs, the Forgotten War to Save the Republic. (William Henry Harrison)." theuswarof1812.org. Accessed 20 Oct. 2020.* *http://theuswarof1812.org/battledetail.aspx?battle=77*

[326] *"The War of 1812 - William Henry Harrison." theuswarof1812.org,* *The Forgotten War to Save the Republic.* The War of 1812 - (William Henry Harrison) (theuswarof1812.org). *Accessed 9 Mar. 2021*

[327] "The War of 1812 - William Dudley." *theuswarof1812.org,* The War of 1812 - (Siege of Fort Meigs) (theuswarof1812.org). Accessed 21 Oct. 2020

[328] "The War of 1812 - Winfield Scott." *theuswarof1812.org*. The War of 1812 - (Winfield Scott) (theuswarof1812.org). Accessed 21 Oct. 2020

[329] *Watkins, Mark A. "Marinda Fox-Ewell-Watkins." 12 Sep 2008,* *Marinda Fox-Ewell Watkins (kykinfolk.com), Accessed 26 Sep. 2020*

[330] *Weaver S. "A Kentucky Baptist in the War of 1812. Thoughts of a Pastor-Historian." 3 Jul. 2012. A Kentucky Baptist in the War of 1812 | Thoughts of a Pastor-Historian. Accessed October 20, 2020.*

Weiser, Kathy. Legends of America –

[331] *"Benjamin Bonneville – Exploring & Defending the American West." Feb. 2020, Benjamin Bonneville – Exploring & Defending the American West – Legends of America. Accessed 26 Oct. 2020*

[332] *"Fremont's Expeditions of the American West." pp.1-2. May 2018, Fremont's Expeditions of the American West – Legends of America. Accessed 5 Nov. 2020*

[333] "The Great Indian Warpath." Dec. 2018, *The Great Indian Warpath – Legends of America*. Accessed 24 Feb. 2021

[334] *"Hall Jackson Kelley – Promoting the Oregon Trail." Feb. 2020, Hall Jackson Kelley – Promoting the Oregon Trail – Legends of America. Accessed 26 Oct. 2020*

[335] *Wensyel JW. "The Newburgh Conspiracy | AMERICAN HERITAGE." Www.americanheritage.com, Apr. 1981 [p.8] The Newburgh Conspiracy | AMERICAN HERITAGE. Accessed 12 Oct. 2020*

[336] *Whitfield, Wm W. "The Coming of the 'Black Robes.'" Ravalli Republic, Ravalli County Museum. 25 Apr. 2020, The coming of the 'Black Robes' | Local News | ravallirepublic.com Accessed 2 Nov. 2020*

Wikipedia Contributors. *en.wikipedia.org,* Wikipedia.

[337] "Charles I of England." 18 Feb 2021. Charles I of England - Wikipedia Accessed 8 Oct 2020

[338] "Daniel Boone." 2019, Daniel Boone - Wikipedia Accessed 10 Oct 2020

[339] "Darien Scheme." 6 Jan. 2020, Darien scheme - Wikipedia Accessed 10 Jan. 2020

[340] "1800 United States presidential election." 26 Feb. 2021, 1800 United States presidential election – Wikipedia. 8 Mar. 2021

[341] "French and Indian War." 19 Feb. 2019, French and Indian War - Wikipedia Accessed 27 Feb. 2020

[342] *"John Foxe." 26 Jul. 2020,* John Foxe – Wikipedia. *Accessed 27 Feb. 2021*

[343] *"John Logan (pioneer)." 27 Sep 2019,* John Logan (pioneer) - Wikipedia. *Accessed 14 Oct. 2020*

[344] "John Murray." 21 Aug 2020, John Murray - Wikipedia. Accessed 11 Oct. 2020

[345] "John Punch (Slave)." 23 Sep. 2019, John Punch (slave) – Wikipedia. Accessed 27 Feb. 2021

[346] "John Smith (explorer)" 30 Apr. 2019, John Smith (explorer) – Wikipedia. Accessed 8 Oct. 2020

[347] "Lord Dunmore's War." 22 Sep. 2020, Lord Dunmore's War – Wikipedia. Accessed 28 Feb. 2021

[348] "Patrick Henry." 27 Feb 2021, Patrick Henry – Wikipedia Accessed 3 Mar. 2021

[349] "Pietism." 8 Oct. 2020. Pietism – Wikipedia. Accessed 9 Oct. 2020

[350] "Roanoke Colony." Roanoke Colony – Wikipedia. 24 Nov. 2018. Accessed 8 Oct. 2020

[351] "1788–89 United States presidential election." 12 Oct. 2020. 1788–89 United States presidential election – Wikipedia. Accessed 13 Oct. 2020

[352] "1792 United States presidential election." 4 Mar. 2021, 1792 United States presidential election – Wikipedia. Accessed 14 Oct. 2020

[353] "1796 United States presidential election." 26 Feb. 2021, 1796 United States presidential election – Wikipedia. Accessed 8 Mar. 2021

[354] "Siege of Lathom House." 13 Aug. 2020. Siege of Lathom House – Wikipedia. Accessed 8 Oct. 2020

[355] "Tennessee." 27 Apr. 2019. *Tennessee – Wikipedia*. Accessed 14 Oct. 2020

[356] *"Thomas Jefferson." 2 Feb. 2019, Thomas Jefferson – Wikipedia. Accessed 12 Oct. 2020*

[357] *"Treaty of Lochaber." 9 Jul. 2020, Treaty of Lochaber - Wikipedia Accessed 11 Oct. 2020*

[358] William Cowbridge. A Date with History. *William Cowbridge – dailybritain.wordpress.com.* 20 Jul. 2015. Accessed 27 Sep. 2020

[359] *Williams, Shauna. "Chapter XVIII Whitman Massacre and Cayuse War." Www.Genealogytrails.Com, Chapter XVIII Whitman Massacre and Cayuse War (genealogytrails.com). Accessed 4 Nov. 2020*

[360] *Williams WJ. Transylvania Company | NCpedia. www.ncpedia.org. Transylvania Company | NCpedia. 2006. Accessed 9 Mar. 2021*

[361] *Wolfe B. Virginia Company of London. Www.encyclopediavirginia.org. 20 May 2013. Virginia Company of London – Encyclopedia Virginia. Accessed 8 Oct. 2020*

[362] *Yellowstone Genealogy Forum. "Yellowstone Genealogy Forum - James Bridger." Sites.Rootsweb.Com, 18 Feb. 2004,* Yellowstone Genealogy Forum - James Bridger (rootsweb.com). *Accessed 5 Nov. 2020.*

IMAGE CREDITS

(1), OpenStax College. "European Colonization on the Atlantic Coast," U.S. History 3.8, 30 Dec. 2014, openstax.org/books/us-history/pages/3-3-english-settlements-in-america#CNX_History_03_03_Settlement. Lic. public Domain. Accessed 27 June 2021.

(2) Mary Boleyn, sister of Queen Anne Boleyn, maternal first cousin of Katheryn Howard. Courtesy of Wikipedia. Lic. free to modify, share and use.

(3) 1939. Fox's on the Mattaponi River. In Ellen Mookler Cocke, "Some Fox Trails in Old Virginia; John Fox of King William County, Ancestors, descendants, and near kin". Frontispiece. Photo taken before 1923.

(4) Fox, Jr., James Royal. "Kentucky Inner and Outer Bluegrass." The Secrets of Benjamin Fox. 25 June, 2020. Lic. for public domain.

(5) Fox, Jr., James Royal. "Buffalo Traces" The Secrets of Benjamin Fox, 27 June 2020. Lic. for public domain.

(6) Wikipedia Contributors. "Daniel Boone." Wikipedia, Wikimedia Foundation, 2019, Daniel Boone – Wikipedia. *Portrait by Chester Harding, 1820. Lic. free to share and use. Accessed 13 Jun. 2021.*

(7) Simpsonhistory.com. "Nathaniel Hart." Copyright © 2010-2021. Lic. free to modify, share and use.

(8) Fox, Jr., James Royal. "Native American Tribes,1783". The Secrets of Benjamin Fox. 25 June, 2020. Lic. for public domain.

(9) Fox, Jr., James Royal. "Western lands of North Carolina (Tennessee)." The Secrets of Benjamin Fox. 24 June, 2020. Lic. for public domain.

(10) Treaty of Paris Map, 1783. Mapssite.com. Maps: Treaty Of Paris Map 1783 (mapssite.blogspot.com). 14 June 2008. Lic. for public domain.

(11) Map of Original 13 Colonies. map from "The Old Northwest, with a view of the thirteen colonies as constituted by the Royal Charters" - PICRYL Public Domain Image. British Library, 1888. Lic. For the public domain.

(12) Daniel Boone Escorting Settlers Through the Cumberland Gap. George Caleb Bingham. The Bridgeman Art Library, object 29102. George Caleb Bingham - Daniel Boone escorting settlers through the Cumberland Gap - Daniel Boone – Wikipedia. *Lic. free to use and share commercially.*

(13) Wilderness Road Into Kentucky. Own work by Nikater, submitted to the public domain. Background map courtesy of Demis. Www.demis.nl. 14 Apr. 2000.

(14) Fox, Jr., James Royal. "Northern Kentucky 1794." The Secrets of Benjamin Fox. 7 Aug. 2020

(15) "Arthur Fox gravestone. Arthur Fox – Washington, KY – American Revolutionary War Veteran Grave." Findagrave. Courtesy of Green, Dena, by permission

(16) By Wyatt, on Thinglink.com. Lewis and Clark Expedition (thinglink.com). Public domain.

(17) "Tecumseh." Www.it.wikipedia.org. Lic. free to share and use commercially. 13 Mar. 2021. Accessed 13 Jun. 2021.

(18) "Battle of New Orleans, 1815." Jean Hyacinthe de Laclotte. Wikipedia. Org. https://en.wikipedia.org/wiki/Battle_of_New_Orleans#/media/File:Battle_of_New_Orleans,_Jean_Hyacinthe_de_Laclotte.jpg. Lic. free to share and use commercially.

(19) Finley, Anthony. "Old Historical State, County and City Maps of Kentucky."Finley's 1827 Map of Kentucky and

Tennessee. Mapgeeks, 9 Dec. 2017, Old Historical State, County and City Maps of Kentucky (mapgeeks.org). *Lic. free to modify, share and use commercially. Accessed 14 Jun. 2021.*

(20) From a National Parks Service lesson plan website. Trail of Tears National Historic Trails. 21 Sep. 2005. www.wikipedia.org. Lic. Free to modify, share and use.

(21) Edmund Burke Bacon. Unknown Artist. 6 Feb. 2020, courtesy of Nora Brashear by permission.

(22) Betsy Eliza Fox. Unknown Artist. 6 Feb. 2020, courtesy of Nora Brashear. Eliza Fox Bacon portrait by permission.

(23) Gravestones of Edmund Burke and wife Eliza (Fox). Ancestry.com. 2 Dec. 2012. Courtesy of Lynn Ware Sprattling by permission.

(24) "Marinda Fox and son." Courtesy of Noraye Sinclaire and Mark A Watkins with permission. 20 Jun 2009.

(25) "Death of Joseph Smith." Wikipedia. Lamb, Adrian. Copy after unidentified artist, circa 1840. National Portrait Gallery, Smithsonian Institution. NPG.73.20. Www.Wikipedia.org. Lic. free to modify, share and use commercially.

(26) Brigham Young. Wikiquote.com. 11 Sep 2020. *Brigham Young – Wikiquote*. *Lic. Free to modify, share and use commercially.*

(27) "Narcissa Whitman." Wikipedia.org. Marcus Whitman – Wikipedia. 24 June 2021. Lic. free to modify, share and use commercially.

(28) Dr. Marcus Whitman. Wikipedia.org, Marcus Whitman – Wikipedia. 24 June 2021. Lic. free to modify, share and use commercially.

(29) "Kit Carson and John Fremont." Unknown photographer. Wikimedia.org. File:Carsonfremont.jpg – Wikipedia. 4 Oct. 2014. Lic. Free to modify, share and use commercially.

(30) Fox Cemetery, Jackson County, TN. Courtesy of G.L. Goolsby, by permission. Findagrave.com. Fox Cemetery in Tennessee - Find A Grave Cemetery.

(31) Benjamin's gravestone in the Fox Cemetery. Courtesy of Allen Bregman, by permission. 12 Mar 2012. FindaGrave.com. https://www.findagrave.com/memorial/38603364/benjamin-k-fox.

(32) Whitman Mission at Waiilatpu. Jackson, William H. HistoryLink.Org, courtesy of National Park Service (SCBL 151). 21 Oct 2014. https://www.historylink.org/File/10954. *Lic. free to modify, share and use commercially.*

(33) 'Tennessee Gentleman', by Ralph E.W. Earl c1831. The Hermitage collection, courtesy of the Tennessee Portrait Project. Tennessee Gentleman portrait of Andrew Jackson by Ralph E. W. Earl - Andrew Jackson – Wikipedia. *Lic. free to modify, share and use commercially.*

(34) Assassination of Joseph Smith. "Corbis". 19th century etching. Wikipedia.org. 10 June 2021. Death of Joseph Smith - Wikipedia.

(35) Map of 54, 40, or fight. Wikimedia Commons. 24 Apr 2006. https://commons.wikimedia.org/wiki/File:Oregon_boundary_dispute_map.PNG#filelinks. *Lic. free to modify, share and use commercially.*

Printed in the USA
CPSIA information can be obtained
at www.ICGtesting.com
LVHW042126040524
779389LV00005B/33